'WE ARE ALL HERE TO STAY'

CITIZENSHIP, SOVEREIGNTY AND THE UN DECLARATION ON THE RIGHTS OF INDIGENOUS PEOPLES

'WE ARE ALL HERE TO STAY'

CITIZENSHIP, SOVEREIGNTY AND THE UN DECLARATION ON THE RIGHTS OF INDIGENOUS PEOPLES

DOMINIC O'SULLIVAN

Australian
National
University

PRESS

For Cara, Lucy and Joey
in Sarah's memory

ANU PRESS

Published by ANU Press
The Australian National University
Acton ACT 2601, Australia
Email: anupress@anu.edu.au

Available to download for free at press.anu.edu.au

ISBN (print): 9781760463946
ISBN (online): 9781760463953

WorldCat (print): 1192996368
WorldCat (online): 1192995059

DOI: 10.22459/WAAHTS.2020

Cover design and layout by ANU Press

Contents

List of Abbreviations

ACCHO	Aboriginal community–controlled health organisation
ATSIC	Aboriginal and Torres Strait Islander Commission
KLP	Kommunal Landspensjonskasse
TRC	Truth and Reconciliation Commission of Canada
UN	United Nations
UPR	Universal Periodic Review
US	United States
the Declaration	The United Nations Declaration on the Rights of Indigenous Peoples
the Intervention	Northern Territory Emergency Response

Acknowledgements

Thanks, as always, to my family for supporting this work, written on Ngunnawal country and with the help of a Charles Sturt University Senior Research Fellowship.

Love and thanks to Cara, my wife, whose own work for a more just world greatly inspires, and whose support for me and my work is forever appreciated.

My daughter, Lucy, and son, Joey, for the distractions, fun and inspiration they bring, for the love and support they give to me and my work, and my daughter Sarah Therese (2006) whose memory is honoured and endures.

My parents, Tui and Vincent, who helped with proofreading and editing, and my uncle Dermot Sullivan (1924–2020), whose conversation, deep knowledge of history and politics, and always knowing where to find a beer, helped develop the interests that led me to write this book.

Introduction

The United Nations (UN) Declaration on the Rights of Indigenous Peoples ('the Declaration', which is introduced in detail in Chapter 1) is a comprehensive codification of indigenous human rights. It was adopted in 2007 by the UN General Assembly by a vote of 144 to four. Australia, Canada, New Zealand and the United States (US) dissented. There were 11 abstentions: Azerbaijan, Bangladesh, Bhutan, Burundi, Colombia, Georgia, Kenya, Nigeria, the Russian Federation, Samoa and Ukraine (UN, 2007c). Over time, the four dissenting states, which are this book's principal focus, withdrew their objections and, in each of these, as well as in other jurisdictions, the Declaration has come to provide political, legal and moral frameworks for thinking about what it means not only for both indigenous and non-indigenous peoples to say that 'we are all here to stay' (*Delgamuukw v British Columbia*, 1997, para. 186), as Canada's Chief Justice Lamer put it in 1997, but also for thinking beyond justice as the simple reconciliation of indigenous presence with the sovereignty of the Crown. Indigenous and non-indigenous populations ought to recognise the other's presence in more substantive terms, which, from the Declaration's perspective, means that the rights and capacities of self-determination are accepted as belonging to indigenous peoples as much as they belong to anybody else.

This book provides a comprehensive critical analysis of what it means in political practice for both indigenous and settler populations to recognise the other's presence and, in particular for indigenous peoples, what it means to enjoy the rights and capacities of self-determination. The book makes its arguments with reference to each of the Declaration's 46 articles. Each is referred to in a specific jurisdictional and policy context so that both the theoretical and practical policy significance of the Declaration's component parts may be examined. This analysis begins with a description of the Declaration's development through the UN system before introducing self-determination as the overarching principle that the Declaration enunciates.

The book then explains that it is their shared British colonial heritage and development into liberal democratic states (the meaning of this term is explained later in this introduction) that allows and rationalises this book's focus on Australia, Canada, New Zealand and the US. These common experiences help to explain the four states' initial objections as well as their subsequent reading down of the Declaration's potential impact, leading to their positions being reversed in 2009 (Australia), 2010 (New Zealand), 2011 (the US) and 2016 (Canada).

The principal theoretical concepts used to inform this book's analysis and develop its arguments are introduced following the discussion of the book's jurisdictional focus. The introduction of these liberal concepts—sovereignty, citizenship and democracy—and their interpretation to form a liberal theory of indigeneity (O'Sullivan, 2014, 2017) are discussed. Their meanings for political relationships in societies like those that dissented are explained. Their interpretations, to reframe debates about the workings of the state to support political relationships grounded in trust, are discussed as the basis for reconciliation (explained later in this introduction)—a political objective often stated but not consistently pursued in the dissenting states. A further and related condition for reconciliation is the operation of public institutions according to values that neither assimilate nor alienate indigenous peoples.

The introduction of the political concepts that this book uses to analyse the Declaration is followed by a description of its structure, which explains how these concepts are systematically applied throughout the text. This description also shows how sovereignty, citizenship and democracy inform the book's ultimate purpose: to examine and propose what the Declaration may mean in both political theory and political practice.

Background to the Declaration on the Rights of Indigenous Peoples

More than 25 years of indigenous advocacy and global cooperation preceded the Declaration's adoption. It is the most comprehensive body of collective indigenous political thought ever and makes it clear that domestic indigenous 'aspirations ... are not out of step with international expectations' (p. 9). It provides a reference point beyond the state for the assertion of indigenous rights and, as this book also shows, the Declaration legitimises and gives international authority to an overarching indigenous claim to self-determination.

The Declaration's genesis in the UN system was a report published in 1981 by the Special Rapporteur to the Sub-Commission on the Prevention of Discrimination and Protection of Minorities. The report of the rapporteur, José Martinez Cobo, on the problem of discrimination against indigenous populations was commissioned by the UN Economic and Social Council in 1971. The report began the UN's systematic interest in indigenous peoples as distinct peoples (Nakata, 2001). Earlier UN human rights instruments, such as the Universal Declaration of Human Rights, adopted in 1948, enunciated principles of human equality— rights to equal protection against discrimination, to collective property ownership and to participate in the affairs of the state (UN, 1948, arts. 7, 17 and 21). However, the 2007 Declaration is more significant still because it foreshadows the interpretation and application of these principles in specific indigenous contexts.

As Martinez Cobo (1981) observed, 'the principles proclaimed in existing international instruments concerning human rights and fundamental freedoms [were] not fully applied in all countries' (p. 79) and not equally applied to all peoples. Therefore, he recommended that 'specific principles should be formulated for use as guidelines by governments of all states in their activities concerning indigenous populations' (p. 79) and that:

> Such principles must necessarily contain any additional and specific provisions which, following careful study, may be deemed necessary for the full recognition and protection of the indispensable rights and freedoms of indigenous populations. (p. 79)

Martinez Cobo presumed that all societies, including states such as Australia, Canada, New Zealand and the US, were morally obliged to accept and defend those 'indispensable' rights and freedoms. The obligation was to ensure that a state's prevailing political systems could attend to those rights and freedoms by recognising the right to self-determination as a right belonging to *all* and not just to *some* peoples.

The right to self-determination and its implications are discussed throughout the book. In particular, it is discussed as a theoretical concept with a potentially transformative impact on how indigenous nations and the states that have emerged over their territories think about the practices of sovereignty and citizenship, and what these considerations mean for the form that democracy takes. This book is a study of the theoretical and practical interrelationships among these concepts and a study of what these relationships mean for the indigenous person's right to live as a member of an indigenous nation and simultaneously, if they wish, as a member of the state with the right to participate in its affairs with substantive and distinctive equality. This idea, that indigenous peoples are entitled to enjoy membership of their own nations and make decisions through their own institutions according to their preferred processes, while also enjoying equal *and* culturally contextualised membership of the state, is introduced below and developed through the book as 'differentiated citizenship'.

In response to Martinez Cobo's (1981) study, the UN Economic and Social Council established the Working Group on Indigenous Populations. The group's mandate was:

- to review developments pertaining to the promotion and protection of human rights and fundamental freedoms of indigenous peoples
- to give attention to the evolution of international standards concerning indigenous rights. (UN, 2001, para. 2)

The group consisted of five experts, appointed by the UN Sub-Commission on the Prevention of Discrimination and Protection of Minorities (now the Sub-Commission on the Promotion and Protection of Human Rights), from Japan, Cuba, Nigeria, Hungary and the United Kingdom. Its meetings were open to indigenous representatives and, in 1985, the UN established the Voluntary Fund for Indigenous Populations to give financial support to their participation. UN member states and nongovernment organisations also participated in the group's deliberations, establishing it 'as a focal point of international action on indigenous issues' (UN, 2001, para. 3) and making it one of the largest UN human rights forums.

During the 1980s and 1990s, the group's annual meetings attracted more than 700 indigenous people 'from the forests of Amazonia to the north of Alaska and Greenland; from the Sami people in Northern Russia to the Masai in Kenya to Australia's aborigines' (UN, 1997, para. 2). The working group released its Draft Declaration on the Rights of Indigenous Peoples in 1993. The draft was approved the following year by the UN Sub-Commission on the Prevention of Discrimination and Protection of Minorities.

The draft declaration's working definition of the indigenous right to self-determination was significant:

> By virtue of [the right of self-determination, [indigenous peoples] freely determine their political status and freely pursue their economic, social and cultural development. (Iorns, 1993, 'Draft declaration', pt. I art. 3)

The subcommission referred the draft declaration to the Commission on Human Rights, which referred it to a further working group of member states and indigenous organisations. Alongside the negotiations that followed, the UN created a Permanent Forum on Indigenous Issues. Established in 2002, the forum comprised indigenous policy experts nominated in equal number by UN member states and indigenous nongovernment organisations. The forum's annual meetings, which were open to representatives of all indigenous peoples, provided an environment for further indigenous advocacy in favour of what was still a draft declaration.

While the working group found that member states and indigenous organisations agreed that the draft provided a sound starting point for negotiation, several states had reservations, especially concerning the scope of the right to self-determination. Some believed that this right could be interpreted to disrupt the territorial integrity of the nation-state by allowing indigenous groups to secede (UN, 1996).

This major point of contention was ultimately resolved for most member states, though within the context of the indigenous organisations' argument that self-determination is a right that belongs to all peoples and that it was already well established. It had, for example, been expressed as a universal right in the International Covenant on Civil and Political Rights (UN, 1966a) and in the International Covenant on Economic, Social and Cultural Rights (UN, 1966b). Indigenous organisations resisted the possibility that the right to self-determination would be limited or qualified only for indigenous populations (UN, 1996). They also resisted the view that what the draft contained were social or political aspirations, but not rights. As a declaration, the instrument would not be legally binding; however, from other state and indigenous perspectives, it would still be politically and morally binding (UN, 1996), which as this book shows, gives the Declaration political value and significance.

Some states were also concerned that the proposed requirement of indigenous consent to resource extraction, and other commercial activities on their lands, would compromise state authority to regulate land use. Some argued that the Declaration needed to define indigenous people and some questioned the propriety of distinctive peoplehood as a right of indigenous populations.

However, indigenous organisations argued that a universal definition would prevent indigenous groups from defining themselves according to their own value systems and would, as such, constrain the right to self-determination. Several governments agreed that retaining this flexibility was essential if, overall, the Declaration was to be universally relevant (UN, 1996). However, there was still a concern among member states that the term 'peoples' may privilege collective rights over the rights of individuals and make indigenous groups subjects of international law with consequent rights over natural resources, for example. Indigenous counterarguments claimed that collective rights are the sum of individual rights so that the two bodies of rights could not conflict (UN, 1996).

For the indigenous organisations, collective rights were central to identity and being. However, some states argued, for example, that the draft framed the collective right to education and to separate indigenous political, legal, economic and social systems in ways that could give rise to discrimination against other citizens (UN, 1996).

The working group tried to resolve these points of contention by negotiation and exhaustive deliberation. However, it was ultimately only the UN member states who would vote when the draft was submitted to the General Assembly, and it was a compromise text adopted by the Human Rights Council in 2006 and referred to the assembly for what was expected to be a final vote in January 2007.[1]

At this point, Namibia, supported by other members of the African Union, successfully moved to have the vote delayed. Their reservation was that most African peoples were indigenous to the African continent and that self-determination only applied to peoples seeking freedom from colonial subjugation (Engle, 2011). To ensure that this argument was not compromised, the African Union wanted further work on the

---

1   For a full summary of the differences between the draft text and the text submitted to the Human Rights Council for referral to the General Assembly see UN (2006b, Annex I).

definition of indigenous peoples. It also wanted further consideration of self-determination, land and resource ownership and the status of distinctive indigenous political and economic institutions. It particularly wanted further consideration of the implications of self-determination for the territorial integrity of the state (Engle, 2011). Further negotiations took place, and among the outcomes was a clause specifically precluding the secession of an indigenous people from an existing state. The final declaration, adopted in September 2007, affirmed a more tightly defined indigenous right to self-determination, though kept it as an essential principle of international law.

The right to self-determination is also of sufficient scope to have significant theoretical implications for sovereignty, citizenship and democracy—concepts that are introduced in this chapter's following section. The various perspectives of states, indigenous nations, scholars and political actors may then be assessed against the optimistic expectations of the Indigenous Australian legal scholar Megan Davis (2007), who argued that the Declaration's adoption:

> was a momentous occasion for Indigenous peoples. It is an important document of developing standards that Aboriginal and Torres Strait Islanders in Australia can use in their day-to-day relationships with all levels of government. It was a long struggle to draft the document and to have it move through the UN hierarchy to adoption by the General Assembly. The UN human rights system confirmed that it is indeed capable of faithfully facilitating substantive standard setting activities for the collective rights of indigenous peoples. [It] symbolises goodwill on the part of states in acknowledging the historical injustice toward indigenous peoples. The Declaration will also go some way to delivering justice to those first peoples whose deprivation of human rights is the very cornerstone of the sovereignty, wealth and power of the most obstructive and argumentative states who voted against the declaration in the General Assembly. (Conclusion section, para. 1)

This book will show how and why Davis's optimism is contested from some indigenous and state perspectives and shared from others, and it will show what these contrasting perspectives mean in both theoretical and practical policy terms.

Self-determination

The Declaration affirms self-determination as a right that belongs to indigenous peoples as much as it belongs to anybody else. It does not introduce new rights. It codifies and contextualises existing ones, and its purpose is to provide a framework for applying them to distinctive indigenous circumstances. As the Declaration codifies it, self-determination is more politically significant than reconciling 'the pre-existence of aboriginal societies with the sovereignty of the Crown' (*Haida Nation v British Columbia (Minister of Forests)*, 2004, para. 17). This is because the Declaration makes assumptions not just about '*who* rules, but [also about] *how* rule is accomplished' (Corrigan, 1990, p. 264, emphasis in original). When self-determination is applied in response, indigenous rights are neither what Corntassel (2012) calls 're-gifted rhetoric' (p. 92) nor restricted by what Carroll (2012) argues is an indigenous–state relationship that must always and everywhere allow states to 'maintain their hegemony as the only true sovereigns' (p. 147).

This book's alternative perspective is that self-determination is an argument for the greatest possible indigenous political autonomy while pragmatically accepting the state's right to govern. However, the right to government is not hegemonic and, if they wish, indigenous persons may actively participate in state affairs to ensure that their perspectives are heard in day-to-day policymaking and to ensure that they are always placed to influence the operation of public institutions. This influence is, in turn, a determinant of the extent to which the right to self-determination is either present or curtailed.

As an intellectual framework, the Declaration allows new ways of thinking about the political capacities that indigenous peoples may (and may not) claim both within their own nations and within the states that have emerged over their territories. Specifically, the Declaration:

> sets out the individual and collective rights of the world's 370 million native peoples, calls for the maintenance and strengthening of their cultural identities, and emphasises the right to pursue development in keeping with their own needs and aspirations. (UN, 2007a, para. 2)

It sets standards and frameworks in relation to indigenous peoples'
political expectations by:

> affirm[ing] that indigenous peoples especially have the right to
> self-determination, recognis[ing] that they have been denied
> enjoyment of the right, and mark[ing] the parameters for processes
> that will remedy that denial. (Anaya, 2009, p. 189)

The Declaration's standards and frameworks maintain that 'Indigenous
peoples are equal to all other peoples … [and there is a] right of all peoples
to be different, to consider themselves different, and to be respected as
such' (UN, 2007b, annex). They also reflect principles of the Universal
Declaration of Human Rights (UN, 1948) that 'All are equal before the
law … All are entitled to equal protection against any discrimination'
(art. 7); 'Everyone has the right to own property alone as well as in
association with others' (art. 17[1]); and 'Everyone has the right to take
part in the government of his country, directly or through freely chosen
representatives' (art. 21[1]).

Self-determination's potential—or ultimate objective—is, then, to
contribute to the development of states that do not intrude on indigenous
lives or appropriate indigenous lands and resources. It protects rights to
political authority, cultural integrity and economic security. It asserts
political agency and reflects international acceptance of minimum
standards for the expression of that agency. For the Australian Human
Rights Commission (2013), for example, the Declaration 'enshrines
[the] right to be different as Peoples and affirms the minimum standards
for the survival, dignity, security and well-being of Indigenous peoples
worldwide' (p. 4). Self-determination is concerned with the political
spaces that indigenous peoples may choose to occupy as peoples entitled
to independent political authority through maintaining and developing
their own political institutions *and* as citizens of the state.

Australia, Canada, New Zealand and the United States: Dissenting Liberal Democracies

Indigenous peoples may seek recourse to the Declaration to support
their right to self-determination anywhere in the world. However, this
book's expansive consideration of what it means, both theoretically and
practically, to say that 'we are all here to stay' is focused on the dissenting

states. Although comparative reference is made to other jurisdictions (in Chapter 6 especially), the focus on Australia, Canada, New Zealand and the US is made because the liberal democratic values that underlie each of their systems of government helps to explain their initial opposition to the Declaration. It also helps to explain why they subsequently reversed their positions and why the Declaration's implications are potentially transformative in those jurisdictions.

Liberal democracy is a form of political organisation based on the primacy of the individual and the protection of personal freedoms. Protecting these freedoms is a principal function of the state. From a liberal democratic perspective, freedom requires that each person is fundamentally equal: that each is equal before the law and has the same rights and responsibilities to contribute to the government of the state. However, the Declaration posed a philosophical challenge to states whose political systems operate on the assumption that each person's liberty establishes an individual right to participate in public affairs through, for example, voting at regular elections and enjoying the same rights, privileges and obligations before the law, but where neither collective rights nor individual rights grounded in culture are routinely admitted. It was from these perspectives (introduced in Chapter 3) that the four states' objections highlighted an ongoing tension over the terms of indigenous political status within, and in relation to, the state. A tension over what it means to be equal and what it means to be an indigenous citizen, especially in relation to the further presumption that the government of the liberal state occurs by the people's consent. A condition that, as this book shows, is rarely, if ever, met in respect of indigenous peoples. As this book explains, this condition is elusive because the presumption of freedom through equality has been interpreted by states and dominant populations as sameness, meaning that political arrangements may proceed without regard to culture, colonialism or the group memberships in which, and through which, freedom is experienced. The Declaration's presumption that states and indigenous peoples ought to work out what, in practice, it means for indigenous peoples to enjoy political freedom makes it a liberal instrument especially suited to the analysis of indigenous rights in the dissenting states.

These states, with their variously assertive indigenous minority populations and shared British colonial heritage, feared that the Declaration would disrupt their territorial integrity and enhance, rather than simply contextualise, the rights of indigenous citizens vis-a-vis all others. These fears, and the reasons that they receded over time, are discussed in detail in Chapter 1.

In short, the Declaration shows how and why there is, in fact, scope within liberal democratic practice for indigenous persons to enjoy both equal and distinctive liberal rights; where equality and difference are compatible, fair and reasonable. In particular, the Declaration illuminates the idea that individual liberty may depend on the recognition of group rights and may only be meaningful with reference to cultural context and colonial experience. In respect of these states, it is instructive to examine the Declaration in relation to liberal ideas of sovereignty and citizenship and for what the Declaration proposes as their practical application—in particular, the presumption that restrictions on liberty must be justified according to some coherent political principle. For example, that one person's freedom does not impinge on the freedoms of another, or that individual freedom may be subject to a wider and broadly accepted public good—but not, as Locke (1887) argued, on the presumption that there are racial hierarchies of human worth that give some groups greater influence than others over the arrangement of public affairs.

The Declaration's liberal character is what makes it a valuable instrument in indigenous claims to self-determination, for it allows such claims to be expressed in the prevailing language of the liberal state in ways that make sense in terms of the values that underlie the national political community and its public institutions. If self-determination is a liberal right, then its claims are more likely to be heard simply because liberalism is either the state's prevailing political order or the political order that the international community wishes to impose.

The dissenting states made liberal political arguments against the Declaration (see Chapter 3 for the systemic development of this point). However, liberalism is not a singular nor absolute political philosophy. There are many interpretations of its essential presumption that 'a liberal is a man who believes in liberty' (Cranston, 1967, p. 459). The ways in which political systems give effect to that objective are also widely interpreted. For the politics of indigenous self-determination, the most important and highly contested point concerns whether each person's liberty must be recognised and expressed in the *same* way or whether they may be *differently* understood and exercised. In particular, whether relationships between group rights and personal liberty may be admitted, and whether there are rights of culture and prior occupancy to be brought into account.

This book's recurrent themes therefore include the Declaration's capacity to contribute significantly to making citizenship a more meaningful political status than many indigenous people have experienced by rethinking democracy's capacity to ensure substantive indigenous voice in public affairs alongside the indigenous right to use their own institutions and political processes to manage their affairs independently of the state.

Sovereignty

The colonial process began in each of the dissenting states in different ways and at different times during the eighteenth and nineteenth centuries. However, in each case, it was rationalised by the assumption of sovereignty's (see Chapter 7) transfer from indigenous nations to the British Crown. From the British perspective, sovereignty was an absolute political authority that allowed its permanent settlement and government of indigenous territories. This book introduces alternative indigenous conceptions of sovereignty and contests the idea that sovereignty is an absolute and indivisible authority vested in a single entity, such as the Crown-in-Parliament. It also argues that sovereignty is not an authority once held exclusively by indigenous peoples, taken and exercised exclusively by the settler state and reclaimable by indigenous people as an absolute power. The authority of sovereignty is more complex, and the Declaration helps to make sense of these complexities by proposing new spaces of political authority—spaces of inclusion in which a new kind of liberal politics can be worked out.

Each of this book's chapters shows how the Declaration may help contemporary societies contest the idea of state sovereignty as colonial hegemony, with its intellectual origins in the writings of the seventeenth-century English political philosopher John Locke.

Locke viewed the liberal values of freedom and authority over one's own affairs as essential political rights. However, he did not believe that these rights applied to everybody. There were exceptions that served to justify the colonial demand for sovereignty over other peoples and territories. For example, the British acquisition of Australia in 1788 was justified with reference to Locke's theory of property, which excluded hunter-gatherer peoples from land ownership. One had to work the land, in an agricultural sense, to claim ownership of it. Unowned land could simply be taken by others, as Locke (1887) explained:

God, when He gave the world in common to all mankind, commanded man also to labour, and the penury of his condition required it of him. God and his reason commanded him to subdue the earth—i.e. improve it for the benefit of life and therein lay out something upon it that was his own, his labour. He that, in obedience to this command of God, subdued, tilled, and sowed any part of it, thereby annexed to it something that was his property, which another had no title to, nor could without injury take from him. (p. 207)

In 1838, the *Sydney Herald* drew on Locke's argument to justify the British claim to sovereignty in Australia, arguing that, to the Indigenous people:

This vast country was to them a common—they bestowed no labour upon the land—their ownership, their rights, was nothing more than that of the emu or the kangaroo. They bestowed no labour upon the land and that—and that only—it is which gives a right of property to it. ('Sworn to no master', 1838, p. 2)

According to Reynolds (1996), such depictions of precontact Indigenous Australia, which amounted to a view of the land as unoccupied or 'terra nullius', were not grounded in fact, but were instead examples of a 'self-serving Eurocentric jurisprudence of convenience' (p. xii).

In contrast to Locke, eighteenth-century Enlightenment philosophers, such as Immanuel Kant (1970), argued against suppressing the liberty of others. Kant's writings can be seen as contesting settler colonialism's attempts to assimilate indigenous peoples into settler cultures to create ethnically homogenous political communities. For example:

Men have different views on the empirical end of happiness, and what it consists of, so that as far as happiness is concerned, their will cannot be brought under any common principle, nor thus under an external law harmonizing with the freedom of everyone. (Kant, 1970, pp. 73–74)

Settler colonialism is an ongoing process that the Declaration aims to circumvent. It is a process involving the gradual and continuing phenomenon of settler populations increasing their relative power vis-a-vis indigenous populations. To be clear, this process did not end when the four states gained political independence from the British Crown. By that time, settler populations were in the majority, had acquired control over large tracts of indigenous land and had established new states according to their own political arrangements and norms of government.

The assimilation of indigenous people into the cultures of the settlers was supposed to ensure that there was no resistance to the development of these new societies. Assimilation is the process through which indigenous cultures were expected to become one with that of the settler population. In Australia, for example, it was pursued through the removal of indigenous children from their families, as official policy, in all states from the early 1900s until the mid-1970s. The Western Australian Protector of Aborigines, AO Neville, described the policy as one of breeding out aboriginality (Neville, 1947). In New Zealand, the policy was more subtle and implemented through Native Schools, which existed between 1867 and 1969 and provided Maori with a lesser curriculum focused on what, in the 1930s, the Director-General of Education explained as 'lead[ing] the lad to be a good farmer and the girl to be a good farmer's wife' so that the Maori mode of living would copy 'the nuclear family of the pakeha social order' (as cited in Hill, 2004, p. 182). Indigenous peoples, across jurisdictions, have seen assimilation as the antithesis of self-determination and of a nondominant, noncolonial or postcolonial political order, where the state does not exercise a controlling authority over indigenous peoples.

Instead, such a political order would mean that indigenous peoples are free to live according to their own cultural values, manage their own affairs and enjoy the land and resource rights that the Declaration promises and which are noted throughout this book in specific jurisdictional and policy contexts. Indigenous peoples would also be free to participate in the affairs of the state *as* indigenous. They would then be positioned to develop just terms of association with the state. Terms of association where, for example, the state accepts that exercising powers of domination over indigenous peoples is unjust and that serious attempts must be made at restitution for the deprivation of indigenous peoples' lands, cultures and political authority, which among other considerations would include seeking agreement on what it could mean to live together differently (Maaka & Fleras, 2005). Just terms of association mean that states act unreasonably if they accord indigenous peoples lesser legal or political status by virtue of their indigeneity; it means working out the terms of a fundamentally equal, even though distinctive, indigenous citizenship.

The terms of association between indigenous peoples and the state may be just when both independent indigenous institutions and state institutions support indigenous people's capacities to make decisions over their own affairs without interference from the state, and when state institutions, like schools, hospitals and policymaking agencies, accept indigenous people's participation in these institutions *as* indigenous. An alternative is to deny that the right to self-determination is inherently bound in culture and to assume that when people go to school or seek help in a hospital that they do so as 'cultureless' beings and to assume that these institutions operate from positions of cultural neutrality. Another alternative is that culture is relevant, but that it is the culture of the postsettler population that properly determines the values under which public institutions operate. In this way, the indigenous person's access to equal schooling or equal health care depends on their willingness and ability to assimilate into the settler culture: to think and understand the world only in terms that make sense in a culture that is not their own.

Colonialism cannot be undone; however, the Declaration's assumption is that its consequences may be mitigated so that, as this book argues, noncolonial political relationships may be imagined. This is because the Declaration raises questions about whether a political order—where the state is the single site of sovereign authority—is a just model for political relationships.

Sovereignty is widely understood as referring to 'supreme authority within a territory' (Philpott, 2016, para. 1). In practice, sovereignty is the authority of governments to govern and to make laws and public policies to regulate the lives of those living in their territories. However, there are limits on a government's capacity to make laws and public policies, including constraints that arise from Locke's (1887) argument that legitimate government occurs by the people's consent; for while Locke's was an exclusive people, the Declaration's is not. This issue is brought into sharp focus by the New Zealand Waitangi Tribunal's finding in 2014 that the Treaty of Waitangi did not involve Maori ceding sovereignty to Britain when the instrument was signed in 1840 (Waitangi Tribunal, 'He Whakaputanga me te Tiriti', 2014). This raises the question: under what circumstances might a society develop in which Maori feel sufficient ownership to consent to New Zealand's overall system of government? This theme of what, from indigenous perspectives, might justify consent for the liberal state recurs throughout this book and is especially important in Australia where there is a well-established possibility that treaties between some states and Indigenous nations may be negotiated in coming years (see Chapters 2 and 3).

Treaties require indigenous nations to consider the terms of their consent to the state. Under what circumstances might consent be given? Withholding consent cannot disrupt state systems of government. However, a treaty's foundational presumption is that it is reasonable for societies to think about the distribution of political authority because, as this book shows, treaties cannot admit absolute, indivisible and incontestable state authority over and above indigenous peoples. The book's purposes therefore include consideration of what possibilities exist, with reference to the Declaration, for the exercise of multiple and sometimes shared sovereignties. It attends to this purpose by establishing the independent indigenous authority that the Declaration rationalises and by examining the capacities that exist and might be developed for indigenous peoples to influence, share and help lead the state and its institutions. The book is thus a systematic examination of how liberal political theory might rationalise and give effect to such objectives and in ways that do not diminish the rights of other citizens.

It is important to ask whether the Declaration supports the development of a politics and liberal theory of indigeneity and whether it can help to substantively improve the lives of indigenous peoples. Might the Declaration help citizenship, in a liberal state, to achieve what Ivison (2002) suggests is among its essential purposes—to give people reasons to believe that the state is theirs because:

> to be at home in the world is to be able to identify with those institutions and practices [of the state], to see the norms and ends as expressed in the public life of the community as ones that are connected to her flourishing. And it is not just about feelings. These institutions and practices should actually help her life go better. (p. 6)

Might the Declaration then support an indigenous right to deliberate in public affairs as equal citizens in ways that indigenous peoples find worthwhile? Is there a form of deliberation not confined to what Watson and Venne (2012) call aboriginal management of 'white political space' (p. 88)? Might indigenous deliberation involve 'white political space' making way for a national political space in which indigenous peoples participate *as indigenous*, setting aside an 'us' and 'them' binary and claim in Australia, for example, 'a bit of blackness in this country's white document [i.e. the Constitution]' (Axelby & Wanganeen, 2017, para. 8)? Is there such a thing as a liberal theory of indigeneity (O'Sullivan,

2014, 2017) that might set aside that binary in favour of more inclusive political arrangements than those possible under New Zealand's bicultural political philosophy, for example?

Biculturalism was the dominant philosophy informing Maori public policy during the 1980s and 1990s. It advocated greater respect for Maori culture in public organisations and facilitated greater Maori involvement in public decision-making. Its presumption was that the Treaty of Waitangi, signed in 1840, was a partnership between Maori and the British Crown—or Maori and Pakeha (New Zealanders of Anglo-Celtic heritage)—as signatories to the treaty. The bicultural presumption was that this partnership ought to guide national social and political relationships. However, in positioning Maori and Pakeha as always and everywhere distinct, biculturalism understated the significance of social, cultural, political and economic relationships between Maori and other New Zealanders. Instead it created an 'us' and 'them' binary, and the terms Crown and Pakeha came to be used interchangeably to describe the non-Maori treaty partner. The interchangeable use of these terms gave the Crown an exclusive ethnic character to mean that, while biculturalism allowed independent Maori authority and supported the development of tribal political institutions, it did not admit space for meaningful Maori influence within the state. The Declaration provides a more expansive framework for thinking about political relationships and self-determination's practical possibilities.

A Liberal Theory of Indigeneity

This book considers the Declaration with reference to a politics of indigeneity involving both political theory and political strategy. When the politics of indigeneity claim spaces of indigenous agency, authority and autonomy, they are concerned with indigenous peoples defining their own terms of belonging to the state—a distinctive belonging as First Peoples and shareholders in the collective sovereignty that the state ought to safeguard on behalf of *all* and not just *some* people. When this occurs, the political and legal precepts that facilitated Britain's colonisation of the dissenting states must be reconsidered. Likewise, the workings of the public institutions and political systems that undermined indigenous forms of government and land tenure, while simultaneously limiting their influence over those systems, must also be reconsidered.

This book's liberal theory of indigeneity rests on the assumption of an extant indigenous political authority, which asks what scope exists for a more expansive politics of inclusion. Consistent with the Declaration, it presumes that the liberty of the indigenous person is not simply an individual right, but one that only makes sense in relation to the cultural and other political rights that the indigenous nation retains. Thus, liberty is culturally contextualised. However, it is also contextualised by a colonial politics whose very logic is liberty's deprivation.

Liberty is attainable only with reference to a political theory that recognises how and why freedom might be constrained; that is, a theory that recognises that liberty can only derive meaning in the cultural context of the persons claiming it. A liberal theory of indigeneity aims, then, 'to create political space for substantive and sustainable reconciliation through self-determination and a particular indigenous share in the sovereign authority of the modern state itself' (O'Sullivan, 2017, p. 35). Such a theory requires a fundamental reappraisal of colonial thought and the displacement of the colonial state by one that is consciously and sustainably postcolonial. The Declaration is not a panacea for this kind of political relationship, but it does legitimise the aspiration and provides supporting principles. It does so by facilitating the juxtaposition of traditional indigenous conceptions of political authority with Western liberal democratic theory. Its potential is to allow 'cultural theorists [to] demand a degree of differentiation not present in almost any developed democracy' (Fleras, 2000, p. 373). This juxtaposition of ideas tests liberalism's inclusive potential, not only of people but also of perspectives on what the state is for and what it ought to achieve in terms of *all* people's rights as distinct from *some* people's interests.

A liberal theory of indigeneity seeks just terms of association between indigenous nations and the state and for indigenous peoples within the state. Its focus on circumventing colonialism's exploitative logic means that its interest in protecting group rights is not the same as a general liberal interest in the rights of ethnic minorities. Prior occupancy means that indigenous people's claim to distinctive status is fundamentally different. Theirs is a claim to exercise political rights through culture and, explicitly, through geopolitical relationships with the colonised land. The usurpation of land, linguistic and cultural rights are transgressions of justice occasioned against indigenous peoples solely because they are indigenous. It is only because of one's membership of an indigenous group that one has experienced the injustice, so it follows that restitution is owed to the group. Personal liberty cannot, then, occur in isolation from the group. If liberalism is concerned with the liberty of all and not just some citizens, it must be attentive to group rights. This is also because culture and prior occupancy provide distinctive terms for indigenous belonging as equal citizens. Consequently, the rights of indigeneity do not arise from a 'conjunction between "culture" and "disadvantage"' (Scott, 2003, p. 94). A liberal theory of indigeneity is not a theory of egalitarian justice; nor is it a theory concerned with the rights of poor people. This is because the rights to language, culture and a distinctive political voice belong to all indigenous people. These rights embody a special moral significance because they are rights that colonialism has usurped. They have not been freely surrendered, so remain as expressions of the right to self-determination.

As a theory, indigeneity is concerned with protecting the right to self-determination (O'Sullivan, 2017). It demonstrates this concern by contesting 'the exclusive sovereignty of the State to pass and enforce laws, define agendas, establish priorities, articulate patterns of entitlement, or demand compliance by decree if not by consent' (Tully, 1999, p. 223). Therefore, an inclusive and meaningful sovereignty that is available to indigenous peoples in cultural and sociopolitical contexts, as much as it is available to anybody else, is presumed. This presumption of the right to participate freely in the political, social and economic affairs of the state carries substantive rights of citizenship. Indigenous peoples' prior deprivation is the foundational cause of their political marginalisation and material poverty. The Declaration's focus is justified, as political domination or denial of the right to self-determination occurs only because indigenous human rights, and sometimes indigenous humanity, have been denied. Thus, indigeneity may have implications for the nature of one's belonging to the state.

Differentiated Citizenship

The ways in which one belongs, or does not belong, to a political community can be understood as an expression of citizenship; likewise, the ways in which one is part of, or excluded from, the sovereign can also be viewed this way. As the embodiment of political capacities, citizenship 'is an ideological and power laden concept [that] can exacerbate, exaggerate or mediate tensions over the distribution of power and authority' (O'Sullivan, 2017, p. 51). Citizenship reflects the ways in which people are positioned in the political community and in relation to its institutions of power. For indigenous peoples, it determines whether they are willing to see the state as 'ours' (i.e. as an inclusive institution) or as 'their' exclusive settler-colonial construct.

The right to conceptualise and exercise one's citizenship of the indigenous nation, and also of the liberal state, in culturally meaningful terms is important. Personal liberty cannot occur in isolation from these relationships. Just terms of association require that indigenous peoples may claim their liberty, as citizens, in ways that are personally meaningful, such as through the right to a culturally meaningful political voice and to representation in public affairs, or through speaking in parliament or judicial proceedings in one's own language. The Declaration affirms these rights and provides guidance on how they might be realised. They are justified in liberal terms because inclusivity 'is compatible with a form of universalism that counts the culture and cultural context valued by individuals as among their basic interests' (Gutmann, 1994, p. 5).

However, settler colonialism means that, in practice, indigenous peoples may not routinely (or ever) experience citizenship as the substantive and important political concept that Aristotle once described. For Aristotle, the citizen was 'he who has power to take part in the deliberative or judicial and administrative power of the state' (Hindess, 2002, p. 94). In this construct, citizenship means that each member of a society has the same opportunity for meaningful influence on public affairs as any other. Equal capacity, as a citizen, requires attention to culture and to sociopolitical contexts. This is reflected in the Declaration's proposal that citizenship and its capacities belong to indigenous people as to any people—that is, inherently: they are not granted by the state's benevolence.

Citizenship's strength is measured by the extent to which people are inclined to use its capacities and their 'desire to participate in the political process … to promote the public good and hold political authorities accountable' (Kymlicka & Norman, 1994, p. 335). Therefore, it is democratically important for indigenous people to see the state as belonging to them, and membership of the state as something worthwhile and capable of contributing to their capacity for self-determination. However, this is not a common indigenous experience. Unless contrary perceptions and realities can develop, self-determination will remain unattainable.

At the same time, ensuring the political capacity of indigenous institutions to manage their own affairs and develop their own societies in ways that are collectively meaningful is important. Indigenous peoples must be able to claim the authority to determine what they want of their own societies and to determine the spheres of influence that they want their societies to enjoy. In some instances, colonialism has diminished that capacity; in others, the sense of indigenous purpose remains strong. In both cases, there is liberal justification for the public recognition of indigenous decision-making systems and for indigenous people's capacities to:

> develop the right to difference in cultural expression, but sameness in political opportunities; difference in forms of land tenure, but sameness in capacity to make decisions about how land will be used; difference in the way one is taught at school, but sameness in terms of educational quality. (O'Sullivan, 2017, pp. 51–52)

These are among the conditions for what Maaka and Fleras (2005) call 'belonging together differently'. Belonging together differently is possible when the terms of association between indigenous people and other citizens, and between indigenous peoples and the state, are grounded in a politics of participatory parity (Fraser & Honneth, 2003).

This concept of participatory parity means that indigenous people may contribute to public affairs with reference to the specific contexts and experiences of colonised peoples and from their own cultural perspectives. They need not express their arguments through the language and epistemologies of the majority population, for to insist on this approach to political participation would be to make indigenous culture a democratic disability—an obstacle to equal and meaningful participation. Measures like guaranteed indigenous seats in parliaments and the proposed voice to parliament in Australia, which are discussed later in this book, are examples of participatory parity, a form of democratic politics that assumes necessarily inclusive processes of public reason will inform public decision-making.

Public reason is the assumption that, to deliberate properly, people must give reasons for their views and expose them to informed scrutiny. Poorly thought out opinions or a refusal to entertain that another may have a reasoned (even if different) view, does not allow democracy to work to its potential. It does not allow indigenous people to defend their priorities and aspirations to an audience that is attentive, respectful and open to the possibility of modifying its own positions. It also means, for example, that indigenous people are not able to scrutinise the opinions of others or argue for the unreasonableness of discriminatory positions. Public reason means that people must deal with disagreement with serious and well-informed argument. Rash opinions are unreasonable because they disregard another's right to be heard and considered.

The processes that are used to make decisions are variables that influence people's capacity to participate and thus influence the moral acceptability of the decision itself. Political values play an important role in policy formation, as they ensure that jurisdictions cannot function in a culturally neutral or acultural fashion. Consequently, liberals cannot argue that cultural preferences are private matters. Culture cannot be kept from public life because political values themselves are deeply rooted in human culture.

As liberal states, the dissenting states' underlying political values are, to varying degrees, compatible with the Declaration's view of the right to self-determination as a right 'based on principles of justice, democracy, respect for human rights, non-discrimination and good faith' (UN, 2007b, annex). However, liberalism is a broad and contested political philosophy. These differences are borne out in the ways that states and indigenous nations, as well as individual political actors, think about concepts such as sovereignty and citizenship.

Differentiated citizenship both lays the foundation for and is a reflection of reconciliation, which is itself preliminary to self-determination. Reconciliation is a process of the state acknowledging colonialism's harm, expressing sorrow and resolving to correct the consequences of injustice and ensure that fairness and respect prevail in future relationships.

The Truth and Reconciliation Commission of Canada (TRC) and New Zealand's treaty settlement process are state attempts at reconciliation. As well as these, the book assesses attempts at reconciliation in Canada and the US and discusses, especially, the TRC's view that the Declaration is an important instrument of reconciliation and essential to the forging of just political relationships between indigenous nations and states and, for indigenous people, relationships within the state itself. Just political relationships require trust and an important measure of the Declaration's value is whether it can be used to promote such relationships. Trust is also preliminary to the conclusion of meaningful treaties between indigenous nations and the state—as indigenous nations in Australia are pursuing.

This book shows the significance of relationships among reconciliation, treaties and trust as preliminary to self-determination. Conversely, when Australia, Canada, New Zealand and the US voted against the Declaration, they reinforced indigenous peoples' mistrust of the state, and it is not yet evident that withdrawing their opposition to the Declaration has made a substantive difference. The relationship between trust and substantive improvement in people's lives is an important one and ultimately the most significant measure of the substance of the right to self-determination and of the Declaration's practical value. Therefore, this book examines why mistrust occurs and the Declaration's potential responses in helping to create societies where indigenous people may exercise meaningful self-determination through differentiated citizenship. The book shows how and why this is an ambitious aspiration that many indigenous peoples do not expect to succeed, but it also shows how and why it is an important goal in relation to the objectives and possibilities of self-determination.

Structure

Chapter 1 shows that the Declaration works against exclusive state sovereignty. This is because political agency should belong to indigenous peoples as much as it belongs to anyone else. There are rights of prior occupancy that indigenous peoples are entitled to retain and which distinguish indigenous claims from those of ethnic minorities as well as from the claims of the materially poor. The Declaration sets out the ways in which these claims can be admitted within the liberal democratic presumptions of the state. Chapter 1 is not an apology for the Declaration; rather, its purpose is to show how, according to the Declaration, liberal democracy can work better. Subsequent chapters critique that capacity.

The Declaration rationalises a liberal theory of indigeneity by proposing a reconsideration of citizenship, democracy, self-determination and sovereignty. It shows that, while these are often conceptualised in ways that exclude indigenous people and perspectives, exclusivity is a political choice rather than an inevitable outcome of the prevailing liberal order. Chapter 2 shows that integrating the Declaration's principles into a liberal theory of indigeneity creates political space for noncolonial political relationships for indigenous people both within the state as substantively equal citizens *and* beyond the state as members of self-determining indigenous communities.

Self-determination is a goal that ultimately presupposes reconciliation between indigenous peoples and the noncolonial state. It is a goal that is not yet realised in the liberal jurisdictions of Australia, Canada, New Zealand and the US, but one that is actively pursued through the Declaration setting out how self-determination might work in practice according to the liberal principles and presumptions that prevail in those jurisdictions. Consequently, while the Declaration does not restore indigenous political authority, it nevertheless demonstrates how the aspiration of self-determination is a reasonable, if contested, liberal claim. Chapter 3 shows how and why self-determination was contested by the four states who voted against the Declaration before 'reading down' its significance and giving it qualified support. It responds to these objections and introduces examples of liberal democratic inclusion.

As an example of the practical tension between the politics of inclusion and exclusion, Chapter 4 considers the Declaration's requirement that indigenous peoples' 'free, prior and informed consent' must be obtained before indigenous lands can be used by others for any kind of development, including resource extraction. This was one of the principal reasons for the four states voting against the Declaration. Their stance was justified with reference to an 'us' and 'them' binary in which mining was presented as always and everywhere in the national interest, and always and everywhere opposed by indigenous landowners. Chapter 4 shows that this simplistic yet powerful misrepresentation was used to position indigenous peoples beyond the nation-state and as unconcerned with the national interest. It is against this backdrop that the scepticism that some indigenous people hold about the Declaration's political value is discussed, especially the argument that imposing liberal human rights presumptions on nonliberal societies is itself a form of neo-colonial assimilation. While acknowledging the logic of some indigenous people's great suspicion of the liberal state, this book does not accept their arguments, and asks under which circumstances an indigenous person would accept a human right as injurious to their own cultural values.

The chapter argues that indigenous arguments against human rights are often arguments of convenience argued by the more powerful in an indigenous nation to cement their personal status over weaker members of the nation, most commonly women and children. The chapter's contrasting position is to accept the idea that self-determination belongs equally to *all* indigenous persons.

Chapter 5 argues that self-determination cannot occur to its fullest potential without indigenous people claiming the dual and differentiated citizenship of both the state *and* the indigenous nation. It introduces the idea of self-determination requiring substantive indigenous participation in a shared public sovereignty. The Declaration provides a framework for identifying the institutional arrangements that need to be made for this kind of substantive self-determination to occur. Chapter 5 considers self-determination's character and purpose. It considers the ways in which the claim to self-determination supports policy aspirations and possibilities across jurisdictions and policy domains and shows how and why self-determination may be thought about not simply as a body of rights but as a body of transformative political capacities.

Chapter 6 examines how the Declaration is understood in other states and considers its interpretation by jurisdictions as diverse as Belize, Bolivia, China, Finland, Denmark, Ecuador, Fiji, Norway, Malaysia and Sweden, all of which voted for its adoption. The Russian Federation, which abstained from the vote, is also considered. The chapter shows that, while cultural rights are generally accepted, the principle of free, prior and informed consent to outsiders' commercial activity on indigenous lands is not. The tension between state and indigenous perspectives supports the rethinking of sovereignty, citizenship and democracy that this book provides.

The comparative focus of Chapter 6 highlights the existence of a range of interpretations of self-determination and definitions of what it means to be indigenous. For substantive and meaningful self-determination, the concept must be acknowledged as a right that allows indigenous people to determine their own affairs and allows their participation in public affairs as distinctively indigenous citizens. Like the role of sustained cultural relationships to land, such considerations are essential to defining indigeneity and creating meaningful political relationships. The chapter shows why defining indigenous peoples as 'dominated' or 'minority' populations privileges politics and demography over culture as the principal determinant of what it means to be indigenous. Making domination a condition of indigeneity excludes the indigenous peoples of Fiji, for example, from the Declaration's protections. This is significant because, although their majority population status is restored, colonial legacy remains an influence on contemporary politics, and indigenous claims to language, culture, land and to economic rights remain insecure. In this case, majority population status is not, from their own perspectives, the indigenous peoples' principal defining characteristic.

Chapter 7 considers the relationship between self-determination and sovereignty. It argues that self-determination requires a kind of liberal public sovereignty that is different from that often assumed in New Zealand, where the domain of the 'Crown-in-Parliament' is always in conflict with *rangatiratanga*, the Maori chiefly authority claimed as an extant right of prior occupancy.

The chapter introduces what it means for the Waitangi Tribunal, a judicial body concerned with the Treaty of Waitangi, to find that in signing the treaty, Maori did not cede their sovereignty to the British Crown. This is an important point, for if sovereignty remains with indigenous peoples, its contemporary character, and whether and how the authority it embodies is relative and relational to other sites of public power, can be explored.

Sovereignty is more complex than an absolute political authority once held by indigenous peoples, taken by the colonial state and reclaimed as the subject of contemporary indigenous politics. Examples from Australia and the US are also used to illustrate these complexities and to show that the Declaration makes presumptions about the nature and location of political power and provides ways of bringing distinctive indigenous authority into the national body politic. Sovereignty can then be understood as an authority *of* the people—not *over* the people. Indigenous peoples must logically and justly be part of that public sovereignty. Therefore, this book develops the idea of dual spaces of citizenship into a theory and practice of differentiated liberal citizenship, which is both consistent with the liberal democratic political organisation of the dissenting states and a defensible framework for giving effect to the Declaration.

Differentiated liberal citizenship, supported by the Declaration, proceeds from shared sovereignty and provides inclusive answers to the question of who belongs to the postsettler liberal state and on whose terms. Differentiated liberal citizenship allows indigenous peoples to reject colonial victimhood and exercise political authority in ways that are distinctive but equal to that reasonably claimed by other citizens. It presumes participatory parity in public affairs; that is, the idea that all people have the right to make important contributions to public debate and to deliberate and share in the formation of public values.

Chapter 8 shows that liberal democracy's capacity for assimilation does not reflect the ways that this system of political organisation must necessarily or logically function. Instead, liberal democracy has the capacity to allow indigenous people to participate equally and distinctively in the affairs of the states that have emerged over their territories. The chapter examines this capacity through theories of participatory parity and public reason that, ideally, allow all citizens to see that their ability to influence public decision making is fair and reasonable because it is equivalent to the capacity for influence that all citizens enjoy. For indigenous peoples, it is equivalent because, among other considerations, capacity is accepted as occurring with reference to cultural priorities and in response to aspirations for noncolonial political practices and relationships. Although the Declaration is not a panacea for the full restoration of indigenous nationhood, it raises liberal possibilities that are worth pursuing for their potential to make self-determination an aspiration of substantive value through differentiated citizenship. At the same time, as Chapter 9 explains, there are well-developed indigenous objections to differentiated citizenship.

Chapter 9 uses a report commissioned by the New Zealand Iwi (Tribal) Chairs Forum to demonstrate how much is given away when a politics of self-determination through separation from the state is proposed. The report, *He whakairo here whakaumu mō Aotearoa*, recommended a constitutional order that maintained rigid distinctions between Maori and Crown authority which are referred to, with reference to the Treaty of Waitangi, as *rangatiratanga* and *kāwanatanga*, respectively. In the report, *rangatiratanga* was depicted as belonging to Maori (i.e. 'us') and *kāwanatanga* to the Crown (i.e. 'them'). Conflated with New Zealanders of Anglo-Celtic descent (i.e. Pakeha citizens) the Crown was thus given an ethnic character that made it the site of only some citizens' political authority.

Rangatiratanga's purpose, among others, is to constrain sovereignty. However, if sovereignty is understood as the people's political authority exercised by, but not belonging inherently to, the 'Crown-in-Parliament', then *rangatiratanga* is part of the sovereign. Thus, rather than constraining sovereignty, it helps to shape it. Understood in these terms, *rangatiratanga* becomes an example of a collective indigenous voice influencing public authority, reflecting the argument that everybody has the right to help determine the political values of the state. At the same time, indigenous people retain the capacity to govern their distinctive affairs in their own ways through their own institutions. Further, they have an inclusive citizenship in which indigenous political authority is independent in one sphere and shared in another; sovereignty is a collective power, and self-determination is a meaningful concept belonging simultaneously to individual citizens and to indigenous nations as an extant power of prior occupancy. The Declaration's ultimate value is that it supports these aspirations as liberal politics. The chapter uses examples from Australia, Canada and New Zealand to examine contemporary attempts at inclusive liberal politics and discusses, theoretically and practically, what these attempts mean and why they are more likely than isolationist approaches to self-determination to contribute to greater indigenous political authority and capacities of citizenship.

1

The Declaration on the Rights of Indigenous Peoples

[There is a] profound question of whether a State built upon the taking of another people's lands, lives and power can ever really be just. (Matike Mai Aotearoa, 2016, p. 29)

Introduction

It may be true that a state built on taking another's lands can never be just. Neither constitutions nor politics can guarantee that justice has pervasive influence. Yet injustice may be mitigated, and there may be broad principles of justice to inform the development of nondominant and noncolonial political relationships that are, pragmatically, worth indigenous people pursuing. Such principles are imbued in the Declaration—an instrument that takes international human rights discourse beyond the individual to the collective. The Declaration's 'essential novelty' (Wiessner, 2009, p. 4) is that it makes collective rights 'indispensable' (p. 41) and an essential consideration for indigenous political capacity. It therefore shows why it is unjust to think about indigenous rights as simply a subset of general ethnic minority rights. The conflation of indigenous claims with those of migrant ethnic minority populations undermines the right to self-determination. It overlooks the distinctiveness of indigenous claims, including that their source is in relation to land and culture. They may be shaped by colonial histories and political disadvantage and may be compounded by minority population status, but these are not indigeneity's defining characteristics.

The Declaration enunciates political capacities belonging to indigenous nations that are grounded in prior occupancy. Relationships to defined territories thus provide an important distinction with the rights of minorities, and, as this book explains, just terms of association require careful attention to those contexts.

The Declaration precludes an exclusive state sovereignty and gives specific context to general principles of non-discrimination. It requires reimagining the liberal state's form and character and the ways that it manages political relationships. In showing that democratic exclusion is not liberalism's inevitable or necessary form, the Declaration responds to the maldistribution of political authority rather than simply the egalitarian concerns of the indigenous poor.

The Declaration imagines forms of self-determination grounded in substantive indigenous agency—the political capacity to realise rights grounded in prior occupancy. However, its enduring value, like that of the Treaty of Waitangi in New Zealand, is its capacity to support just terms of association between indigenous nations and the liberal state. It supports these terms of association by acknowledging that indigenous peoples rightly exercise the capacities of citizenship *as* indigenous. This could mean having a distinctive voice within the political system, the right to learn at school in cultural context or to influence the provision of health services with reference to cultural imperatives, among other such rights.

This chapter argues that the Declaration's value in contemporary liberal states, like those that dissented from the Declaration's adoption, lies not only in its challenge to prevailing political values and institutions but also, and ultimately, in its potential to remake public institutions in ways that create scope for substantive indigenous agency. The limits and moral shortcomings of the Declaration are examined from both state and indigenous perspectives in later chapters. This chapter's purpose is to introduce the possibilities that the Declaration raises for a more inclusive state. Those possibilities are usefully assessed in relation to a liberal theory of indigeneity that finds practical expression in differentiated liberal citizenship. A liberal theory of indigeneity may, if societies wish, provide ways of thinking inclusively about citizenship, sovereignty and democracy. One of this book's recurring observations is that reconsidering these concepts allows indigenous politics to think beyond an exclusive non-indigenous state or Crown as the sole or inevitable repository of public authority.

Indigenous Peoples and the Liberal Paradigm

Moreton-Robinson (2003, 2004) and Watson and Venne (2012) have shown why indigenous peoples do not routinely look to the liberal paradigm to address collective claims. However, a distinctive liberal theory of indigeneity can be read into the Declaration. That theory shows that the restrictive practices that these Indigenous Australian scholars identify are not essential to liberal philosophy. They are practices that can be challenged to provide a philosophical path beyond the 'framework of liberal individualism versus corporatism' (Holder & Corntassel, 2002, p. 127): a framework that limits indigenous peoples' full enjoyment of their universal human rights as indigenous peoples. It is at least partly to these ends that the Declaration sets out new possibilities for relational justice. For example, the Canadian Assembly of First Nations (2017) pursued relational justice with the state by establishing principles to guide political relationships and by providing 'ways to measure and assess [how] states are respecting and implementing the rights of indigenous peoples' (para. 1). The reports of UN special rapporteurs on the rights of indigenous peoples, and country and nongovernment organisation reports to UN bodies, such as the Committee on the Elimination of Racial Discrimination, inform such efforts, which may, over time, enable the Declaration to acquire persuasive value in domestic legal proceedings, as discussed in Chapter 3.

Meanwhile, Carroll (2012) has argued that the Declaration 'presented the global state community with a political litmus test that exposed … the unique relationships between indigenous peoples and the states into which they have found themselves subsumed' (p. 143). Self-determination requires that these unique relationships must be developed to privilege indigenous political agency meaning that, in turn, Holder and Corntassel (2002, p. 141) err in referring to settler states as the 'host states' of indigenous peoples who occupy the same territories. In using the concept of 'host', Holder and Corntassel (2002) position indigenous peoples as the 'other'—as beyond the state and therefore beyond the legal entity whose decisions materially influence their capacities for self-determination.

The term 'host' implies a voluntarily accepted relationship. One is only 'hosted' if one so chooses. Agency requires a different approach—one of genuine democratic inclusivity broadly accepted by indigenous peoples. It is to support aspirations for democratic inclusivity that one of this book's principal aims is to contest the legitimacy of the idea that:

> The formal theory of the unitary and exclusive sovereignty of the Crown-in-Parliament has endured as a vestigial orthodoxy, relatively unperturbed by theories denying the Crown's unitary character or its formal supremacy. (Kingsbury, 2002, p. 119)

In New Zealand, this understanding of sovereignty informs a common Maori acceptance of a Crown–Maori, 'them' and 'us', binary, the implications of which are systematically discussed in Chapter 9 (see also O'Sullivan, 2007). This book draws an alternative and liberal political framework from the Declaration to transcend that binary. It does so by acknowledging that the Declaration provides for more inclusive conceptions of sovereignty, citizenship and democracy, which then makes it realistic to contemplate an alternative view of Crown sovereignty where the Crown is:

> an inclusive institution [that] forges a sense of the population as bound together in a common enterprise. The Crown, as a mediating institution, is the addressee of demands and complaints made by different groups, enabling the country to avoid a dangerously ethnicised politics in which Maori and non-Maori confront each other directly and repeatedly. (Kingsbury, 2002, p. 119)

A liberal theory of indigeneity is a theory of autonomy, but as a theory concerned with democratic inclusivity, it also aims to minimise the circumstances under which confrontation is likely to occur. It describes the conditions under which indigenous peoples might acquire maximum independence and authority *within* the state, while retaining the attributes of independent authority in and over their own affairs. Citizenship must then be understood as embodying a set of political capacities that belong not just to individuals but also to indigenous nations. A liberal theory of indigeneity is concerned with the state's political character. This is a wider and deeper concern than governments simply acting fairly or determining a 'special duty' owed to indigenous people. Rather, it describes the political conditions under which indigenous peoples might do justice to themselves, thereby securing what they owe to themselves as indigenous citizens of an inclusive liberal society. This is important because it provides an indigenous political theory responsive to Benhabib's (1996) questions about democracy's character and what that character might mean for indigenous self-determination:

> Does democracy rest on homogenising models of identity? What does the body of the 'body politic' look like? Can the ideal of universal citizenship accommodate difference? What institutional, cultural, and representational channels are there for the expression of difference? How much difference is compatible with the ideal of the rule of law under fair and equal conditions? (p. 5)

This book examines how the Declaration helps to conceptualise a state in which indigenous people have the same capacities as anyone else to influence the values and purposes that public institutions are developed to serve. It contrasts this inclusive ideal with the philosophical objections to a liberal theory of indigeneity that arise from theories of democratic exclusion. Under these theories, homogeneity is privileged as the democratic ideal. Justice is equated with sameness. The presumption is that culture has no place in the public realm and that substantive claims to restitution or recognition may not be justly entertained. If each person's political rights and obligations are the same, then they are recognisable and exercisable only in the same ways. However, the principle of justice through sameness is incomplete if sameness can obstruct fairness.

If public relationships among citizens are fair, differences in context and aspirations will have been taken into account. Personal liberty makes such differences legitimate. The circumstances that distinguish any person's present are shaped by the past: the consequences of the past endure. If the past includes the subjugation of political authority, just relationships do not simply emerge in the present; they can occur only as the product of considered choices about how people belong to the contemporary state. If all are to belong on equal terms, one has to consider the political capacities that allow equality.

The alternative may be that belonging is 'inextricably tied to white possession' (Moreton-Robinson, 2003, p. 137), which becomes the 'definitive marker of citizenship' (Moreton-Robinson, 2004, p. 79). It is then an oversimplification of indigenous political experience and expectation to argue that:

> the general duty of a government to do justice to all people is [not] trumped by any special duty it owes to those of the inhabitants who can claim indigenous descent. (Waldron, 2003, p. 30)

What is needed is a political order that allows all people to exercise the rights and obligations of humanity in ways that are personally meaningful, an objective that is reflected in the Declaration itself:

1. Indigenous individuals and peoples have the right to enjoy fully all rights established under applicable international and domestic labour law.

2. States shall in consultation and cooperation with indigenous peoples take specific measures to protect indigenous children from economic exploitation and from performing any work that is likely to be hazardous or to interfere with the child's education, or to be harmful to the child's health or physical, mental, spiritual, moral or social development, taking into account their special vulnerability and the importance of education for their empowerment.

3. Indigenous individuals have the right not to be subjected to any discriminatory conditions of labour and, inter alia, employment or salary. (UN, 2007b, art. 17)

In Australia, for example, respect for these human rights would have prevented policies separating Indigenous children from their families, prevented land alienation, ensured education and health care equivalent to that available to other members of the community, prevented discrimination in criminal justice and the labour market, precluded the closure of remote Indigenous communities, prevented the Western Australian Government's refusal to engage with Indigenous communities in reaching policy decisions in this context and made the Northern Territory Emergency Response ('the Intervention') impossible.[1] Instead, and as subsequent chapters discuss, the Declaration supports an indigenous political focus on good health, education, housing, employment and land rights; affirms the negotiation of treaties to mark formal recognition of indigenous people's prior occupancy; and shows how human rights may have prevented colonisation, a process that undermines the political rights of *all* indigenous people, not just the material claims of the indigenous poor.

---

1   The Intervention was an 'emergency' policy response to alleged widespread sexual abuse of children in the Northern Territory, Australia, in 2007. There was no indigenous participation in developing the policy response, which required the suspension of the Commonwealth *Racial Discrimination Act 1975*.

Prioritising concern for the indigenous poor reflects a kind of distributive justice that separates individual liberty from the cultural contexts and collective environments in which people actually live. Material disadvantage is a public policy outcome; it is not in itself the source of indigenous claims. Indigenous people might be interested in class politics, but indigeneity is a different politics concerned with the maldistribution of political authority. Indigenous peoples' conscious democratic exclusion arises from 'institutionalised patterns of cultural value' (Fraser, as cited in Fraser & Honneth, 2003, p. 30) that are not indigenous and that indigenous people may not have sufficient democratic opportunities to contest.

Exclusion contributes to policy failure (Banks, 2007), which is often explained by a 'power narrative' (Altman, 2009, p. 43) of indigenous inadequacy—specifically, the failings of culture and of personal responsibility. By contrast, democratic inclusion might occur through what Hunt and Blackman (2009) call 'active and informed participation', resulting in both 'non-discrimination' and 'cultural acceptability' in policy outcomes (p. 9). This objective is beyond the concerns of liberal egalitarianism.

Beyond Liberal Egalitarianism

Liberal egalitarianism is concerned with poverty alleviation through the fair distribution of material resources. However, egalitarian justice is not equipped to consider claims to culture, language, collective resource ownership, substantive political authority or just terms of association. These essential constituents of a liberal theory of indigeneity explain the limits of undifferentiated liberal citizenship. Instead, the Declaration maintains that:

1. Indigenous peoples have the right to practice and revitalize their cultural traditions and customs. This includes the right to maintain, protect and develop the past, present and future manifestations of their cultures, such as archaeological and historical sites, artefacts, designs, ceremonies, technologies and visual and performing arts and literature.

2. States shall provide redress through effective mechanisms, which may include restitution, developed in conjunction with indigenous peoples, with respect to their cultural, intellectual, religious and spiritual property taken without their free, prior and informed consent or in violation of their laws, traditions and customs. (UN, 2007b, art. 11)

A liberal theory of indigeneity develops these rights not as claims to privilege over others or a 'birthright to the upper hand' (Brash, 2004, para. 7), but as claims to relational justice within the sovereign citizenry. Whatever its form, sovereignty ought to serve all citizens equally, including those for whom an indigenous collective identity is important. It should not 'reproduce a space for politics that is enabled by and rests upon the production, naturalization and maginalization of certain forms of "difference"' (Shaw, 2008, p. 9), but should be stable, clear, ordered and obviously inclusive. These are determinants of the political space that is required for the right to self-determination to have practical meaning and improve the lives of indigenous peoples—determinants of a political space where public sovereignty is shared.

Sharing public sovereignty means that public institutions should not be 'theirs', as in an 'us' and 'them' binary, but should reflect all people's right to contribute to the formation of public values and the ways in which public institutions work. If, as Benhabib (1996) argued, the 'claims of culture' are limited by their consistency with prevailing norms and values, then indigenous peoples must enjoy meaningful opportunities to shape those norms and values. This is the assumption of New Zealand's Te Kotahitanga research and professional development program for school teachers (see Chapter 5), which seeks to ensure that Maori achievements at school are not dependent on their putting their own values and ways of life to one side. Te Kotahitanga's underlying pedagogic principle is that Maori should be able to bring their culture into the classroom and that culture should not be an impediment to success (Bishop, O'Sullivan & Berryman, 2010). This acknowledges the reality that, when people claim membership of a group:

> What they are saying … is not just that they are strongly attached
> to this spiritual view or background; rather it is that this provides
> the frame within which they can determine where they stand on
> questions of what is good. (Taylor, 1989, p. 27)

Culture helps to frame people's expectations of citizenship, including schooling and, more broadly, of what it means to be a free and politically equal person. Given culture's political importance, it is idealistic to argue that, for the resolution of conflict, 'there must be some standard by which to determine the goodness or badness' of competing claims, and that 'whatever that standard is, there can be but one' (Mill, 1843, p. 951).

Instead, the Declaration provides an international standard for assessing indigenous claims as distinctive claims, and for assessing the counterclaims of the state.

The Declaration precludes indigenous people—and by extension their cultures—from deliberate and systematic exclusion from substantive citizenship. While it does not prescribe the form that indigenous inclusion should take, the presumption that inclusion should always and everywhere occur if that is the indigenous wish is significant.

Admitting indigenous ways of being human into state law complements the native Canadian argument that the Declaration imposes a responsibility to 'live up to the concept of being a self-determining human … it is a new way to reform and empower our traditions and versions of humanities' (Henderson, 2017, p. 13).

Self-determination is present when 'responsibility-based' (Corntassel, 2008, p. 123) movements reflect self-determination as a body of political capacities and not simply a body of rights. In this way, self-determination 'de-center[s] the state from discussions of indigenous political, social, economic, and cultural mobilization' (Corntassel, 2008, p. 123). Self-determination is then a reflection of political space; specifically, the space 'to function well if one so chooses' (Nussbaum, 1987, p. 20) and in ways that are personally meaningful. This book shows, in the discussions that follow, that these aspirations are reasonable and realisable because 'discourses of difference … are part of the liberal tradition' (Little, 2003, p. 25). In particular, indigenous values and political processes should influence the conduct of public affairs.

Rather than be subservient to those of the state, indigenous political philosophies should legitimately influence public affairs so that space is created 'for [indigenous] right[s] to be distinct, on [their] own path, and free from interference' (Garrow, 2012, p. 182). This argument rationalises differentiated liberal citizenship's concern for protecting language and culture in public institutions *and* in traditional spheres. However, the right to self-determination cannot be limited to matters of culture, for culture is maintained only by economic security and substantive participation at all levels of the political process. Substantive political participation is both 'instrumental and constitutive' (Ruger, 2006, p. 298) of a fair policy process, including economic policies that are conducive to indigenous economic security. This is democratically important because 'at the core of the modern liberal democratic project ... [is] the capability of persons to determine and justify their own actions' (Held, 1995, p. 149).

In jurisdictions like Canada and New Zealand, inclusion remains contested. However, in Australia, inclusion is a new and radical proposition. In 2017, the UN special rapporteur criticised the Australian Government's Indigenous Advancement Strategy's shifting of service delivery contracts away from Indigenous providers as well as its reduced budget for Indigenous policy programs (UN, 2017b). The government defended the Indigenous Advancement Strategy (UN, 2017a) even though its own audit office found wider problems remained in its administration. The audit office report provides a brief but instructive insight into the nature of indigenous public policy failure:

> The implementation of the Strategy occurred in a short timeframe and this affected the department [of the Prime Minister and Cabinet]'s ability to establish transitional arrangements and structures that focused on prioritising the needs of Indigenous communities. (Australian National Audit Office, 2017, p. 8)

The audit office also found that:

> The department's grants administration processes fell short of the standard required to effectively manage a billion dollars of Commonwealth resources. The basis by which projects were recommended to the Minister was not clear and, as a result, limited assurance is available that the projects funded support the department's desired outcomes. Further, the department did not:
> - assess applications in a manner that was consistent with the guidelines and the department's public statements;
> - meet some of its obligations under the Commonwealth Grants Rules and Guidelines;
> - keep records of key decision; or
> - establish performance targets for all funded projects. (Australian National Audit Office, 2017, p. 8)

The report showed that the conditions for informed policy could not be presumed:

> The performance framework and measures established for the Strategy do not provide sufficient information to make assessments about program performance and progress towards achievement

of the program outcomes. The monitoring systems inhibit the department's ability to effectively verify, analyse or report on program performance. The department has commenced some evaluations of individual projects delivered under the Strategy but has not planned its evaluation approach after 2016–17. (Australian National Audit Office, 2017, p. 8)

In 2018, the Department of the Prime Minister and Cabinet released an *Annual Evaluation Work Plan* for the Indigenous Advancement Strategy. Greater attention was to be paid to ensuring indigenous engagement in implementing the strategy and to what was known about what actually works in indigenous policy—there was to be 'a culture of evidence-based thinking and practice' (Commonwealth of Australia, Department of the Prime Minister and Cabinet, 2018a, p. 1).

Implementing a regime in which effective policy is routinely and systematically supported by widely accepted knowledge of what works represents a significant procedural shift in Australian indigenous public policymaking. For example, the causes of preventable premature indigenous deaths are well known and the relative importance of each cause has been identified and provides policy direction in the development of solutions (O'Sullivan, 2015), yet budgetary allocations to supportive measures have been reduced (UN, 2017a).

According to Vos, Barker, Begg, Stanley and Lopez (2009), 11 risk factors explain the life expectancy differential of Australia's Indigenous people: 'tobacco, alcohol, illicit drugs, high body mass, inadequate physical activity, low intake of fruit and vegetables, high blood pressure, high cholesterol, unsafe sex, child sexual abuse and intimate partner violence' (p. 474). Another risk factor, which is consistent with surveys showing that up to 79 per cent of Indigenous Australians have experienced racism in the health system (Paradies, 2006), is people's reluctance to seek medical advice. One South Australian hospital worker told Dwyer et al. (2011) that:

> We're seeing people here who actually haven't accessed the system so their cancers are very, very advanced. We've seen [Aboriginal people] who have got... major carcinoma that's disfiguring, just distorting their body shape... so they've obviously been in pain ... for a long time and that suggests to me that... they're reluctant or reticent or unable to access systems for whatever reason. (quotation is as it appears in the source, p. 18)

One response may be to admit, systematically, that there is a right to *be* indigenous when one goes to hospital—to admit that there is a right to culture—which requires indigenous participation in decisions about how health systems operate and who works in them. This is because health outcomes are not the product of clinical competence alone. They are influenced by health workers' philosophical dispositions towards providing equally effective care to indigenous patients (O'Sullivan, 2015). The marked presence of racism in the health system indicates that effective and culturally respectful care is not always the indigenous experience. Efficacious health care may, then, require fundamental political equality.

Towards Political Equality

The Declaration is not concerned with special rights but with the codification of liberal democratic rights in historical, political and cultural context. It is 'one law for all' grounded in human equality and cognisant of culture's unavoidable centrality to equality. However, the Declaration is not a panacea for achieving just terms of association. Its limits occur because power is not absolute. For example, the Declaration will not absolutely 'assimilate the colonizer into Aboriginal processes of power-sharing', as Watson and Venne (2012, p. 89) desire, yet implementing the Declaration does presume meaningful political recognition, especially—and most importantly—of the right to exercise citizenship in a differentiated form. The Declaration makes this possible by establishing that indigenous persons are 'peoples' and thus entitled to collective recognition (UN, 2007b).

The rights that the Declaration enunciates are grounded in internationally established norms of human equality. They give human rights a collective character that challenges their traditional understanding as belonging only to the individual. Inclusive group rights allow indigenous peoples to reconceptualise their view of the contemporary state not as a *Leviathan*-like entity but as a body structured, in part, on a liberal theory of indigeneity in which *all*, and not just *some*, people share sovereign public authority (O'Sullivan, 2014).

In this way, the Declaration raises the aspirations of indigenous peoples and states alike. For example, it represents the international community's rejection of terra nullius, which presumed that indigenous societies lacked the institutional, intellectual and social capacity for nationhood. In Australia, this rejection had allowed Justice Brennan to propose, in his *Mabo v Queensland [No. 2]* (1992) judgment, that:

> It is contrary both to international standards and to the fundamental values of our common law to entrench a discrimination rule which, because of the supposed position on the scale of social organisation of the Indigenous inhabitants of a said colony, denies them a right to occupy their traditional lands. (para. 42)

The Declaration also rejects the proposition 'that settlers are citizens because they possess what Indians lack: the capacities for rational self-government and legal institutions of private property, both of which define legal personhood' (Dahl, 2016, p. 17). Dahl continued:

> Insofar as citizenship is legally 'defined through the natural right to own property' and rests on the self-ownership of the possessive individual, Indians negatively define settler citizenship by representing the negation of the proprietary self in the absence of dominant conceptions of private property. To the extent that American democracy depends on the propertied independence of citizens, the enclosure of land in private property mirrors the enclosure of settler sovereignty, both of which enact the exclusion of Indians from citizenship. In highlighting the constitutive exclusions of settler democracy, Indian nullification operates less as an institutional feature of constitutional design than as a rhetorical mode that captures the foundational division of settler democracy, the structuring of citizenship along a settler-indigene divide. (Dahl, 2016, p. 17)

Its inclusive emphasis means that, even as an aspirational document (as opposed to an instrument of customary international law), the Declaration is politically and morally valuable. As well as challenging state hegemony over indigenous peoples, it challenges state dominance of international relations and reshapes the ways in which one is able to think about the possibilities and scope of international law and politics. As Mazzuoli and Ribeiro (2015) asserted, this is because human rights 'change the hermeneutics of international law' (p. 1713). Taking this argument further, Patton (2005) argued that:

> Against the background of a more comprehensive understanding of the nature and effects of colonial administration, reparation might be described simply as an attempt to constitute a moral and political community where before there was none. (p. 265)

The idea of a 'moral and political community' is differentiated liberal citizenship's ultimate purpose.

Differentiated citizenship is the condition that the Declaration may create—a condition that allows the politics of indigeneity to test the substantive and practical value of the ways in which liberal democracies work. The Declaration is a robust and considered framework for thinking about the character of differentiated citizenship, the political cultures it might require and the values that it might assume.

The Declaration takes the terms of indigenous peoples' relationships *with* and *within* states beyond the realm of domestic law. Its principles endure the vicissitudes of domestic politics and prejudices of local laws and public policies. Under international human rights law, states do not have unconstrained authority. State institutions lie between the constraints of domestic politics and international law—they are bodies that sometimes exist in a state of philosophical conflict over the merits of self-determination. In providing a measure for the international evaluation of domestic policy principles, the Declaration provides a way through this conflict.

The Declaration confirmed *all* indigenous peoples' place in international law. In doing so, it tried to make indigenous peoples 'subjects rather than objects of international law' (Schulte-Tenckhoff, 2012, p. 76). The effect was to reconceptualise debates about the right to self-determination: to whom did it belong, how might it be exercised and why? The Declaration's extension of the right to self-determination to groups as well as individuals is highly significant for indigenous groups because they have the characteristics of peoplehood: common ancestry, common culture and sustained geopolitical attachments to the same place. This allows a people to organise itself politically in subnational forms, as explained in the Declaration:

> States shall consult and cooperate in good faith with the indigenous peoples concerned through their own representative institutions in order to obtain their free, prior and informed consent before adopting and implementing legislative or administrative measures that may affect them. (UN, 2007b, art. 19)

The Declaration presumes that indigenous rights proceed from an overarching right to self-determination, belonging equally to men and women (UN, 2007b, art. 44), and 'should be interpreted in accordance with the principles of justice, democracy, respect for human rights, equality, non-discrimination, good governance and good faith' (art. 46[3]). It proposes that the specific rights of women are matters of concern for both states and indigenous nations and makes no distinction between people residing within tribal boundaries and diaspora populations. The right to self-determination is held equally by all indigenous people; the right to belong to one's indigenous community privileges culture over blood quantum.

The Declaration seeks to diminish the state's constraining influence by simultaneously strengthening indigenous nations and ensuring substantive indigenous inclusion in the public life of the state. It promotes indigenous political authority beyond the state through indigenous political institutions, which weakens the state by increasing indigenous entities' relative power. Conversely, the Declaration proposes an inclusive democratic state in which indigenous peoples are guaranteed a substantive voice that, though it serves the state's integrative function, is not assimilationist but, rather, balances the state's authority with the explicit expectation that indigenous peoples can enjoy national citizenship in distinctive ways. This has major implications for democracy and the meaning of indigenous belonging to the state.

The Declaration's challenge to liberal theories of 'belonging' is a 'serious conceptual one' (Gover, 2015, p. 349). It allows indigenous peoples to assert a culturally contextualised and politically independent belonging to the state. Henderson (2008) described the politics surrounding the Declaration as:

> a cognitive struggle, a challenge to existing ways of thinking about humanity. It was a manifestation of *shared persuasion* [emphasis added]. The new emergent consciousness displaces the old discriminatory models of imperialism and colonialism based on racism. (p. 10)

Though nonbinding, the Declaration is a document of 'considerable moral import' (Belanger, 2010, p. 2). Binding status may eventually be acquired through its persuasive legal influence and practical influence as an instrument for public advocacy (Wiessner, 2009). In the meantime, the politics that might be drawn from it should be understood as significant rather than revolutionary—a politics responding to a 'distinctive settler-state political theory' that 'usefully show[s] where existing liberal democratic theories, including those underpinning human rights

43

frameworks, "run out" and must be adapted to the particular circumstances of settler societies' (Gover, 2015, p. 348). The Declaration shows how such adaptation is possible and why it contributes to an indigenous politics of liberal possibility and indigeneity. According to Anaya (2010):

> the Declaration has a significant normative weight grounded in its high degree of legitimacy ... a function not only of not only the fact that it has been formally endorsed by an overwhelming majority of UN Member States, but also the fact that it is the product of years of advocacy and struggle by indigenous peoples themselves ... The norms of the Declaration substantially reflect indigenous peoples' own aspirations, which after years of deliberation have come to be accepted by the international community. (para. 5)

Liberal Inclusivity

Rawls (1999) has argued that a complete 'conception of justice' is one that is 'able to order all the claims that can arise' (p. 115). However, it is often a self-serving desire to exclude based on the presumption of inherent superiority that encourages non-indigenous people to imagine that indigenous claims might affront what they are themselves owed in justice. For indigenous peoples, the state is an imposed institution of extraordinary coercive power. It is real, omnipresent and constraining. However, it is not fixed or constant in the functions it maintains nor in its distribution of power; it need not perpetually include or exclude the same people. Liberal theory can, but need not, assume that a majority is always and everywhere 'more likely to be substantively right than a minority' (Mansbridge, 1996, p. 57).

Liberal theory accepts that a decision is neither just nor efficacious simply because it is the majority position. The political process is not an end in itself, for its underlying values influence the fairness of its outcomes. The Declaration presumes that the state must include indigenous peoples who will, as a matter of course, influence the terms of their inclusion. Further, the Declaration recognises and affirms that:

> indigenous individuals are entitled without discrimination to all human rights recognized in international law, and that indigenous peoples possess collective rights which are indispensable for their existence, well-being and integral development as peoples. (UN, 2007b, annex)

The Declaration assumes that liberal democracy can provide a political framework responsive to indigenous needs, rights and aspirations including, especially, a broad and comprehensive right to self-determination. From this perspective, the state need not be a 'message of domination—an ideological artefact attributing unity, structure, and independence to the disunited, structureless and dependent workings of the practice of government' (Abrams, 2006, p. 97). Instead, the state's coercive capacity may be directed towards indigenous good. The state can sometimes rise above the constraints that popular prejudice might otherwise impose. For example, while there is deep-seated public prejudice against settlements for Crown breaches of the Treaty of Waitangi and against the treaty's policy influence, sustained leadership from both sides of the New Zealand Parliament has moderated this resistance.

In New Zealand today, it is unlikely that treaty settlements and guaranteed Maori seats in parliament would receive support in a popular vote. Similarly, Canada's TRC, and Australia's Human Rights and Equal Opportunity Commission's National Inquiry into the Separation of Aboriginal and Torres Strait Islander Children from Their Families, would not have occurred without the state confronting popular prejudice. However, these examples do not diminish the case for a more transformative politics to give postsettler states a secure and inclusive structure that recognises that indigenous peoples are entitled to occupy distinct political spaces within the liberal state. The claim of Indigenous Australians to a constitutionally guaranteed voice in the Australian Parliament is an example, as are claims in New Zealand for better protected independent institutions of Maori political authority. These are discussed in later chapters. In both cases, the possibility of success is enhanced if the proposals are shown as having a liberal justification and the potential to make democracy work better. However, as is also explored in later chapters, making democracy work better is not always an indigenous objective, and other kinds of political relationships may be understood as more consistent with the right to self-determination.

Nevertheless, the Declaration itself presumes that self-determination through differentiated liberal citizenship ought to be structured into domestic political arrangements. This presumption has significant transformative potential. Juxtaposing liberal and indigenous political theories establishes differentiated citizenship as the source of a political language for thinking about and responding to indigenous claims.

The Declaration provides a comprehensive body of political principles to assist in the development and usefulness of that language—a standard of justice against which institutional arrangements can be measured.

The Declaration also provides a set of principles through which a postcolonial politics might recognise that 'Our children should have the opportunity to live more Indigenous lives than we do' (Alfred, as cited in Corntassel, 2012, p. 99). The purpose is to ensure that the indigenous affairs narrative is not one of victimhood, but one that promotes people living in self-defined equality and dignity. In this regard, the 'hard issue' the Declaration may help to address is 'how to articulate local ideas of peoplehoods, on the one hand, with regional or nationwide ideas about citizenship, on the other' (Bowen, 2000, p. 13). The Declaration addresses this issue by showing the depth of liberal democracy's capacity for differentiated inclusion, thereby allowing the expression of civic rights and responsibilities in a culturally preferred manner. Its point of distinction is that it can acknowledge distinctive indigenous participation in public affairs without restricting the liberal rights of others.

The Declaration assists the politics of indigeneity to work out ways of creating 'legitimate authorities—sovereignties—within and across spatial, temporal and discursive conditions that may be at odds with those that have enabled modern state sovereignty' (Shaw, 2008, p. 5). This means that the state alone is precluded from defining political agendas and entitlements. Instead, meaningful public sovereignty is inclusive, contestable and responsive to the geopolitically contextualised experiences of peoples who did not freely agree to the transfer of political authority to settler states. It is responsive to collective rights as constituents of personal liberty.

However, liberal democracy, as it prevails in Australia, Canada, New Zealand and the US, can struggle to see relationships between collective rights and individual liberty—that is, between sociopolitical experience and personal freedom. Liberal democracies can also find it philosophically difficult to acknowledge culture's place in shaping people's experience of liberty: where, how and why liberty exists, and where, how and why it is constrained.

Liberal democracy may not easily admit that liberty makes sense only in cultural context and for culturally framed reasons. However, the Declaration's liberalism is an inclusive one that positions the individual as a bearer of substantive political rights and obligations in common with others. It places the individual in cultural context and gives effect to relationships between personal liberty and the cultural context in which liberty may be defined. Its purpose is to reconfigure the state to ensure that indigenous peoples are part of it, if they wish, and may influence its values, purpose and form.

The political objective is to transform the postsettler states in which indigenous peoples reside such that they lose their colonial character. The presumption is that all people have the right to participate in their government. The state ought not be perpetually the domain of non-indigenous citizens, with indigenous citizens relegated to a less influential indigenous domain. The Declaration's liberal potential is to 'undercut government attempts to assert the moral high ground' and presume 'coercive paternalism' (Dorfmann, 2015, p. 13).

The Declaration provides the liberal political language for indigenous peoples to express their aspirations in ways that are recognisable by the state and consistent with international legal principles. In this way, the Declaration facilitates public reason as an expression of equal capacity for citizenship (discussed in further detail in Chapter 6). The Declaration's liberalism—its assumption that liberty belongs to *all* and not just *some* people and that liberty is realised through both collective *and* individual human rights—is its distinguishing pragmatic value. By such means, it provides a conceptual and practical framework for developing a liberal theory of indigeneity in which indigenous people actively participate in determining the form and purpose of the state.

The Declaration codifies state obligations across policy domains. However, its most important contribution to domestic politics is that it brings philosophical certainty to the question of what it means for an indigenous person to belong to the nation-state. It seeks to ensure that power is distributed in ways that allow the state to become a site in which indigenous self-determination can substantively and systematically displace colonial political relationships. To achieve this, it sets out the attributes of indigenous political authority and its relationships with broader public sovereignty and shows the ways in which public sovereignty is not an unconstrained authority vested only in a non-indigenous government or Crown.

The Declaration does not go so far as to prescribe Watson and Venne's (2012) aspiration for a decolonised political order. It cannot override alternative political values, but it may challenge them. It may support Watson and Venne's (2012) argument that:

> For a real act of decolonization to occur we need to regain an Aboriginal centre – that is, an Aboriginal centre that engages in its own decolonization and repair from the effects of colonialism – and to enable that centre to occupy the spaces of political power, rather than let it become assimilated into colonial processes of power-sharing. (pp. 88–89)

As Corntassel (2012) argued, one must be careful not to accept the 'illusion of inclusion' (p. 92) or complacently accept that the Declaration's possibilities will be realised through state benevolence. Just as some policy actors overstate the capacity of New Zealand's Treaty of Waitangi to prescribe processes and outcomes in all areas of public life (O'Sullivan, 2007, 2008), there may be a propensity to expect more from the Declaration than its scope and content allow. It is important that people do not expect that the UN can 'somehow "gift" rights to indigenous peoples': while indigenous rights instead 'inherently flow from customary rights' (Beatty, 2014, p. 49), they must still be actively sought by indigenous peoples who must be clear about what they want and why.

The Declaration pays special attention to state obligations to indigenous citizens. However, it also allows indigenous peoples to make their own claims over and above the nation-state. It provides authoritative guidance to indigenous peoples on how rights might be asserted in both law and politics. Although recourse to international courts, tribunals and committees may not lead to legally binding rulings, their findings can lend moral authority to arguments for certain claims to be accepted as rights.

The 'interpretive standards' (Trask, 2012, p. 334) that the Declaration provides can be used to develop legal arguments and to assist courts and other bodies to interpret instruments of binding effect. In bringing clarity and coherence to the international legal arrangements that indigenous peoples may use to conceptualise and assert their claims, these have the potential to transform the ways that relational justice and just terms of association are understood. It is also significant that, under the Declaration, indigenous peoples enjoy greater opportunity to have an act or omission of the state declared a contravention of a fundamental right. For example, in 2016, the Australian Capital Territory's *Human Rights Act 2004* was amended to make specific reference to the Declaration:

> Aboriginal and Torres Strait Islander peoples hold distinct cultural rights and must not be denied the right—
>
> a. to maintain, control, protect and develop their—
>
>   i. cultural heritage and distinctive spiritual practices, observances, beliefs and teachings; and
>
>   ii. languages and knowledge; and
>
>   iii. kinship ties; and
>
> b. to have their material and economic relationships with the land and waters and other resources with which they have a connection under traditional laws and customs recognised and valued.
>
> *Note:* The primary source of the rights in [this section] is the United Nations Declaration on the Rights of Indigenous Peoples, art 25 and art 31. (s. 27[2])

Conversely, and significantly, the *Human Rights Act* confined its reference to just two of the Declaration's articles whereas the full substance of the right to self-determination requires regard for the instrument as a whole. In Canada, this was the purpose of legislation, introduced but defeated in parliament, that would have required all Canadian federal legislation to be consistent with the Declaration ('Bill C-262', 2018 [Canada]). If passed, the legislation could have become a blueprint for the Declaration's implementation, not just in Canada but also in jurisdictions like Australia, New Zealand and the US.

Conclusion

The Declaration is potentially transformative. While there remain both state and indigenous objections to the principles it establishes (see Chapters 3 and 4), its drafting by indigenous peoples from all parts of the world gives it significant and distinctive political status. The Declaration positions indigenous peoples' collective interests within international human rights discourses and challenges the nature of state sovereignty. Although it is a liberal document, it enunciates a different kind of liberal democracy to that used by postsettler states like Australia, Canada, the US and New Zealand to exclude indigenous peoples from substantive and equal citizenship. The Declaration provides a framework for rethinking citizenship, democracy, self-determination and sovereignty. It supports, and is supported by, a liberal theory of indigeneity concerned with just terms of association and political relationships of indigenous agency. However, the Declaration is not a panacea for recognising the right to self-determination. It will not restore indigenous political authority to its precolonial form. Instead, it imagines meaningful indigenous political authority inside the state and beyond it in indigenous institutions operating for indigenous purposes and according to indigenous values.

As the following chapter argues, the Declaration enunciates self-determination as the foundational right from which all other indigenous rights proceed. Chapter 2 shows how self-determination, as normative politics, is a necessary outcome of reconciliation. It also shows the significance of political trust to reconciliation and self-determination. Trust requires the substantive political inclusion that the Declaration intends.

2

Reconciliation, Trust and Liberal Inclusion

Introduction

Self-determination presumes the spirit and substance of reconciliation; it supposes trust and political inclusivity. Reconciliation provides a foundation for just terms of association. This foundation involves recognising injustice and taking steps to ensure that it does not recur. Reconciliation is neither simple nor uncontested. For some, it is a necessary condition for just political outcomes; for others, it is shallow symbolism; for others still, it does not propose measures of sufficient substance to transform political relationships in meaningful and far-reaching ways. For its proponents, reconciliation's underlying presumption is that, if the truth is known, and the perpetrators of injustice acknowledge that truth, then societies may correct the consequences of injustice and accept a different kind of politics.

The Declaration may contribute to reconciliation by providing principles to inform a politics of respect including respect for self-determination as a right that belongs to all and not just some. Reconciliation requires relationships of trust, and it requires that indigenous people can find reasons to trust political institutions and systems. Relationships of trust are preliminary to the noncolonial political order that the Declaration seeks. These relationships require that indigenous peoples have the political capacity to influence the cultures, values and operations of public institutions to reflect their own priorities and ways of working. Reconciliation requires substantive indigenous inclusion, participation and meaningful leadership in the policy process.

Treaties are potential instruments of trust, and their contemporary discussion in Australia may draw the relationship between reconciliation and self-determination into public discourse. Conversely, exclusive policy measures, such as the Intervention, along with discriminatory welfare and education policies, position indigenous peoples as opponents in an 'us' and 'them' binary. Democratic exclusion is reconciliation's powerful opposite; it is a philosophy of fundamental political inequality that entrenches mistrust and in turn prevents effective public policy. Reconciliation shows how democratic exclusion can be contested.

Reconciliation

For indigenous politics, reconciliation is the idea that state sorrow and atonement for transgressions of justice provide the foundation for working out new, just and durable terms of association. Reconciliation requires 'awareness of the past, acknowledgement of the harm that has been inflicted, atonement for the causes, and action to change behaviour' (TRC, 2015, pp. 6–7). Although it is acknowledged that 'reconciliation will take some time' to realise (p. vi), the Declaration provides guidance on what reconciliation should achieve for indigenous peoples:

> States shall provide effective mechanisms for prevention of, and redress for:
>
> a. Any action which has the aim or effect of depriving them of their integrity as distinct peoples, or of their cultural values or ethnic identities;
>
> b. Any action which has the aim or effect of dispossessing them of their lands, territories or resources;
>
> c. Any form of forced population transfer which has the aim or effect of violating or undermining any of their rights;
>
> d. Any form of forced assimilation or integration;
>
> e. Any form of propaganda designed to promote or incite racial or ethnic discrimination directed against them. (UN, 2007b, art. 8[2])

Corntassel depicted the process as one of 'forgive and forget' (2012, p. 92).

While reconciliation is not a matter of 'shaming and pointing out wrongdoing' (TRC, 2015, p. vi), forgiveness cannot logically involve forgetting. Instead, the TRC focused on 'truth determination' to 'lay the foundation for the important question of reconciliation' (p. vi).

For the commission, the 'important question' centred on the Indian residential school system established by the state: 'Now that we know about residential schools and their legacy, what do we do about it?' (p. vi).

Reconciliation means that the 'forgiven' party commits to restitutive measures and to relational justice in future encounters. It cannot simply preserve or legitimise the 'status quo', as Corntassel (2012) feared—nor can it occur without reparation nor restitution. Reparation is owed:

> [when] one infringes on [another's] … right to pursue and possess what he values … [unfairly thwarts their] legitimate attempt to do or possess something … [or] makes it impossible for [them] to pursue a legitimate goal, even if [they] never actually attempt to achieve that goal. (Boxill, 1995, p. 110)

From this perspective, the only argument that can be raised against reparation is that the alleged transgression was, in fact, just.

It is premature to accept Wiessner's (2008) argument that the Declaration is a 'milestone of re-empowerment' that may 'reverse colonialism' to make indigenous peoples 'sovereign again, masters of their own fate' (p. 1142). However, the Declaration is potentially an instrument of reconciliation and political clarity about self-determination and its possibilities (O'Sullivan, 2017). The TRC (2015) drew on the Declaration in its account of reconciliation, observing that:

> [Reconciliation] requires that the paternalistic and racist foundations of the residential school system be rejected as the basis for an ongoing relationship … It also requires an understanding that the most harmful aspects of residential schools have been the loss of pride and self-respect of Aboriginal people, and the lack of respect that non-Aboriginal people have been raised to have for their Aboriginal neighbours … Virtually all aspects of Canadian society may need to be reconsidered. (p. vi)

The TRC was preceded by the Royal Commission on Aboriginal Peoples, which proposed reconciliation as a policy aspiration. The royal commission 'opened people's eyes and changed the conversation about the reality for the Aboriginal people in this country' (TRC, 2015, p. 7).

Similar roles were played in Australia by the 1987–1991 Royal Commission into Aboriginal Deaths in Custody and 1995–1997 National Inquiry into the Separation of Aboriginal and Torres Strait Islander Children from Their Families. Along with the 1992 *Mabo* and 1996 *Wik Peoples v Queensland* decisions of the High Court of Australia (see O'Sullivan, 2005), they contributed to the emergence of the 1990s as a decade of significant transformation in Indigenous public policy. The inquiry into the removal of Indigenous children was distinctive because of its recommendation that state, territory and federal parliaments make apologies for the removals (Human Rights and Equal Opportunity Commission, 1997). It focused public consciousness on Indigenous people's place within the national political community. Having played a role in the removals, Christian churches were vocal in their support for reconciliation. For them, secular reconciliation flowed from the concept's foundation in sacramental theology in which broken relationships between God and the penitent were corrected through sorrow, atonement and forgiveness, which was conditional on a demonstrated resolve to desist from further transgressions of justice. However, secular reconciliation's momentum was not sustained beyond the 1990s (O'Sullivan, 2005).

There was, for example, ideological resistance to public sorrow so that, while each of the state parliaments accepted the royal commission's recommendation to pass a motion of apology for the removals, the Commonwealth Parliament did not do the same until 2008. As Ian Anderson (2004) has argued, the Howard Government's (1996–2007) refusal to say 'sorry' reflected the wider contradictions of its indigenous policy:

> Its disavowal of indigenous self-determination rested upon the denial of the ongoing existence of an indigenous polity. In part, this reflected an atomised understanding of society – indigenous people being preferably constructed as a population of individuals rather than socially organised, interconnected groups of families and clans. However, in setting indigenous health and social disadvantage as a policy priority, the neo-liberal state reconstituted the collectivity it sought to deny through the measurement of disadvantage and the development of institutional responses. (Ian Anderson, as cited in Mazel, 2016, p. 20)

The lesson for jurisdictions like Canada was that reconciliation requires a strong and unbreakable connection between sorrow and policy outcomes—between rhetoric and substance. Reconciliation needs to make people's lives better. It imagines significant political transformation, but it is a difficult and ongoing task grounded in relational justice. It is not clear or certain that one can ever say that society is forever 'reconciled'. However, as Newhouse (2016) put it in relation to Canada, reconciliation requires that 'we will have to confront our history, our governance processes and our understandings of Indigenous peoples and their capacity to govern themselves' (p. 2).

In Canada, the TRC recommended the establishment of an independent Reconciliation Council to report annually on policy consistency with reconciliation, providing a public record of the progress made towards implementing the commission's 94 'calls to action' to which the Canadian Government, led by Justin Trudeau (2015–), had committed (Tasker, 2016). This commitment reflected a significant evolution in political thought from Pierre Trudeau's first government (1968–1979), which had sought to develop federal relationships with indigenous nations. From a Métis perspective, these efforts were attempts to recognise 'special needs' not 'special rights'. In 2003, the Canadian Supreme Court overturned that philosophical premise by recognising the Métis as a 'rights bearing people' (Métis Nation, 2017, p. 2) with protections under the Canadian Constitution.

While significant, the Supreme Court's decision remains distant from the Métis River Settlement's aspiration in 1869 to be recognised as a separate province in the Canadian federation. This 'dream for a self-governing Métis nation within the Canadian federation' has 'faded with time', but it has 'never died' (Métis Nation, 2017, p. 1). In 2015, as part of its election promise, Trudeau's Liberal Party of Canada observed that:

> Canada must complete the unfinished work of Confederation by establishing a renewed Nation-to-Nation relationship with the Métis Nation, based on trust, respect and co-operation for mutual benefit. A Liberal government will work in partnership with the Métis Nation, on a Nation-to-Nation basis, to further Métis self-government. (as cited in Métis Nation, 2017, p. 3)

Once in government, the Liberal Party affirmed its position, establishing a 'Permanent Bilateral Mechanism' with each of the First Nations, Inuit and Métis peoples. In 2017, the federal Minister of Justice and Attorney General, Jody Wilson-Raybauld, observed an important relationship between the Declaration and Canada's reconciliation efforts, both of which required 'a set of new laws, policies, institutions, structures and patterns of relationships that fit together and acknowledge and integrate Indigenous knowledge, perspectives and legal traditions' (Wilson-Raybauld, 2017).

In 2015, Justin Trudeau told the national Assembly of First Nations that:

> It is time for a renewed nation-to-nation relationship with First Nations Peoples.
>
> One that understands that the constitutionally guaranteed rights of First Nations in Canada are not an inconvenience but rather a sacred obligation. (Trudeau, 2015, paras. 23–24)

Nation-to-nation relationships recognise indigeneity's political distinctiveness. They establish nationhood—rather than race, ethnic minority status or relative material poverty—as differentiation's purpose and justification. In response to Trudeau, the assembly's national chief, Percy Bellegarde (as cited in Sweetgrass, 2015), remarked:

> We are being heard and I believe understood like never before.
>
> We are opening doors in Ottawa to facilitate the work of all First Nations, on the implementation and recognition of our rights and title, treaty enforcement and implementation, and realizing self-determination for Indigenous Nations. (paras. 14–15)

Fitzgerald and Schwartz (2017) observed that Canada may indeed 'be on a path toward reconciliation with Indigenous peoples' (p. 1). If so, engagement with the Declaration represented 'an opportunity to explore and reconceive the relationship between international law, indigenous peoples' own laws and Canada's constitutional narratives' (p. 1). This engagement required a reappraisal of political relationships, such as the federal parliament's retention of jurisdiction over 'Indians and lands reserved for Indians' (UN, 2014, p. 6). For example, indigenous jurisdiction over social policy, especially the care and protection of children, competes with state assumptions of knowing better, state control of public budgets and the hegemonic value to the state of positioning indigenous peoples as deficient in the care and safety of their children. The Canadian *Indian Act 1876*, a powerful symbol of the 'we know best' position, remains an obstacle to reconciliation and thus self-determination (Wilson-Raybauld, 2017).

The *Indian Act* was intended to 'civilise' the indigenous populations. In 2014, the UN Special Rapporteur on the Rights of Indigenous Peoples recorded a series of human rights violations under the Act: 'A rigidly paternalistic law at its inception, it continues to structure important aspects of Canada's relationship with First Nations today, although efforts at reform have slowly taken place' (UN, 2014, p. 4). Referencing this paternalism, it is significant that the National Aboriginal Economic Development Board proposed that, in constructing nation-to-nation relationships, the Canadian Government refrain from a 'we know best' approach to policy development (Public Policy Forum, 2017).

Reconciliation's ability to eliminate the marginal political status of indigenous people relies on substantive indigenous participation, yet the TRC (2015) only recommended 'consultation':

> We call upon federal, provincial, territorial, and municipal governments to fully adopt and implement the United *Nations Declaration on the Rights of Indigenous Peoples* as the framework for reconciliation. (p. 325)

> We call upon the Government of Canada to develop a national action plan, strategies, and other concrete measures to achieve the goals of the *United Nations Declaration on the Rights of Indigenous Peoples*. (p. 325)

> We call upon the Government of Canada, on behalf of all Canadians, to jointly develop with Aboriginal peoples a Royal Proclamation of Reconciliation to be issued by the Crown. The proclamation would build on the Royal Proclamation of 1763 and the Treaty of Niagara of 1764, and reaffirm the nation-to-nation relationship between Aboriginal peoples and the Crown. The proclamation would include, but not be limited to, the following commitments:

> i. Repudiate concepts used to justify European sovereignty over Indigenous lands and peoples such as the Doctrine of Discovery and *terra nullius*.

> ii. Adopt and implement the *United Nations Declaration on the Rights of Indigenous Peoples* as the framework for reconciliation.

> iii. Renew or establish Treaty relationships based on principles of mutual recognition, mutual respect, and shared responsibility for maintaining those relationships into the future.

> iv. Reconcile Aboriginal and Crown constitutional and legal orders to ensure that Aboriginal peoples are full partners in Confederation, including the recognition and integration of Indigenous laws and legal traditions in negotiation and implementation processes involving Treaties, land claims, and other constructive agreements. (p. 199)

Reconciliation requires just terms of association in every field of public life. The commission was 'convinced that [the Declaration] ... provide[d] the necessary principles, norms, and standards for reconciliation to flourish in twenty-first-century Canada' (TRC, 2015, p. 21). Further, the commission proposed that public institutions should operate in ways that are consistent with the Declaration, 'which Canada has endorsed' (p. 21).

Reconciliation is yet to do for Australia what the TRC urges for Canada—that is, 'inspire Aboriginal and non-Aboriginal peoples to transform Canadian society ... [to] live together in dignity, peace, and prosperity on these lands we now share' (TRC, 2015, p. 8), which requires trust grounded in inclusive and respectful political relationships.

Trust and the Politics of Inclusion

As well as providing a foundation for just terms of association, reconciliation's purpose is to bring trust to political relationships. Procedural integrity is preliminary to just policy outcomes. Truth is important—not simply truth about the content of a given policy proposal but a deeper truth about the history that lies beneath political relationships. Reconciliation requires that parties accept the other's legitimacy, its right to be present in the body politic in its own way and for purposes that might differ from one's own.

Relationships of trust are difficult to achieve, though as determinants of a noncolonial political order, they are vitally important. As one non-aboriginal witness to the TRC (2015) explained:

> I really understand the reticence of some First Nations people about wanting to accept offers of friendship and possibilities of interaction. I understand why that is and I hope that in time we will be able to gain trust and some kind ways of interacting with one another that will be mutually beneficial. ... I think we're moving. ... I think civil society, non-governmental organizations, church organizations, Aboriginal organizations are moving in the direction of openness ... and I think we have a long way to go. (quotation is as it appears in the source, p. 308)

Trust presumes substantive indigenous inclusion in decision-making. However, Canada is yet to develop processes to ensure that inclusion in national citizenship.

Citizenship and self-determination are not only bodies of rights but also the assurance of political capacity. For example, it is important to be present when decisions are made about the policy settings and budgetary allocations that influence self-determining opportunities. An indigenous presence in public institutions 'indigenises' the bureaucracy (Maaka & Fleras, 2009) by allowing indigenous people to participate at all levels of the policy process: from the executive to the legislative, and from the school to the police station. It allows indigenous people to be involved in setting, implementing and evaluating policy priorities. Indigenous presence reduces the political gap between decision-makers and those who experience those decisions when they engage with public institutions. Trust is an essential precursor to legitimacy.

The long history of indigenous mistrust of government has many explanatory variables—for example, the practice of approving development projects on indigenous lands against a community's wishes. Beck's (2016) comparison of the approaches to water management consultation of the governments of Alberta and the Northwest Territories in the Mackenzie River Basin highlighted the differences between Alberta's minimalist approach to engagement and the Northwest Territories' more participatory approach, and emphasised the 'important implications for moving [free, prior and informed consent to development] from an international norm to a domestic template for action in Canada' (p. 487). Beck's study serves as an example of von der Porten, Lepofsky, McGregor and Silver's (2016) claim that, in Canada:

> The time of Indigenous 'inclusion' into state-led marine policy making is ending. Indigenous peoples are increasingly asserting their rights to *primary* roles in policy- and decision-making that affect the traditional homelands, freshwater bodies and oceans. (p. 68)

Participation implies serious and secure opportunities for indigenous peoples to influence the outcome of negotiations and supports reconciliation by providing reasons for trust.

Creating reasons for trust motivates contemporary Australian debates about treaties and an Indigenous voice to parliament. In 2019, the Victorian and Northern Territory governments engaged in treaty negotiations with Indigenous nations, and the New South Wales Opposition (the Labor Party) indicated that it would do the same if it was able to form government after that state's next election.[1]

One would expect such treaties to recognise prior Indigenous occupancy of Australia and to accept that this provides grounds for at least some degree of Indigenous intranational self-determination. In return, the state may expect recognition of its own legitimacy. The question for the Indigenous nations is whether and to what extent this is reasonable, and, if it is not reasonable, the points on which the state should concede to create moral legitimacy. Part of the difficulty is that there is no precedent for a treaty or treaties in Australia. Canada's modern treaties and New Zealand's Treaty of Waitangi were signed in such different contexts that the guidance they could provide may be limited.

Modern Canadian treaties are settlements of land claims not otherwise able to be settled. In 2014, 24 modern treaties affecting 95 indigenous communities and 40 per cent of the Canadian landmass were in place (UN, 2014). However, according to the UN special rapporteur, the conclusion of land settlement agreements appeared to have occurred in a confrontational context in which the government perceived 'the overall interests of Canadians as adverse to aboriginal interests, rather than encompassing them' (UN, 2014, p. 16).

Whereas in New Zealand the Treaty of Waitangi was signed before colonisation commenced, the Australian treaties are proposed more than 200 years after the event. Treaty policy is well developed in New Zealand but not fully settled. The UN Committee on the Elimination of Racial Discrimination (2007) suggested that New Zealand 'continue the public discussion over the status of the Treaty of Waitangi, with a view to its entrenchment as a constitutional norm' (para. 13).

In 2017, the New South Wales Aboriginal Land Council argued that a treaty was needed to 'codify and provide certainty about the relationship between the State Government and Aboriginal peoples' (para. 4). The council expected such a treaty to support 'five key goals – protecting our culture and heritage, pursuing our full Land and Water rights, driving economic independence and prosperity, supporting our peoples and

---

1   At the 2019 state election, the Liberal and National Party coalition government was returned and had no stated interest in pursuing treaties.

securing our future' (New South Wales Aboriginal Land Council, 2017, para. 8). While in Australia, official interest in addressing disadvantage has strengthened since the Howard Government's defeat in 2007, this interest has been principally one of egalitarian justice rather than substantive self-determination justifying any redistribution of political authority, such as that which a treaty might secure.

Any trust generated from these egalitarian concerns is inevitably compromised by Australia's otherwise poor record of achievement and inattention to the recognition of meaningful indigenous political authority. In 2017, the UN Permanent Forum on Indigenous Issues could cite only three instances of policy success from the Council of Australian Governments' Closing the Gap in Indigenous Disadvantage policy:[2] a decline in child mortality rates, an increase in final year secondary school completion rates and a reduction in mortality from chronic diseases (UN, 2017a, p. 2).

The requirement that the prime minister report annually to parliament on progress towards Closing the Gap policy targets ensures that there is at least scope for public accountability, which the UN special rapporteur argued ought to be complemented by a systematic process for Indigenous people themselves to monitor progress (UN, 2017b). In 2018, this principle was recognised in a small though potentially significant way with the appointment of the first Indigenous Commissioner to the Productivity Commission. The commissioner's duty is to lead Indigenous evaluations of Closing the Gap. Indigenous-led policy evaluation may help to close the relational gap between Indigenous peoples and the policy process. It may also help to raise Indigenous trust and confidence in the intent of public policy.

Closing the gap in political disadvantage is also important. Calls for a constitutionally guaranteed Indigenous voice to the national parliament reflect the argument that democratic institutions ought to hold indigenous peoples' confidence. Trust and confidence cannot be assured unless it is apparent to indigenous peoples that their values have the capacity to

---

2   Closing the Gap is a policy measure of the Council of Australian Governments. It aims to close statistically measurable gaps in Indigenous disadvantage in areas such as health and education. It has been largely unsuccessful and critiqued for not sufficiently including Indigenous people and perspectives in its development. Governments have, in part, tried to address these critiques. The policy contrasts with the more holistic and inclusive approach to disadvantage in civil society's Close the Gap policy approach; see O'Sullivan (2015) for an account of the distinctions between the two.

influence and that their citizenship is meaningful. This contrasts markedly with the approach taken by the Howard Government in 2007, which explicitly excluded Indigenous consultation in drafting the Intervention. The Intervention used the military to 'restore order' after an official report identified high levels of child sexual abuse across Indigenous communities in the Northern Territory (Northern Territory Government, 2007). Its stated purpose was to address a 'crisis of community dysfunction' (Explanatory Memorandum, Northern Territory Emergency Response Bill 2007 [Cth], pt. 8 para. 14) and human rights obligations in respect of child safety.

The sense of injustice that the Intervention raised among many Indigenous people was grounded in the long history of public indifference towards the sexual violation of Indigenous women by white men. In its review of this history, the Human Rights and Equal Opportunity Commission (1997) demonstrated the striking hypocrisy of the Intervention for Indigenous people whose:

> removal as children and the abuse they experienced at the hands of the authorities or their delegates have permanently scarred their lives. The harm continues in later generations, affecting their children and grandchildren. (p. 4)

The Intervention required suspension of the *Racial Discrimination Act 1975* (Cth), which meant that:

> Persons subject to the Northern Territory Intervention are prevented from challenging, on the basis of racial discrimination, its measures through existing domestic law and are prevented from seeking any remedy. (Merkel, Newhouse & Schokman, 2009, para. 266)

Significantly, there were no Indigenous members of the Australian House of Representatives at the time the legislation was passed. In setting aside self-determination's essential presumptions—that is, 'the rights to freedom from discrimination and participation in decision-making' (Cowan, 2013, p. 280)—the power of democratic exclusion was clear.

Differentiated liberal citizenship may have prevented the Intervention by preventing the states' presumption of absolute power. Instead, the Intervention further diminished Indigenous citizenship. For example, welfare payments were sequestered and the Intervention became the catalyst for the trial of a cashless welfare card in the Northern Territory and other largely Indigenous parts of Australia. Under the trial, a proportion of a beneficiary's payment from the state was placed on to a bank card that could not be used to purchase alcohol or tobacco. In this way, *some* but not *all* citizens' capacity to make their own spending decisions was removed. The racial make-up of a community was the criterion for inclusion in the trial.

The cashless welfare card trial showed that an obstacle to Indigenous policy development was the quality, and sometimes even the presence, of valid evaluative data. For example, a government report proclaiming the trial's success was not independent and appeared to have been written to support a predetermined outcome. Clarke (as cited in Davey, 2017) explained that:

> Surprisingly there is no use of statistical methods to test the significance of any observable trends, so it's hard to know what can be concluded even on a descriptive level … Given the issues with the design, it is difficult to see how they will have evidence of the program's impact on which to base an informed policy decision. (para. 27)

Despite extensive community consultation during the scheme's development and review, the then Minister for Human Services overstated the case in claiming consultation as 'an element likely contributing to its early success' (Tudge, as cited in Davey, 2017, para. 32). Indigenous opinion was divided. However, consensus on future policy proposals is more likely to emerge if all concerned have access to the same robust and reliable evaluative data, and time and space to deliberate. The appointment of the Indigenous Productivity Commissioner is a step in that direction.

Mistrust and Policy Racism

The UN special rapporteur has described the legacy of Indigenous Australian marginalisation as a subtle form of racism (UN, 2017b). The failure to recognise the historical and ongoing significance of this legacy has had a compounding effect. In this context, the Intervention was not only an explicit defence of racial discrimination and justification of political inequality but also helped to explain why some Aboriginal people feel that they 'are born with one foot in the grave' (Axelby & Wanganeen, 2017, para. 10).

One cannot reduce sexual, drug and alcohol abuse, violence and/or parental neglect to a unidimensional explanation grounded in individual moral weakness (Collingwood-Whittick, 2012). Nor is it useful to examine more complex and multifaceted explanations unless they add to what is already known about likely solutions. Especially as indigenous mistrust of the state obstructs effective policymaking, the key is to identify institutional arrangements and values that lend themselves to the implementation of known solutions. As Canada's TRC and Australia's Inquiry into the Separation of Aboriginal and Torres Strait Islander Children from Their Families show, schools, hospitals and welfare agencies have been used systematically and deliberately to undermine indigenous societies. This history continues to interfere with the development of indigenous respect for the state and confidence in the honour of its intentions. Given this context, the UN special rapporteur recommended that Australia's Closing the Gap policy targets be extended to include reductions in the rates of imprisonment, child removal and violence against women (UN, 2017b). He had earlier expressed the view that Aboriginal peoples' concerns merited 'higher priority at all levels and within all branches of government' (UN, 2014, p. 20).

Mistrust contributes to poor outcomes in education and health. In Australia, Indigenous people discharge themselves from hospital against medical advice at 13 times the rate of other citizens (Australian Institute of Health and Welfare, 2009) and many Indigenous children find school unsatisfactory—mistrust helps to explain why. Lee, Fasoli, Ford, Stephenson and McInerne (2014) explained that 'We should not be surprised if even very young children find school learning programs so unrewarding they sometimes decide to stay away' (p. 231).

Mistrust arises from decisions like the one to reduce bilingual schooling in the Northern Territory in 2008. The policy was in response to poor results in national school assessments. Blame was apportioned to the children themselves and to the bilingual nature of their schooling, yet there were (and are) remote schools in the Northern Territory that did not have a resident teacher (Lee et al., 2014). It is likely that the decision to reduce bilingual schooling was ideologically inspired, as only 20 per cent of the Northern Territory's children were schooled in bilingual programs. Further variables contributing to low achievement were not properly considered, nor was the Australian state's proper contribution to indigenous language retention as a matter of relational justice brought into account (Lee et al., 2014). This oversight was especially striking in light of the UN Permanent Forum on Indigenous Issues's proposal for an International Year of Indigenous Languages to draw political attention to language preservation and revitalisation as a matter of urgency for many indigenous peoples (Pop Ac, 2017).

It is inaccurate for school pedagogies to presume that English is the indigenous child's first or dominant language. Standard English is not the principal means of communication for most Indigenous children in the Northern Territory, and English needs to be taught as an additional language (Lee et al., 2014). Although standard English is a prerequisite for entry into the middle class, in which access to political authority disproportionately lies, it cannot, efficaciously, be the school system's only language. Nor, as a matter of justice, can it alone define the knowledge that the system legitimises. According to Devlin (2009), 'there is a deeper meaning' to bilingual schooling, as:

> a tool for survival in a fast changing, often confusing world. It can open up new, inspiring perspectives as learners from one culture come to grips with the metaphors, the core concepts, the key insights, the poetry, the art and music of the other culture. (p. 3)

Language is the means through which culture is expressed and developed, and the means through which relationships and environments are understood. Languages are basic rights of humanity. The undermining of indigenous languages by the state is a routine colonial strategy.

Signalling institutional racism, Lee et al. (2014) observed that, in Australia, teacher training programs are not responsive to the linguistic context of classrooms that require Indigenous children to learn in a language in which they are not proficient. They argue that Indigenous children are not presented with the same opportunity to learn as non-native English-speaking migrant children for whom additional English language instruction is available, yet the Declaration requires that schooling give all citizens equal opportunity. Citizenship requires that school systems aim to give all school leavers the capacity for social participation.

In Australia, Year 12 completion rates are improving (Belot & Laurence, 2017). Closing the gap in Year 12 completion rates is arguably the most important of the seven Closing the Gap targets, as failure against all others is ultimately a function of poor education; yet, and often explicitly, educational success has not been the system's aspiration for indigenous peoples. Schooling for indigenous peoples exists in a political and cultural context that distinguishes it from schooling for other citizens. Public schooling's role in the usurpation of indigenous political authority and its cooption by the state as a coercive force in the assimilation of indigenous peoples gives it a morally, as well as politically, important contemporary role in reconciliation by contributing to the restoration and maintenance of self-determination.

Self-determination requires that public schools adopt a 'culturally sustaining pedagogy' (McCarty & Lee, 2014, p. 101). This has particular relevance in the US, where almost 90 per cent of Native American children attend public schools despite the existence of private charter schools (McCarty & Lee, 2014). Although their success is mixed, American charter schools are intended to support indigenous peoples' authority to make decisions about their children's education (McCarty & Lee, 2014). This philosophical presumption, which is absent in the Australian system, might help to increase indigenous people's trust and confidence in the education system as one that exists for them as much as for anyone else.

The Native American Community Academy in Albuquerque, New Mexico, is more successful than public schools in terms of student retention and achievement (McCarty & Lee, 2014). It has a curriculum based on 'respect, responsibility, community/service, culture, perseverance and reflection' (McCarty & Lee, 2014, p. 108). The school privileges relationships in ways that are not possible in mainstream public schools. As one teacher explained to McCarty and Lee (2014):

> The relationship that we're gonna have in this classroom—I'm gonna treat you like one of my nieces or nephews, so that it does not end once we are out of this class. It does not end once you've graduated from [Native American Community Academy]. (p. 109)

Relationships within schools, and between schools and their communities, are important determinants of scholastic achievement (Bishop et al., 2010). Schooling ought to enhance and secure cultural identity. It should also help to increase indigenous access to the middle class, for that is where economic security and the capacity to deliberate in public affairs is disproportionately found. Effective schooling is also important for realising the demographic dividends that indigenous population structures in Australia, Canada, New Zealand and the US allow.

Demographic dividends are the opportunities that arise from a youthful population structure. As Jackson (2011) explained, the differential in Maori educational attainment may decline 'simply because' a disproportionate number of Maori are of an age at which qualifications are most likely to be completed. The median age of Maori is 15 years lower than the median age for non-Maori people. Maori aged 15–24 years comprise 31 per cent of the Maori working age population (Jackson, 2011), which, on its own, ought to contribute to a reduction in the income differential as this cohort's income rises with age and experience. At the same time, participation rates for secondary schooling and university enrolments among Maori have increased. Between 2008 and 2017, the rate of university enrolment for Maori increased by 16 per cent, and postgraduate enrolments for Maori increased by 19 per cent (Universities New Zealand, 2018). Contributing factors included an increase in the number of Maori attaining the required school level qualifications for entry to university, the Maori age structure and increasing financial support from iwi (tribes) to their members.

Almost half the indigenous Canadian population is under the age of 25 years. This creates opportunities of the kind and scope that Jackson (2011) imagined for New Zealand, in which 'the importance of recognising and proactively investing in the dividend years for Maori … to transform them to economic windfalls cannot be overemphasised' (p. 70). Similarly, from 1991 to 2016 in Australia, the number of Indigenous university graduates increased from fewer than 4,000 to 30,000 (Grant, 2016), creating scope for a significant demographic dividend. However, demographic dividends do not always extend to economic dividends (Jackson, 2011). This requires deliberate policy measures and systematic indigenous-led policymaking to eliminate mistrust as an obstacle to effective education, for example, and which an Indigenous voice to parliament would facilitate. Indigenous-led policy evaluation to inform policy development is similarly important and is the outcome that the appointment of an Indigenous Productivity Commissioner is intended to facilitate.

As the UN special rapporteur has recommended, policy processes ought to 'value and prioritise the [policy] leadership of Aboriginal and Torres Strait Islander people' (UN, 2017b, Closing the Gap and health, para. 4). This is fundamental to the trust that reconciliation requires and is an example of the participation in public affairs that self-determination requires.

Conclusion

The Declaration 'offers a positive framework for state-indigenous relations, but much more theoretical and political work remains' (Maciel, 2014, p. 39). This book's purpose is to contribute to a theoretical account of what the Declaration might mean for the conduct of contemporary indigenous–state relations and for securing indigenous belonging to the state. Reconciliation, trust and inclusivity are essential to that discussion. As it is for the Declaration itself, reconciliation's ultimate test is its capacity to contribute to a democratic form that raises indigenous quality of life and political authority.

For reconciliation to occur, indigenous people must find reason to accept that the postsettler state is at least capable of legitimacy. Equally, the act of reconciliation must be of sufficient substance to make the state worthy of trust—for without trust, self-determination is impossible.

Trust may follow if the Declaration is engaged to show how indigenous rights are not just acceptable in liberal theory but also required. In this regard, the Declaration's overarching potential is to rationalise a liberal theory of indigeneity that may, for some indigenous peoples, give moral integrity to the modern state. However, trust is difficult partly because state acceptance of the Declaration by Australia, Canada, New Zealand and the US is reluctant and conditional.

The following chapter discusses Australian, Canadian, New Zealand and US perspectives on the Declaration; their shifts from opposition to acceptance of its value as an 'aspirational' document; and liberal theory's capacity to support both indigenous inclusion and exclusion.

3

The Declaration and the Postsettler Liberal State: Perspectives from Australia, New Zealand, Canada and the United States

Introduction

Australia, Canada, New Zealand and the US have politically assertive and well-organised indigenous minority populations. In each case, their votes against the Declaration strengthened indigenous mistrust of the state. These countries objected to the Declaration on the grounds that it could threaten the territorial integrity of the state and undermine liberal democratic values. The latter objection contrasts with indigenous reservations, raised in Chapter 4, that the Declaration would impose universal liberal values on societies that were not liberal and that sought to retain their own political systems. This chapter responds to the first set of objections and shows that, in the end, its acceptance by the four states was not so much a change of position but a 'reading down' of its contents to make it more consistent with their prevailing laws, practices and institutional arrangements (Gover, 2015). Presenting an indigenous view of this acquiescence, Astenhaienton (as cited in Holder & Corntassel, 2002) observed that 'It's easy for us [indigenous peoples] to agree. The hard part is to get governments to see the Declaration as necessary and not so threatening' (p. 141). Therefore, Wiessner (2008), who described the Declaration as a 'milestone of re-empowerment' (p. 1142), may have overstated the case in suggesting that the international community had, in substantive terms, arrived at a consensus on the Declaration (p. 1141).

Beyond the state, some liberals objected to the Declaration's presumption that it is sometimes just to treat people differently, yet as this chapter demonstrates, these objections reflect but one strand of liberal possibility and do not foreclose all others. The Declaration, in fact, gives indigenous aspirations the political support that comes from being able to express ideas in liberal terms in the prevailing language of international human rights.

The Declaration also affirms legal pluralism in the ways that disputes between indigenous nations and the state are resolved. Pluralism is a liberal principle that helps to make state systems of law and politics work more fairly and inclusively; it responds to self-determination's relative and relational character. However, the Declaration remains a controversial instrument, and significant objections remain from both indigenous and state perspectives. This chapter sets out and responds to state objections, and the following chapter considers indigenous arguments and shows how these arguments are responses to indigenous mistrust of the state.

The Declaration and the State

Fears that the Declaration would disrupt the territorial integrity of existing states arose from the draft document's definition of self-determination as the right of indigenous peoples to 'freely determine their political status and freely pursue their economic, social and cultural development' (UN, 2007b, annex). Explaining such fears, Kingsbury (1992) proposed that existing state indigenous policy objectives reflected a conflict between the values of justice and order. National integrity grounded in homogeneity is simple and orderly: it ensures that majority populations retain control of the political community. However, this kind of order conflicts with justice because 'legitimacy is a function of the norm-creating process and of fairness and efficacy in implementation' (Kingsbury, 1992, p. 493). In fact, and in contrast, order is also preserved by the limits that the Declaration places on self-determination's scope. For example, it cannot be 'construed as authorizing or encouraging any action which would dismember or impair, totally or in part, the territorial integrity or political unity of sovereign and independent States' (UN, 2007b, art. 46[1]). Thus, the Declaration does not threaten territorial integrity, but in other respects it presents a powerful challenge to state conceptions of order.

This book's argument is that justice requires distinctive and secure indigenous shares in public sovereignty. This aspiration is expressed in the Declaration in liberal democratic language; yet according to Carroll (2012), under the Declaration, 'the perceived place of indigenous nations continues to be below that of the states in which they reside' (p. 144). As an instrument of the UN, the Declaration focuses on the obligations of the state. Its foundational positions are not the political capacities of indigenous peoples. Its value lies in the constraints it places on state power and its assumption that indigenous people have the right to participate in public affairs and to maintain independent political authority.

Canada argued that the UN Working Group on Indigenous Populations, which drafted the Declaration, was unnecessary because existing laws and agreements met the just and reasonable rights of indigenous Canadians (Thompson, 2017). Canada found the Declaration 'too sweeping and open-ended' (Coates & Holroyd, 2014, p. 7):

> Canada does not want to see the traditional concept of self-determination used to attack the territorial integrity of a sovereign, non-colonial state. Since Canada is such a state, it does not agree that the concept of self-determination is applicable to Indigenous populations within Canada. (Department of Indian Affairs and Northern Development, as cited in Thompson, 2017, p. 30)

Positioning Canada as a 'non-colonial' state is not consistent with indigenous experience. Nor is it consistent with Gover's (2015) explanation of Canada's, Australia's, New Zealand's and the US's attempts to legitimise the postsettler state. These countries sought legitimacy by giving an assimilationist interpretation to 'the rule of law, principles of neutrality, equality and non-discrimination' (p. 346).

New Zealand argued that the Declaration was inconsistent with the Treaty of Waitangi and undermined the individual rights of universal citizenship. No evidence has emerged to support this view, nor have authoritative Maori arguments been raised to suggest any inconsistency between the Declaration and the treaty. The problem, Gover (2015) argued, is that negotiated political settlements, such as New Zealand's treaty settlements, are well advanced and sanctioned in domestic law. It was feared that the intrusions of international law could undermine these arrangements and prevailing political relationships, which New Zealand believed were working well:

> to accede to some expressions of indigenous 'rights' in international law, even when domestic agreements give effect to norms that are consistent with such rights, because of the possibility that these rights could disrupt or undermine local bargains, allow non-discrimination principles to be used to challenge settled claims, empower settler judiciaries to enforce or refer to those rights at the expense of domestic executive prerogatives and obligations and, in so doing, perhaps bring the discursive processes of bargaining to a premature close. (Gover, 2015, p. 347)

In Australia, Indigenous rights have traditionally been peripheral to mainstream politics. The Declaration was adopted at a time when Indigenous policy reflected the assimilationist presumptions and rhetoric of the outgoing Howard Government (1996–2007). The Liberal Party's 1988 election campaign theme song encapsulated this rhetoric: 'Son you're Australian; that's enough for anyone to be' (Brett, 2005, p. 25). The idea that there might be subnational units of identity undermined the government's view of equality grounded in sameness. The Declaration's affirmation of indigenous groups as 'peoples' who were capable of nationhood challenged this deeply held view.

Australia argued that self-determination 'is not a right that attaches to an undefined subgroup of a population seeking to obtain political independence' (as cited in Gover, 2015, p. 367). Canada argued that the right to self-determination should be exercised through 'negotiations between states' and the various indigenous peoples within those states as a 'necessary component of exercising the right of self-determination' (as cited in Gover, 2015, p. 367). Both countries believed that indigenous rights were not inherent but were the subject of political negotiation. Rather than self-determination, it was 'the prospective liberalism of human rights and the constitutive liberalism of state-indigenous bargaining that could be made to co-exist in the text of [the Declaration]' (Gover, 2015, p. 361). Recognising indigenous rights relies on recognition that sovereignty is shared.

The US argued that, rather than refer to 'indigenous peoples', the Declaration ought to address the rights of 'persons belonging to indigenous groups' (as cited in Gover, 2015, p. 365). Like the other objecting states, its position was that:

> We strongly support the full participation of indigenous people in democratic decision-making processes but cannot accept the notion of a sub-national group having a 'veto' power over the legislative process. (as cited in Carroll, 2012, p. 144).

The idea that the Declaration provided a veto over certain policy decisions was shared among the four states. The veto power was read into the requirement that development activities on indigenous lands require indigenous consent (UN, 2007b, art. 10). Such power was also read into Article 26 of the Declaration, which attracted special objection because of its commitment to the indigenous right to 'the lands, territories and resources which they have traditionally owned, occupied or otherwise used or acquired' (UN, 2007b). Where this aspiration could not be met, the article provided for compensation by way of 'lands, territories and reserves equal in quality, size and legal status' (art. 28[2]). The problem, as the US explained, was that 'almost the entirety of the United States was once owned, occupied or used by American Indians, Alaska Natives and Hawaiian Natives or within the ambit of the phrase' (as cited in Gover, 2015, p. 321). Therefore:

> [The US could not] agree with a blanket statement that all existing legal rights of others to lands 'traditionally occupied' by indigenous persons at some much earlier time should in all cases be set aside regardless of the circumstances. (as cited in Gover, 2015, p. 371)

The four opposing states were concerned that the Declaration would require them to return land that was already alienated and transferred to private interests and that this would undermine social cohesion and public support for the principle of negotiated settlements.

Canada's position was that the Declaration 'might not fully accord with the norms and precedents that have been established through judicial decisions and negotiations on land claims and self-government' (Canadian Human Rights Commission, as cited in Boyer, 2014, p. 12). However, the Declaration's focus is broad. Although it implies an unavoidable relationship between rights and policy outcomes, as Coates and Holroyd (2014) asserted, judicial interpretations do not suggest that the Declaration will have constitutionally disruptive effects:

> While those indigenous political thinkers and leader [*sic*] who argue for full Aboriginal sovereignty have found new strength in the UNDRIP, it is not likely to upset or redefine the law of the land. (p. 9)

This is partly because, in a liberal democracy, there is no such thing as 'full sovereignty'. Public sovereignty is widely dispersed and constrained by its relative and relational character. Sovereignty is constantly reconfigured and reshaped.

New Zealand and Canada feared that the Declaration would give indigenous individuals preferential access to education (Gover, 2015). However, rights to language and culture, which are essential constituents of education, only make sense as group rights—one cannot speak to oneself. Indigenous rights are distinctive because human rights can only be exercised in context. Prior occupancy and (usually violent) displacement contribute to that context, which is why Schulte-Tenckhoff (2012) is wrong to have argued that the:

> culturalization of indigenous rights … stresses cultural identity and distinctiveness over historical and legal-political aspects, such as the effects of colonialism [such that] the recognition of cultural rights comes at the price of the right of self-determination understood as a group right. (p. 67)

Culture *is* a group right; it is also a political right—a right that provides all others with their source and context.

The four UN member states who voted against the Declaration were also concerned that the recognition of collective land rights 'could constitute racial discrimination against non-indigenous persons' (Gover, 2015, p. 369). Their objections were not to collective rights per se but that these rights may carry benefits not available to other citizens (Gover, 2015). However, indigeneity is not concerned with rights or privileges *over* other citizens. Instead, it differentiates rights to make them contextually relevant. Rights to indigenous languages, cultures and resources carry no meaning for other people. Indigeneity means that indigenous rights belong in a distinctive form. The relationship between land and religious freedom is an example of that distinctiveness.

Land's spiritual dimension occurs alongside its economic purpose. The two purposes are not ordinarily in conflict for indigenous peoples. Conflicts over rights emerge when state policies privilege the economic development of non-indigenous commercial interests over the spiritual interests of an indigenous population. In such cases, the bounds of liberal toleration are put to the test and resolving the disagreement can be a mark of society's acceptance of religious freedom.

There is also a relationship between participation in environmental decision-making and opportunities for good health, which Black and McBean (2016) argued creates a case for 'the decolonization of environmental decision making' (p. 1). There is a well-understood causal relationship between 'socio-economic and environmental decisions' (p.1), and indigenous knowledge in environmental protection can have important policy significance. In this sense, indigenous participation is a 'need' as much as it is a 'right' (p. 1).

'Soft' Law

Ultimately, the Declaration was acceptable to the dissenting states as an instrument of 'soft' law—as a document that would not disrupt the territorial integrity of the state. However, 'soft' law can 'harden' (Villeneuve, 2016). It may be incorporated into domestic legislation and influence judicial interpretations of existing law. It can also influence the form and context of subsequent binding instruments. For example, the Canadian Federal Court has found the Declaration a persuasive instrument (Boyer, 2014, p. 13). International law can then 'substantiate' traditional rights (Gupta, Hildering & Misiedjan, 2014, p. 26).

According to Gover (2015), the Declaration is not 'a suitable basis for the development of a binding treaty or of rules of customary international law' (p. 355). In light of this, in 2016, Australia's position was that:

> Some principles in [the Declaration] remain unsettled in international law, particularly those relating to self-determination and free, prior and informed consent. Consistent with the principles of [the Declaration] … Australia recognises the importance of engaging in good faith consultation with Indigenous peoples in relation to decisions that affect them. Australia argues that free, prior and informed consent does not include a right of veto. (Charge D'Affaires, Australian Permanent Mission, 2016, p. 1)

Canada reversed its initial opposition to the Declaration because it came to interpret the document as a 'non-legally binding [one] that does not reflect customary international law nor change Canadian laws' (Canadian Human Rights Commission, as cited in Cultural Survival, n.d., para. 6). One might suggest, then, that Ottawa's initial fears 'were overblown' (Thompson, 2017, p. 33) and that the country's refusal to support the Declaration was 'incongruous' with its previous policy positions (Belanger, 2010, p. 7). New Zealand's stance was similarly inconsistent with its gradual developments towards Maori self-determination, at least since the *Treaty of Waitangi Act 1975* (NZ), which established the Waitangi Tribunal as a judicial body to hear allegations of Crown breaches of the treaty. In the Canadian and New Zealand cases, it is important to acknowledge that their objections to the Declaration, followed by their conditional support, 'does not negate [their] former [and subsequent] recognition of Indigenous rights' (Belanger, 2010, p. 7).

The US agreed that the Declaration was nonbinding yet continued to view it as a 'moral and political force' (as cited in Gover, 2015, p. 55). The US's revised position reflected its:

> commitment to work with tribes, individuals, and communities to address the many challenges they face. The United States aspires to improve relations with indigenous peoples by looking to the principles embodied in the Declaration in its dealings with federally recognised tribes, while also working, as appropriate, with all indigenous individuals and communities in the United States.
>
> Moreover, the United States is committed to serving as a model in the international community in promoting and protecting the collective rights of indigenous peoples as well as the human rights of all individuals. (United States of America, 2011, The Declaration and U.S. Initiatives, para. 1)

In 2012, the UN special rapporteur argued that the Declaration should:

> serve as a beacon for executive, legislative and judicial decision-makers in relation to issues concerning the indigenous peoples of the country. All such decision-making should incorporate awareness and close consideration of the Declaration's terms. (UN, 2012a, p. 19)

In the US, the Declaration followed measures such as the *Native American Languages Act of 1990*, which, according to the UN special rapporteur, 'reflect[ed] a significant level of dedication on the part of the Government to indigenous concerns within the self-determination policy framework' (UN, 2012a, p. 9). However, at other times, that dedication has not been apparent in a complex, contested and unsettled policy environment.

For example, the *Alaska Native Claims Settlement Act* extinguished aboriginal title and hunting and fishing rights in favour of individual shares in corporations established to administer indigenous assets. Cultural rights and opportunities were traded for commercial shares (UN, 2012a) in the face of significant native Alaskan opposition. A further example concerns the conflict of political authority and values between the US and the Great Sioux Nation over the Keystone XL gas pipeline (discussed in Chapter 4).

Australia accepted a case for 'internal' self-determination, and the US acknowledged a right to 'self-governance' (Gover, 2015, p. 367). Their respective positions recognised that land rights:

> by necessity, entails a degree of 'de facto' self-governance because the collective must decide on the intra-group allocation of rights among members of the group. The state must determine rules for the governance of transfer, succession and conservation of 'inter se' property rights.(Gover, 2015, p. 369)

However, the argument that self-determination is only an internal right of self-governance implies that it cannot simultaneously occur *within* the nation-state to give effect to differentiated liberal citizenship.

Self-government may presume an isolationist and unsustainable nationhood. It requires large and discrete population bases and politically cohesive institutions. This may be ideal for some indigenous populations, but it is often not supported by the infrastructural capacity of smaller communities. Nor is isolable self-government desirable for those who enjoy strong political, financial, personal and familial relationships outside the indigenous nation.

Rather than re-evaluate citizenship's structure to make it inclusive, Australia, Canada, New Zealand and the US indicated that they would entertain '"special measures" intended to overcome indigenous disadvantage' (Gover, 2015, p. 362). However, 'special' or 'affirmative action' measures are limited in scope and effect. They are concerned with the temporary redistribution of resources to address the immediate consequences of material disadvantage. They do not consider the more significant imperative—namely, the removal of the political causes of relative disadvantage.

WE ARE ALL HERE TO STAY'

States adopt special measures to achieve social equity. However, to accept these measures as just substitutes for political equality is to set aside meaningful rights of prior occupancy. This is why indigeneity is not a theory of egalitarian distributive justice. Material prosperity does not diminish an indigenous person's claim to existence as a member of a distinct people. Indeed, public policies grounded only in distributive justice are assimilationist. They require that indigenous peoples 'forgo the full normative implications of their claims and … accept forms of assimilation into state institutions as restitution' (Woons, 2014, p. 5). To prevent settler self-interest being the framer of policy debate—which is the risk when policies that do not address political equality are favoured—policy negotiations should 'begin with indigenous accounts of what is fair and reasonable' (p. 5).

Liberal Objections to the Declaration

There remain liberal objections to distinctive recognition. Liberals—such as the former leader of the New Zealand National and ACT parties, Don Brash, and former Australian prime minister John Howard—have maintained, often to significant public approval, that liberal egalitarianism alone assures indigenous people of their fundamental human equality. According to them, distinctive recognition is unnecessary—an illiberal privilege that is offensive to the proper recognition of other citizens (O'Sullivan, 2007).

According to Kymlicka (1995), the tension between liberal inclusivity and a liberalism concerned only with the rights of the acultural individual comes from the view that:

> ethnic identity, like religion, is something [that] people should be free to express in their private life, but it is not the concern of the state to attach legal identities or disabilities to cultural membership or ethnic identity. (p. 4)

Waldron (2003) gives further theoretical expression to this argument: from his perspective, the universal rights of liberal citizenship impose a common obligation on all people to act justly to one another. This means that one must always act with the same regard for indigenous citizens as for all others. The claim to special recognition then becomes unnecessary and unjustified.

However, historic injustices cannot so easily be superseded by a 'principle of proximity where justice is owed to all who are, as Kant puts it, "unavoidably side by side in a given territory irrespective of cultural or national affinity"' (Waldron, 2003, p. 30). The present has emerged from somewhere. Justice requires attention to context. It cannot assume that history has endowed all citizens with equal contemporary political capacity. The colonial past conditions the colonial present. The present could potentially supersede the past, but there are numerous conditions that must first be met. For example, indigenous conceptions of justice enjoy a broader and more long-term focus than simply settling entitlements to land (Patton, 2005).

Relational justice is important and is only superseded when colonialism itself is superseded. It is erroneous to presume that, even though a right might be unjustly alienated, the injustice can still be extinguished with time and circumstance, and that no compensation is reasonably owed. Restitution is not, from this perspective, preliminary to the creation of ongoing just terms of association. For example, if a people's disconnection from land as a source of economic sustenance has been replaced over time by some other source, then the presumption is that the claim to the original property right may have been superseded.

There is a causal link between the alienation of indigenous land, whenever it occurred, and contemporary economic disadvantage (O'Sullivan, 2017). Restitutive justice requires measures that allow indigenous peoples to eliminate that disadvantage. In this way, restitutive justice is both preliminary to just terms of association and a condition of its continuance. As Justice Brennan noted in relation to the acquisition of Indigenous land in Australia, Indigenous people 'underwrote the development of the nation' (*Mabo v Queensland [No 2]*, 1992, para. 82). These principles are recognised in New Zealand's Treaty of Waitangi settlements. The first significant treaty settlement, which took place in 1995, included an apology from the Crown for the Invasion of the Waikato in 1863–1864 and its 'crippling impact on the welfare, economy and development of Waikato [people]'. Further:

> The Crown recognises that the lands confiscated in the Waikato have made a significant contribution to the wealth and development of New Zealand, whilst the Waikato tribe has been alienated from its lands and deprived of the benefit of its lands. (*Waikato Raupatu Claims Settlements Act 1995* [NZ], s. 6.5)

In contrast, Waldron (2004) argues that supersession is just because, 'unlike their ancestors', the descendants of the first colonists generally 'have nowhere else to go' (p. 268). However, the possibility that restitutive measures could occasion injustice to colonial descendants does not supersede indigenous claims. The possibility ought to be proven in specific circumstances and each injustice balanced against the other. Colonial descendants' rights to self-determination are relative and relational to the rights of others. They are not morally superior to the rights that indigenous peoples claim. Indeed, there are no cases in Australia or New Zealand in which these people have been required to surrender what is justly theirs. Indigenous peoples are not asking others to go away. Therefore, the question is not which rights are superseded, but which rights justly belong to indigenous peoples, and how are they realisable in the interests of a substantive and durable self-determination?

Colonialism was the underlying aggression. Consequently, it is reasonable that it is the colonised (not the coloniser) whose claim to self-determination is the first heard. To support the inverse—in which indigenous rights are given secondary and morally lesser consideration—would be to perpetuate the colonial order.

Waldron's (2004) supersession argument is further undermined by his own concession to the ongoing significance of religious and cultural connections to land:

> The claim that the lost lands form the centre of a present way of life—and remain sacred objects despite the loss—may be as credible a hundred years on as it was at the time of the dispossession. (p. 72)

Colonialism is an ongoing relational injustice. It was not a single event 'done' to indigenous peoples. It is a system of political values that rationalise political subjugation, and a system under which justice cannot occur. Its essential presumption is that indigenous peoples have no claim to self-determination. This presumption arises from Locke's (1887) theory of property, which, as noted in the introduction, holds that sovereign authority in relation to land is acquired only by working the land for agricultural production. In Australia, early British observers concluded that Australia's Indigenous peoples did not work the land in such ways and this in itself justified their displacement.

Colonialism means that political structures, relationships and values exclude some people. A human desire or will to 'do justice' to all is not a value that people will always and everywhere accept. Political conflict arises in situations in which there is a difference between what people consider just for themselves and what they accept as just for others. In postsettler societies, conflict arises when non-indigenous actors demand a standard of justice for themselves that they are not willing to extend to indigenous peoples.

Waldron (2004) sets aside the significance of context to justice. Moreover, like Hegtvedt (2005), he failed to account for indigenous peoples' right and responsibility to 'do justice' to themselves. 'Doing justice' requires political capacity, and liberal egalitarian equality is not the same as self-determination's substantive equality. It is from the perspective of capacity that it is best to consider what makes indigenous claims just. Only then can one 'draw attention to the rightful role of the group in understanding justice' (Waldron, 2004, p. 121) because, as Hegtvedt (2005) correctly explained:

> Understanding how people perceive the boundaries of groups that are the recipient of benefits or burdens facilitates predictions of when conflict may emerge and, potentially, how individuals will respond to differences in what is perceived as just. (p. 41)

According to Waldron (2004), indigeneity's focus on 'the priority of certain entitlements' (p. 6) means that the concept is 'used to transform what would otherwise be a forward-looking discussion of social justice' (p. 8). However, indigeneity privileges the past, such as connections to land, not as an end in itself but as preliminary to understanding the present. The past gives the present social and cultural—as well as political—context, which is a necessary foundation for participating in those 'forward-looking discussion[s] of social justice' that Waldron imagines.

Significantly, and in answer to Waldron's (2004) fears, there are liberal protections ensuring that indigenous claims 'on grounds of historical priority' cannot 'repudiate and marginalise the claims of others' to create 'a very grave moral danger' of 'impervious[ness] of the needs of others' (p. 26). Instead, the human rights of others may moderate the claim to self-determination, although not to the extent of making the claim ahistorical or apolitical as Waldron's supersession thesis would suggest.

Conceptions of justice more broadly inclusive than Waldron's (2004) depend on the strength of the just terms of association that indigenous peoples enjoy within the state. Measures of that strength may include the extent to which indigenous peoples enjoy a substantive deliberative agency. The public recognition of language and culture is also important. Ultimately, however, it is indigenous peoples' capacity to work out for themselves what it means to be a citizen of the state that is self-determination's most significant measure. That capacity is a path to indigenous people leading lives that they have reason to value (Sen, 1999a).

Just terms of association depend on property rights but are not guaranteed by that recognition alone. Broader questions of the terms of indigenous belonging to the state are important and inform ideas about how indigenous peoples might express their share in public sovereignty.

Sharing public sovereignty, or being present as a decision-maker, is important because:

> It belongs to the excellent legislator to see how a city, a family of human beings … share in the good life and in the happiness that is possible for them. (Aristotle, 2010, p. 201)

Democracy retains neo-colonial possibilities, but these are the product of how societies determine democracy's functioning; they are not inherent to the concept itself. Democracy can restrain majoritarian authority, yet states still try to limit the Declaration's full potential.

Conversely, given that the Declaration's principal right is the right to self-determination, it follows that indigenous peoples—not states—ought to conceptualise that potential. They ought to lead political strategies for its implementation, with states examining liberal possibilities for 'a more reparative and constitutive project—the goal of properly constituting a settler body politic and completing the constitution of the settler state by acquiring indigenous consent' (Gover, 2015, p. 346).

Consent means that shared sovereignty is more than a democratic idea; it is an essential constituent of moral legitimacy. The Treaty of Waitangi explains a distinctive Maori view about the legitimacy of the nation-state. If the state's legitimacy is accepted, thought must logically be given to the position that an indigenous group ideally wishes to occupy within the state. It is democratically reasonable that *all* not just *some* citizens contribute to determining 'the conditions under which and the practices through which authority is constituted and legitimised, and what these constitutions and legitimations enable and disable' (Shaw, 2008, p. 1).

Consent requires all citizens' critical engagement in public affairs. Inclusive democratic government ought to mean that public institutions are not discriminatory, which is why, as a matter of restitutive justice, state education systems may play an important part in language revitalisation and allow the coercive powers of state education to yield in some ways to education's transformative capacity, as the TRC (2015) proposed:

> We call on the federal government to draft new Aboriginal education legislation with the full participation and informed consent of Aboriginal peoples. The new legislation would include a commitment to sufficient funding and would incorporate the following principles:
>
> i. Providing sufficient funding to close identified educational achievement gaps within one generation.
>
> ii. Improving education attainment levels and success rates.
>
> iii. Developing culturally appropriate curricula.
>
> iv. Protecting the right to Aboriginal languages, including the teaching of Aboriginal languages as credit courses.
>
> v. Enabling parental and community responsibility, control, and accountability, similar to what parents enjoy in public school systems.
>
> vi. Enabling parents to fully participate in the education of their children.
>
> vii. Respecting and honouring Treaty relationships. (pp. 320–321)

The commission also noted that the relationship between education and health has particular context for Canadian First Nations people:

> We call upon the federal, provincial, territorial, and Aboriginal governments to acknowledge that the current state of Aboriginal health in Canada is a direct result of previous Canadian government policies, including residential schools, and to recognize and implement the health-care rights of Aboriginal people as identified in international law, constitutional law, and under the Treaties. (TRC, 2015, p. 322)

Gunn (2017) extended these claims beyond the expectations they create of the state by arguing that the Declaration's most important legal implication is its insistence that 'rights are defined according to Indigenous peoples' own legal traditions' (p. 35). However, definition is meaningless without participation in the implementation of rights. As Gunn (2017) herself observed:

> If Canada were to begin to embrace just rights of participation, then many more decisions (including resource development decisions) would take into consideration Indigenous laws on land and resource use. (p. 36)

However, in consideration of the problems that might arise when state courts attempted to interpret indigenous laws, Gunn (2017) proposed that 'Indigenous law [might be treated] as foreign law in Canadian courts' (p. 36). Such treatment is the antithesis of self-determination. Indeed, this proposition provides a strong example of the scope of influence that is forgone if indigenous peoples choose not to be part of the state. This book's counterargument is that if there is a need for courts to interpret indigenous laws, then there is also a need for legal pluralism as a constituent of just terms of association that would include appropriately qualified indigenous judges and counsel.

Plurality

Legal pluralism (rather than separation) reflects self-determination's character as a relative and relational power. Recognising legal pluralism requires:

> that matters unfold through dialogue, as each source of legal and political authority must be *persuaded* to act, since *ex hypothesi* no one source of authority enjoys binding authority over all others. (Christie, 2017, pp. 49–50)

Benhabib (1996) argued that democracy works better when there is cultural contestation in public institutions and in civil society. She further claimed that 'constitutional and legal pluralism' (p. ix) can be defended as long as these institutions are impartial.

Legal pluralism requires indigenous access to a politically meaningful sovereignty. However, political and institutional arrangements are always preceded by ideologies—that is, by collective values that, among other considerations, make judgements about people's relative worth and thus the relative capacities they ought to enjoy as citizens. The Declaration requires inclusive public institutions; it may also require transforming the state. It is an important tool for analysing the moral legitimacy of state policies and their underlying values. However, state institutions need not provide the only proper repositories of the people's sovereignty according to an 'ideology of legal centralism' (Duthu, 2013, p. 3). Instead, there is scope for plurality with indigenous civil society contributing as it does to public service delivery in health, education and other social services.

Alfred (2005) is correct to have argued, with reference to the past, that sovereignty was 'an exclusionary concept rooted in adversarial and coercive Western notions of power' (p. 59). However, sovereignty's contemporary character depends on how it is interpreted as a relative and relational concept. It is not dependent on indigenous peoples matching 'the awesome coercive force of the state' (p. 59), as Alfred feared, but on indigenous peoples sharing in the political authority of the state. This may occur through indigenous leadership in the development and delivery of state functions to give cultural focus and independence to the delivery of public services such as schooling and health care.

The Declaration's capacity to influence these matters is a product of prevailing ideas about relationships between state power and indigenous self-determination across jurisdictions. For example, the UN special rapporteur proposed that the US Congress consider affirming the Declaration as 'the policy of the United States' (UN, 2012a, p. 22). However, in not outlining exactly what this meant in legal and practical policy terms, the rapporteur left open the possibility for locally contextualised interpretations of the right to self-determination (UN, 2012a).

In New Zealand, the Declaration affirms the Treaty of Waitangi. It is consistent with Maori accounts of self-determination but, like the treaty, is 'a tool, not a panacea' (Beatty, 2014, p. 49), yet the comparison remains instructive, as Maori have used the Declaration to strengthen treaty claims. The treaty has not become secondary to the Declaration, nor has the Declaration narrowed its scope. Instead, the Declaration establishes principles from which new policy ideas may emerge.

In Australia, the rights that the Declaration asserts extend native title's significance and lend authority to broader claims of citizenship. Religious freedom is a further right that the Declaration upholds. This right adds context and purpose to land claims. It is also important because it was in defence of religious freedom that liberalism developed as a political theory.

According to Coates and Holroyd (2014), the Declaration has 'had [a] profound impact on Canadian politics' (p. 5). Indeed, they described it as 'one of the most significant international political achievements of this generation' (p. 5). However, questions remain about how the Declaration's full adoption and implementation would appear in a liberal society.

The Declaration has helped to normalise indigenous claims in Canada; however, it has not had this effect in Australia, New Zealand or the US. The situation in Canada is different because 'Canada has historically demonstrated a moral (if not always practical) commitment to key international [human rights] agreements' (Coates & Holroyd, 2014, p. 7). For example, the *Canadian Charter of Rights and Freedoms*, as set out in that country's *Constitution Act 1982* (*Canada Act 1982* [UK] c. 11, sch. B pt. I), guarantees that:

> Certain rights and freedoms shall not be construed to abrogate or derogate from any aboriginal, treaty or other rights or freedoms that pertain to the aboriginal peoples of Canada including ... any rights or freedoms that now exist by way of land claims agreements or may be so acquired. (s. 25)

Canada's *Constitution Act*, which is contained in the *Canada Act 1982* (UK), mentions 'The existing aboriginal and treaty rights of the aboriginal peoples of Canada' (*Canada Act*, sch. B pt. I s. 35). This gives constitutional protection to self-government agreements (Coates & Holroyd, 2014). The constitution protects aboriginal title and is supported by an evolving and comprehensive jurisprudence (UN, 2014). In doing so, it reflects Tully's (1995) argument that a constitution is ideally:

> an intercultural dialogue in which the culturally diverse sovereign citizens of contemporary societies negotiate agreements on their forms of association over time in accordance with the three conventions of mutual recognition, consent and cultural continuity. (p. 30)

Yet there remains a 'political stalemate' between the Government of Canada and indigenous peoples over the ways in which the Declaration ought to influence domestic politics (Mitchell, 2014, p. 1). The residential schools' legacy remains strong. It is similarly difficult to remove the presumptions of the statement of the Government of Canada on Indian policy (Government of Canada, Department of Indian Affairs and Northern Development, 1969) from contemporary influence.

On the grounds that treaties would not be relevant to exterminated peoples, the 1969 statement proposed terminating all treaties with aboriginal nations (TRC, 2015). However, under the Declaration:

1. Indigenous peoples have the right to the recognition, observance and enforcement of treaties, agreements and other constructive arrangements concluded with States or their successors and to have States honour and respect such treaties, agreements and other constructive arrangements.

2. Nothing in this Declaration may be interpreted as diminishing or eliminating the rights of indigenous peoples contained in treaties, agreements and constructive arrangements. (UN, 2007b, art. 37)

In this way, the Declaration contributes to an established indigenous politics of resistance and transformation, supporting what Corntassel (2012) has termed 'regenerating indigenous nationhood' (p. 86). Regeneration means that:

> Through our everyday acts of resurgence, our ancestors along with future generations will recognize us as Indigenous to the land. And this is how our homelands will recognize us as being Indigenous to that place. (p. 99)

Resurgence is a politics of 'reconnection' (Corntassel, 2012, p. 97). It is especially significant that the Declaration recognises that the 'right to lands, territories and natural resources is the basis for [indigenous peoples'] collective survival and thus [is] inextricably linked to their right to self-determination' (Daes, 2008, p. 8). Corntassel's (2012) argument not only supports a politics of small-scale or grassroots resistance—understood as a willingness to exercise responsibility—but also recognition of the political capacities that responsibility requires. He asserted that:

> By resisting colonial authority and demarcating their homelands via place naming and traditional management practices, these everyday acts of resurgence have promoted the regeneration of sustainable food systems in community and are transmitting these teachings and values to future generations. (p. 98)

Conclusion

Australia, Canada, New Zealand and the US were the only UN member states to see the Declaration as a threat to their territorial integrity: a threat to the prevailing liberal order to which they wished to continue limiting indigenous access. Their objections revealed the deep conflict that exists over the nature of indigenous belonging in the postsettler liberal state. However, after 'reading down' the Declaration's legal significance, the four states came to accept it as an 'aspirational' document.

Yet, in these and other jurisdictions, indigenous peoples have used the Declaration to help frame their political aspirations and for legal and political purposes. At the same time, there are strongly argued indigenous objections to the Declaration. As the following chapter shows, these are grounded in the view that human rights, and liberal political rights more broadly, are not consistent with indigenous understandings of self-determination. Such objections are motivated by mistrust of the state and state positioning of indigenous peoples as antagonistic towards the public interest in matters such as mining.

The following chapter examines the creation by the state of exclusive public discourses in which indigenous 'demands' conflict with 'reasonable' public interests. These discourses exclude the indigenous from the public. Conversely, some indigenous people see no benefit in inclusion. They do not see themselves as part of the state and argue that democratic inclusion can be assimilationist, as it can involve the imposition of liberal values on nonliberal societies and can be experienced as an expression of colonial power. While this book does not accept these arguments, it acknowledges their importance because they help to explain indigenous mistrust, and, as Chapter 2 argued, being able to set aside that mistrust is an important aspiration. This is because, while indigenous nations may choose to position themselves beyond the liberal state, in doing so, they position themselves beyond the alternative liberal politics of inclusion rationalised by the Declaration.

4

Plurality, Human Rights and What's Wrong with Liberal Inclusion?

Introduction

Liberal states like Australia, Canada, New Zealand and the US respond to indigenous claims with great caution. They may be accepted to a point—until they interfere with the idea that non-indigenous interests deserve moral priority. Political exclusion, from which indigenous mistrust of the state is perpetuated, is the consequence. Arguments that the national interest must always trump indigenous rights to culture position indigenous peoples as beyond the nation—not citizens but binary opponents of the settler public whose demands have prior claim.

Mining and other policies concerned with natural resource use show states wanting to limit plurality in the distribution of political influence and authority. In such contexts, indigenous exclusion can be explicit and unapologetic. For example, to make the Declaration acceptable, the four dissenting states 'read down' the principle of 'free, prior, and informed consent' to one of limited effect, thereby transforming their view of the Declaration into one where the instrument was not, in fact, so favourable to indigenous interests. However, consent should imply a more meaningful political authority than consultation. It should imply an indigenous share in public sovereignty, meaning that indigenous interests cannot be pitted against the common good, because they are part of that 'common', whose collective interests economic development ought to serve. However, from some indigenous perspectives, such a share in public authority is not worthwhile or even morally defensible nor are liberal human rights such as those which the Declaration enunciates.

Just as this chapter examines the state's positioning of indigenous people beyond the public, it considers the reasoning of those indigenous people who, in fact, have no wish to be included. The chapter considers these matters by examining indigenous arguments against the Declaration's underlying liberal foundation—in particular, that its liberal values are inconsistent with indigenous aspirations and therefore inconsistent with the right to self-determination as a collective right.

The possibilities that indigenous peoples find in the Declaration are largely considered elsewhere in the book. However, this chapter's focus is to critique and contest the argument that liberal human rights per se are inconsistent with indigenous rights and to critique and contest the argument that, when human rights privilege the individual, they undermine the collective indigenous good. The chapter shows how indigenous arguments against individual rights have been used to defend sexual violence against women through contested, and often self-serving, interpretations of cultural values. Finally, the chapter shows that the denial of individual human rights means that cultural values are not open to internal contest and may only reflect the will of the physically more powerful. In doing this, it demonstrates the value of international human rights to the right to political voice within the state *and* the indigenous nation.

Mining and the Politics of the Liberal 'Public'

Liberal states have worried that the right to free, prior and informed consent constitutes a veto over land development or resource extraction. Indeed, this reservation was an important factor in the initial reluctance of Australia, Canada, New Zealand and the US to support the Declaration (Banks, 2007). State mining policy often relies on separating indigenous peoples from the 'public' through an overly simplified binary politics in which the 'public' interest favours mining and indigenous interests oppose it. However, indigenous peoples do not speak with one voice on this issue: there are differences of opinion within indigenous nations on mining and other natural resource proposals. There are many examples of resource development and extraction occurring after informed indigenous consent and with significant benefit to indigenous communities (Langton & Longbottom, 2012). However, as the UN special rapporteur has noted in relation to Canada, these presuppose that land title is secure and that the indigenous group is able to participate in negotiations for consent with genuine authority.

Indigenous resistance to extractive industries contests the presumption of terra nullius that allowed colonial states to do as they pleased. Keim and Reidy (2015) argued that Australia's Native Title Tribunal responds to this indigenous resistance with a jurisprudence maintaining that 'a healthy mining industry is synonymous with the public interest' (p. 1). This argument separates indigenous people from the public and discounts the possibility that resistance may be to the specific characteristics of a proposal rather than to mining per se. It also discounts differing opinions within the indigenous nation on the merits of a given proposal.

In Australia, mining incomes have contributed to the rise of an Indigenous middle class and have extended greater prosperity to unskilled and manual workers (Langton & Longbottom, 2012). Yet it is also the case that Australian governments have allowed mining in some areas without Indigenous consent. The corporate imperative to maximise profit as quickly as possible means that there is not automatically an alliance of common interest between miners and indigenous land owners. There are alliances of principle that must also be worked out, and when these are not possible, there can be no consent. However, if there is no requirement for consent, the indigenous property right is not of the standing that liberalism would ordinarily defend. Fundamentally, the displacement of an indigenous people to accommodate a mining venture from which they derive no benefit is unjust. It is reasonable that indigenous peoples are cautious about another party's attempt to use their lands for their own benefit when land alienation is the underlying cause of cultural dislocation and relative material poverty. Coercion, by the will of a more powerful section of the community, is a routine experience for many indigenous citizens.

Indigenous resource rights are, for example, vulnerable unless they are acknowledged through formal and enforceable agreements (Gupta et al., 2014, p. 26). Yet the former UN special rapporteur James Anaya argued that consent was not in fact a veto. He may be correct when good faith negotiations prevail; however, if an indigenous property right is a substantive one, the possibility of veto must always exist, even though it cannot be exercised until good faith negotiations have failed.

Consent raises the standard from consultation to participation. Consultation allows indigenous peoples to react to others' proposals, whereas participation allows them to raise their own.

Robust mining impact assessments are required to inform indigenous consent. Indigenous people have the right to expect some benefit from a project—to be part of the public whose interests mining apparently always and everywhere serves (UN, 2016a). Conversely, Boutilier (2017) argued that 'the duty to consult and accommodate is the closest thing to [free, prior and informed consent] in Canadian constitutional law' (p. 5). Consent is justified because 'a law exists only for the one who has made it himself or agreed to it; for everyone else it is a command or an order' (Rousseau, 1984, p. 97).

Yet the Canadian Supreme Court ruled that aboriginal consent for development is not required when development is in the 'public interest':

> the development of agriculture, forestry, mining, and hydroelectric power, the general economic development of the interior of British Columbia, protection of the environment or endangered species, the building of infrastructure and the settlement of foreign populations to support those aims, are the kinds of objectives that are consistent with this purpose and, in principle, can justify the infringement of aboriginal title. (*Delgamuukw*, 1997, para. 165).

In New Zealand, the *Foreshore and Seabed Act 2004* represented the most significant usurpation of a Maori property right in at least a generation, bringing the question of property rights from historic conflict into the political present. The then New Zealand prime minister Helen Clark, with the opposition's support, positioned herself on 'New Zealand's side' in a battle against 'haters and wreckers' ('Clark defends refusal', 2004). This rhetoric positioned Maori and New Zealand as holding distinct and irresolvable conflicting interests. The presumption was that the New Zealand 'public' was morally more deserving than Maori, who were positioned as outsiders—beyond the public and beyond the political. In contrast, the UN special rapporteur argued that the *Foreshore and Seabed Act* was not 'in line with international standards regarding the rights of indigenous peoples to their traditional lands' (UN, 2011, p. 16). The Act was repealed in 2011, shortly after New Zealand reversed its opposition to the Declaration in 2010. However, the Act's repeal did not reverse all its discriminatory aspects, leading the UN special rapporteur to remind 'the [New Zealand] Government that the extinguishment of indigenous rights by unilaterally, uncompensated acts is inconsistent with the Declaration' (UN, 2011, p. 16). It was inconsistent with a politics of consent.

The Politics of Consent

The UN's guiding principles on business and human rights insist that states are responsible for 'ensuring a regulatory framework that recognises an indigenous peoples' rights over lands and natural resources' (UN, 2016a, p. 4). The regulatory framework 'requires legislation or regulations that incorporate international standards of indigenous rights' (UN, 2016a, p. 4). The maintenance of such a framework requires indigenous participation. Liberal democracy privileges personal agency over the possibility that the state will simply act benevolently to secure indigenous rights.

The Keystone XL pipeline in the US is an example of the indigenous right to consent being set aside in ways that contravene the Declaration and broader human rights norms. The pipeline was intended to carry oil from Alberta, Canada, to Nebraska, US, where it would join an existing pipeline to oil refineries on the US Gulf Coast. As well as contravening Article 26 of the Declaration (see Chapter 3), the pipeline contravenes the following articles:

> States shall consult and cooperate in good faith with the indigenous peoples concerned through their own representative institutions in order to obtain their free, prior and informed consent before adopting and implementing legislative or administrative measures that may affect them. (UN, 2007b, art. 19)

> Indigenous peoples have the right to maintain and strengthen their distinctive spiritual relationship with their traditionally owned or otherwise occupied and used lands, territories, waters and coastal seas and other resources and to uphold their responsibilities to future generations in this regard. (UN, 2007b, art. 25)

> 1. Indigenous peoples have the right to the conservation and protection of the environment and the productive capacity of their lands or territories and resources. States shall establish and implement assistance programmes for indigenous peoples for such conservation and protection, without discrimination.

2. States shall take effective measures to ensure that no storage or disposal of hazardous materials shall take place in the lands or territories of indigenous peoples without their free, prior and informed consent.

3. States shall also take effective measures to ensure, as needed, that programmes for monitoring, maintaining and restoring the health of indigenous peoples, as developed and implemented by the peoples affected by such materials, are duly implemented. (UN, 2007b, art. 29)

The Standing Rock Sioux community in the US received international indigenous support for its opposition to the pipeline. This international indigenous solidarity has been politically important. For example, the Sami Parliament of Norway's intervention contributed to the decision of pension fund Kommunal Landspensjonskasse (KLP) to divest its shares in companies contracted to build the Dakota Access Pipeline. KLP's decision was 'due to an unacceptable risk of contributing to serious or systematic human rights violations' (KLP, 2017, p. 1). Its further reasoning was that the pipeline required the flooding of land, protected under the 1851 Treaty of Fort Laramie, from which the Standing Rock Sioux Tribe had been improperly alienated, according to the US Supreme Court (p. 3). The pipeline was intended for the transportation of oil; however, Sioux people argued that it would interfere with access to sacred sites and safe drinking water. The UN special rapporteur found that the pipeline had been approved without 'adequate social, cultural or environmental assessment'. It was also approved in 'the absence of meaningful consultation or participation by the tribes' (UN, 2017c, para. 11).

The Great Sioux Nation objected to the negotiations on the US's behalf being conducted by junior officers of the Army Corps of Engineers. It viewed their lack of seniority as an affront to Sioux sovereign nationhood (KLP, 2017). The UN special rapporteur identified significant dishonesty in the Army Corps's environmental assessment; in particular, that negotiations were not conducted in good faith. For example:

> Maps in the draft environmental assessment omitted the reservations, and the draft made no mention of proximity to the reservation or the fact that the pipeline would cross historic treaty lands of a number of tribal nations. (Heim, 2017, para. 7)

For its part, KLP (2017) placed 'significant weight on the UN Special Rapporteur's assessment of the situation' (p. 8). KLP noted that the requirement under US law for 'government-to-government consultation had not occurred' (p. 9). The pension fund was further influenced by Article 32.2 of the Declaration, which provided that:

> States shall consult and cooperate in good faith with the indigenous peoples concerned through their own representative institutions in order to obtain their free and informed consent prior to the approval of any project affecting their lands or territories and other resources, particularly in connection with the development, utilization or exploitation of mineral, water or other resources. (UN, 2007b, art 32.2)

KLP's approach highlighted the Declaration's moral persuasiveness.

In Australia, mining requires the negotiation of land use agreements between mining companies and native title holders. Agreements must be registered by the Native Title Tribunal. However, the tribunal is not required to satisfy itself that the agreements represent the wishes of native title holders, nor is it required to consider whether the collective wish has been determined in a fashion acceptable to the group. Agreement by way of an accepted process is the intent, though not always the practical application, of the *Native Title Act 1993* (Cth):

> acts that affect native title should only be able to be validly done if ... every reasonable effort has been made to secure the agreement of the native title holders through a special right to negotiate. (preamble, para. xi)

However, it is procedurally unjust for a mining company to define the negotiating process. Therefore, the Declaration sets out principles to strengthen indigenous negotiating positions:

> States shall establish and implement, in conjunction with indigenous peoples concerned, a fair, independent, impartial, open and transparent process, giving due recognition to indigenous peoples' laws, traditions, customs and land tenure systems, to recognize and adjudicate the rights of indigenous peoples pertaining to their lands, territories and resources, including those which were traditionally owned or otherwise occupied or used. Indigenous peoples shall have the right to participate in this process. (UN, 2007b, art. 27)

Further:

> Indigenous peoples have the right to have access to ... just and
> fair procedures for the resolution of conflicts and disputes with
> States or other parties, as well as to effective remedies for all
> infringements of their individual and collective rights. Such
> a decision shall give due consideration to the customs, traditions,
> rules and legal systems of the indigenous peoples concerned and
> international human rights. (UN, 2007b, art. 40)

While some land use agreements elicit significant benefits for native title
holders (Langton & Longbottom, 2012), the *Native Title Act* does not
require an equitable negotiation process. Agreements do not necessarily
satisfy the requirement for free and informed consent.

Indigenous consent to Adani Australia for its proposed Galilee Basin coal
mine was (and is) contested. As a matter of justice, saying 'no' should be a
simple and straightforward process. It is true that economic development
is in the national interest; however, Australia's economic development
does not depend on a single project. It is a false dichotomy to present
that national imperative as a matter of conflict with the Indigenous right
to culture. They may be mutually exclusive in some cases, but, in a large
and diverse First World economy, the two do not always and necessarily
need to conflict.

The international mining industry is developing standards for the
acquisition of consent. It would be hugely ironic if the mining industry
were to take more seriously the moral argument for free, prior and
informed consent than nation-states. However, Adani is not a member
of the International Council on Mining and Metals and thus has not
committed to the international mining industry's view that free, prior and
informed consent means that the industry ought to:

- respect the rights, interests, special connections to lands and
  waters, and perspectives of indigenous peoples, where mining
  projects are to be located on lands traditionally owned by or
  under customary use of Indigenous Peoples
- adopt and apply engagement and consultation processes
  that ensure the meaningful participation of indigenous
  communities in decision making, through a process that is
  consistent with their traditional decision-making processes
  and is based on good faith negotiation

- work to obtain the consent of Indigenous Peoples where required by this position statement. (International Council on Mining and Metals, 2013, Overview, para. 1)

The Adani case is an extreme one; its environmental and cultural impact is profound, and its economic case is weak. By December 2017, 25 commercial banks had declined loans to support the project (Slezack, 2017).

Good reasons to consent are culturally informed and politically contextualised by colonialism, which is a unique determinant of political experience. The Declaration not only imagines safeguards to protect indigenous interests but also values arrangements that give meaning to the withholding of consent by indigenous peoples. The ability to withhold consent is a matter of political capacity. According to the UN (2016b), 'consultation and consent are not a single event, but should readily occur at all stages of a project from exploration to production to project closure' (p. 5). This is because consent without deliberation could reflect a genuine lack of interest in a policy decision. It could also reflect an individual's lack of confidence in the prevailing decision-making arrangements.

The criteria for reaching publicly reasonable decisions are substantive as well as procedural. Arguments are valid only 'in terms of whether they advance the common good of citizens and the justice of the political society' (Christiano, 1997, p. 243). Therefore, denying indigenous peoples' authority over their lands requires one to argue that such denial is in the interests of the common good, including the good of the indigenous people to whom the argument is being directed. The test is high: 'my proposal P is justified only if, supposing all members of the public were rational, all would accept it' (Gaus, 1997, p. 209). If a prejudicial position must be defended and open to challenge by the reasonableness of others, its intellectual foundation will be exposed.

Democracy might then reappraise public sovereignty to include indigenous peoples and perspectives in the national public. The relationship between the distribution of political capacity and political outcomes makes participation a requirement of justice. The Declaration helps liberal postsettler societies find ways of ensuring the influence of indigenous conceptions of fairness and rationality in the deliberative process. Mitchell (2014) suggested that one would not find conflicts over the commercial exploitation of indigenous natural resources if the right to self-government was secure. This does not mean that resource extractions, or other usages, by non-indigenous corporations could not occur; rather, that there would have to be benefits to indigenous landholders, and that the landholders themselves would decide the acceptability of any associated costs. Secure land rights would ensure indigenous landholders' decision-making capacity. Decisions would be made with respect to the landholders' conceptions of the common good, with themselves part of the 'common'.

To presume that indigenous interests are always and everywhere inconsistent with those of a separate public, and that commercial resource exploitation is always and necessarily in the public interest, is erroneous. As Bohman and Rehg (1997) argued, 'the political process involves more than self-interested competition governed by bargaining and aggregative mechanisms' (p. x). Indigenous conflict with resource development is not inevitable. However, conflict is always likely to occur when the 'public interest' is exclusively defined and when it presumes that development always and everywhere serves a non-indigenous interest with moral priority.

Article 28 of the Declaration contests the presumption of non-indigenous moral priority. However, its far-reaching implications, and postsettler states' rejection of these, have caused some indigenous people to be wary of the Declaration's value. Like all articles in the Declaration, Article 28 is aspirational. The knowledge that it is unlikely to be implemented may compromise its value to indigenous people seeking self-determination's fuller expression. It states:

1. Indigenous peoples have the right to redress, by means that can include restitution or, when this is not possible, of a just, fair and equitable compensation, for the lands, territories and resources which they have traditionally owned or otherwise occupied or used, and which have been confiscated, taken, occupied, used or damaged without their free, prior and informed consent.

2. Unless otherwise freely agreed upon by the peoples concerned, compensation shall take the form of lands, territories and resources equal in quality, size and legal status or of monetary compensation or other appropriate redress. (UN, 2007b, art. 28)

The Declaration and Liberal Human Rights: Indigenous Objections

Indigenous scholarly objections to the Declaration sometimes understate the relative and relational character of self-determination. While some emphasise an isolationist politics, others privilege polemic arguments against universal human rights as a concept of value to indigenous cultures. The latter follow Kulchyski's (2013) presumption that self-determination is incompatible with a liberal human rights framework and insistence that a 'human rights agenda must inevitably dismiss aboriginal cultural distinctiveness' (p. 73). Such critics of the Declaration presume that rights discourses compromise indigenous aspirations by locating them within a state-centred politics. These objections do not accept liberalism's capacity to create a politics of nondomination. They make indigeneity contingent on a political status of perpetual victimhood rather than aspiring to make domination a temporary state.

Later chapters will show that there is a larger and broader indigenous scholarship that more readily finds value in the Declaration as an instrument of political authority. They will show that there are strong indigenous alternatives to the view that 'nothing in this Declaration is likely to shift power imbalances [that] exist, and [that] continue to determine the future of Indigenous Peoples' (Watson & Venne, 2012, p. 91). For example, there is a body of scholarship on indigenous potential that rejects the presumption of perpetual victimhood. Instead, it recognises the power of resilience and agency and presents indigenous peoples' claims to self-determination in ways that help people to create lives that they have reason to value (O'Sullivan, 2017). The counterpoint is that such discourses run the risk of 'seeking political and/or economic solutions to contemporary challenges that require sustainable spiritual foundations' (Corntassel, 2008, pp. 115–116). Further, Garrow (2012) asked whether the Declaration should be used at all to support indigenous claims to the restoration of political authority. In his view, the Declaration lacks legitimate purpose because, as an instrument of Western human rights law, it does not acknowledge indigenous accounts of sovereignty.

Howard-Hassman (2014) described the Declaration's value as limited because it is not a treaty. With reference to Canada, Maciel (2014) suggested that an 'ontological conflict' between the state and indigenous claims obstructed the Declaration's implementation. In the Australian context, Mansell (2011) argued that:

> The fundamental values that make up Australia are based on the belief of white supremacy ... that notion is likely to ensure the Declaration does not become part of domestic law. (p. 659)

Other indigenous commentators reject the Declaration's capacity for meaningful implementation: 'To the extent that we litigate our right to sovereignty through this legal framework, we have lost the true essence of our sovereignty' (Coffey & Tsosie, as cited in Carroll, 2012, p. 146). This is because 'The politics of recognition in its contemporary form promises to reproduce the very configurations of colonial power that Indigenous peoples' demands for recognition have historically sought to transcend' (Coulthard, 2007, p. 437).

Champagne (2013) proposed that, rather than being an instrument of self-determination, the Declaration is a 'sophisticated form of assimilation' (p. 9). It 'treats indigenous peoples either as citizens of nation-states or as ethnic minorities with certain collective political, cultural and economic rights and historical claims' (p. 11), thereby redefining 'indigenous peoples into citizens and ethnic groups' (p. 11). For Ward (2011):

> The only substantive result ensuing [from the Declaration] is that the very structure of relations Indigenous peoples sought to challenge through the processes of the UN have been legitimated in law, the terms of the law itself having been subverted to accommodate legitimation. (p. 549)

Carroll (2012) also read an assimilationist effect into the Declaration, arguing that its inability to:

> recognize formally indigenous political institutions or to restructure indigenous peoples' political relationships with 'the States' reinforces the established construction of geographical scale (and indigenous nations' place on this scale) at international law. (p. 146)

Going even further, Corntassel (2012) described the Declaration's consideration of resource rights as assimilationist: 'the word resource is a way of commodifying and marketizing Indigenous homelands; in contrast Indigenous peoples view their homelands and communities as a complex web of *relationships*' (p. 92, emphasis in original).

Watson and Venne (2012) argued that the Declaration focuses not on 'the rights to self-determination under international law' but on indigenous rights as 'human rights issues within their respective colonised states' (p. 90). Indigenous peoples are therefore 'further encumbered: rather than retaining the rights of peoples as emphasised in the UN Charter, [indigenous peoples] have become objects of local human rights issues' (p. 90). In their view, self-determination is meaningless if it is concerned only with 'gaining political space without indigenous content' (p. 88). They argue that the Declaration's inattention to political space makes it a 'human rights instrument rather than an instrument [that] would provide a mechanism for advancing Indigenous Peoples' rights as nations and peoples' (p. 91).

Watson and Venne (2012) questioned whether the Declaration's dual focus on human rights and collective rights means that the 'individual identity position works to erode that of the collective' (p. 93) and argued that '[i]n an important way, human rights diminish the collective rights of Indigenous Peoples because they concern individuals within the paradigm of the particular state' (p. 96). They worried that allowing the UN Convention on the Rights of the Child to take priority over the Declaration gave states, rather than indigenous peoples, the authority to determine the child's best interests. The final Declaration did not include the draft declaration's statement preventing 'the removal of indigenous children from their families and communities under any pretext' (Iorns, 1993, 'Draft declaration', pt. II art. 6).

The context is clear: in the past, the pretext for removal has been genocidal. However, the final Declaration's seventh article does provide strong safeguards against the removal of children on that pretext:

1. Indigenous individuals have the rights to life, physical and mental integrity, liberty and security of person.
2. Indigenous peoples have the collective right to live in freedom, peace and security as distinct peoples and shall not be subjected to any act of genocide or any other act of violence, including forcibly removing children of the group to another group. (UN, 2007b, art. 7)

Watson and Venne (2012) objected to Article 7, claiming that it elevated 'the rights of the individual over the collective' (p. 97). However, as a work of indigenous peoples internationally, the Declaration remains an authoritative expression of indigenous peoples' political aspirations. Despite not gaining universal approval, its level of indigenous support shows a strong confidence in human rights as both a legal concept and political philosophy.

Watson and Venne (2012) also objected to the Declaration's equal application to men and women because equality undermined male and female distinctiveness in indigenous cultures and undermined an indigenous culture's capacity to define that distinctiveness for itself. Article 44 of the Declaration is explicit: 'All the rights and freedoms recognized herein are equally guaranteed to male and female indigenous individuals' (UN, 2007b, art. 44). Elsewhere, the Declaration maintains that:

1. Particular attention shall be paid to the rights and special needs of indigenous elders, women, youth, children and persons with disabilities in the implementation of this Declaration.
2. States shall take measures, in conjunction with indigenous peoples, to ensure that indigenous women and children enjoy the full protection and guarantees against all forms of violence and discrimination. (UN, 2007b, art. 22)

In a perspective that contrasts with Watson and Venne's, Kuokkanen (2012) argued that self-determination movements pay inadequate attention to violence against women and that:

> One can only conclude that it is prevailing and persistent gender injustice in both indigenous and mainstream societies that lies at the heart of the problem of indigenous women's human rights, not the conflict between individual and collective (or between universal and local) rights. (p. 237)

In the Australian context, violence against women is the most common offence for which Indigenous men are imprisoned (Australian Human Rights Commission, 2017). In the US, one in three indigenous women are raped. In 86 per cent of cases, the perpetrator is a non-indigenous man on a reserve and his non-indigenous status prevents prosecution by reserve authorities (Kuokkanen, 2012). Violence logically and necessarily obstructs women's self-determination (Kuokkanen, 2012; Raya, 2006; Smith, 2013); this shows the importance of self-determination as a right of individuals as much as for groups.

The National Congress of Australia's First Peoples consciously attends to women's self-determination by ensuring equal male and female representation. In contrast, in the Northern Territory, Australia, in 2012, in what the Chief Justice described as an 'extremely difficult case', the Supreme Court accepted cultural values as a mitigating factor in a 55-year-old man's nonconsensual sexual encounter with a 14-year-old girl:

> You [the defendant] believed that traditional law permitted you to strike the child and to have intercourse with her ... The Crown accepts that you believed that intercourse with the child was acceptable because she had been promised to you [at the age of four] and had turned 14 ... The Crown also accepts that, based on your understanding and upbringing in your traditional law, notwithstanding the child's objections, you believed that the child was consenting to sexual intercourse. (Chief Justice Martin, 2005, para. 17)

In accepting the defendant's explanation of his actions, the Court accepted the complainant's lesser humanity and lesser right to participate in the settlement of a contested cultural value. The claim that sexual contact is a cultural right that extinguishes the need for explicit consent can only hold if there is uncontested agreement about the practice in the indigenous nation in which the claim is made. In this context, the view that collective values are prior to individual values is no more than an argument that physical force determines cultural values. Neither principle nor broad acceptance is relevant to the construction of a cultural practice. In contrast, a liberal theory of indigeneity is concerned with all persons as repositories of a right to self-determination and with all persons' right to deliberate in the formation of shared values. Self-determination does not make sense if it is the preserve of the physically more powerful at the exclusion of the collective values and preferences of other members of a community.

If an indigenous person is prevented from claiming priority for their own culture—if they cannot say 'your cultural value is not mine'—their equal humanity is effectively denied. It follows that if one accepts unequal human worth in an indigenous community, one must accept the logic that justified colonialism: a hierarchy of human worth.

In the absence of an individual right to self-determination, the powerful are able to dominate others and frame their domination as reflecting the collective will—the collective construction of the values by which all must live. However, one cannot object to colonialism's inherent violence then also claim extant cultural values in defence of one's own violence. Indeed, a report on violence by the International Indigenous Women's Forum argued that 'it is not "culture" that lies at the root of violence against women, but practices and norms that deny women gender equity, education, resources, and political and social power' (Raya, 2006, p. 30). When the self-interested cultural conceptions of the physically powerful are privileged:

> analyses can run the risk of an idealised cultural determinism, especially if they focus exclusively on the semantics of cultural translation and provide wholly cultural answers to what are fundamentally political questions. (Wilson, 2008, p. 310)

It is unjust and illogical for violent men to propose that it is they alone who determine the cultural practices that all must share.

Pauktuutit, the Inuit women's association of Canada, made violence its most important priority. Commenting on the need for such measures, Kuokkanen (2012) noted, 'It appears that, for indigenous self-determination, violence against women is considered neither an indigenous rights issue nor a human rights issue' (p. 238). Violence is a contravention of another's capacity for self-determination. Borrows (2017) observed that '[i]t would be tragically ironic if nation-states began recognising and protecting the rights of Indigenous individuals, while Indigenous governments did not take the same action' (pp. 25–26).

As Kuokkanen (2012) argued, to suppose conflict between collective and individual indigenous rights 'is spurious as it appears to apply only to women's rights' (p. 227). The supposition is grounded in essentialist and grossly simplified accounts of Western and indigenous political philosophies. It requires an absolute and simplistic distinction between the two. Indeed:

> since Native women are the women most likely to be killed by domestic violence, they are clearly not surviving [as peoples]. So when we talk about survival of our nations who are we including? (Smith, 2013, para. 5)

In Maori thought, sexual abuse is more than violation of the individual, it is violation of all 'past and future generations' (Pihama et al., 2016, p. 9). Although its significance is broader than a human rights discourse can admit, this does not make the right to personal safety invalid or culturally alien.

The right to protection from violence is not a private affair. The argument that individual rights are inconsistent with, and subservient to, collective rights is a self-serving one used by individuals claiming moral authority for their own interests by claiming them as the uncontested values of the collective. Violence against women is an important case study in human rights discourse. One must take care not to remove the indigenous from the human in developing conceptions of self-determination. Recognition of the rights of indigenous women means that one must 'conceive both indigenous peoples' rights and indigenous women's rights as human rights [that] exist in a continuum' (Kuokkanen, 2012, p. 249) where 'securing indigenous women's rights is inextricable from securing the rights of the peoples as a whole' (p. 236).

Watson and Venne's (2012) view that 'the rights of the individual are often at odds with those of the collective' (p. 96) diminishes the reciprocal nature of individual–collective relationships. If the collective does not serve its members, it has no purpose and thus no durability. For these reasons, Watson and Venne's argument illustrates why the liberal rights of citizenship are worth claiming. For most people, the transfer of power from the state to indigenous elites is not self-determination.

Like Watson and Venne (2012), Boldt and Long (1984) failed to convincingly address the question of which liberal human rights people would deny themselves as incompatible with, or obstructive of, their values. Boldt and Long described the individual as the:

> repository of responsibilities rather than … a claimant of rights. Rights can exist only in the measure to which each person fulfils his responsibilities towards others. That is, rights are an outgrowth of every person performing his obligation in the cosmic order. In such a society there is no concept of inherent individual claims to inalienable rights. (p. 166)

It is important not to overemphasise indigenous objections to the Declaration. Wider indigenous support suggests that such objections reflect a minority view. At the same time, such objections are philosophically interesting for the questions they raise about relationships between the nation and the person. They are also important because, as McIvor (2004) argued, discrimination against women is by necessity an obstacle to indigenous self-government: 'after 135 years of sex discrimination by Canada, we were afraid of self-government. Why would neo-colonial Aboriginal government, born and bred in patriarchy, be different from Canadian governments?' (p. 128).

Until 1985, indigenous Canadian women's Indian status was revoked upon marriage to a non-indigenous man. Yet the reverse did not apply: not only could Indian men retain their status on marriage, but their non-Indian wives were also automatically accorded membership of the Indian nation (Kuokkanen, 2012). The state, not indigenous peoples, determined who was or was not Indian. The test of indigeneity was not a cultural one determined according to indigenous norms and values but one enshrined in state law to foster the destruction of indigenous communities. As Kuokkanen (2012) explained, 'For Indian women, "marrying out" literally meant a reality of exile from the communities, and hence from their rights and ties to their families, cultures, and identities' (p. 233).

In 1974, the Supreme Court of Canada rejected a challenge to the validity of the *Indian Act* (*Attorney-General of Canada v Lavell*, 1974). However, the Act was subsequently amended after the UN Human Rights Committee found that revoking indigenous women's status on marriage violated their human rights. This established an important international precedent for appealing to authorities beyond the state. However, the amendment still precluded those who had 'married out' from passing on their Indian status to their children. Indigeneity was not to be a matter of culture or ancestry but the marital status of one's mother. Further appeals saw minor amendments to the law (Kuokkanen, 2012). The indigenous women who mounted these cases and their supporters were 'harshly criticized for being anti-Indian and accused of betraying the self-determination struggles and of cooptation into colonial, Western discourses of individualism' (Kuokkanen, 2012, p. 235). However, such objections can only hold if women have no legitimate voice in the construction of collective self-determination.

Cultural maintenance cannot occur in women's absence. The codification of the right to self-determination in liberal terms is especially significant for women and children. The Declaration's presumption of equality is the underlying value that makes it an instrument of self-determination.

On the other hand, liberal democracy conflicts with the view that 'our [indigenous] rights are unconditional, not subject to mediation, and not susceptible to being settled by legislative or adjudicative mediation or compromise' (Garrow, 2012, p. 195). International human rights may then require a political trade-off that some indigenous peoples are not willing to accept. Human rights may override certain collective rights and conceptualising rights within a liberal paradigm may expose them to political contest in a non-indigenous arena. However, the alternative may be that indigenous peoples wish to exist in closed communities beyond the nation-state as holders of a singular citizenship pursuing an isolable self-determination. In contrast, as Chapter 6 explains, the First Peoples of Fiji may find it problematic that they are excluded from prevailing international definitions of 'indigenous' and thus from the provisions and protections of the Declaration.

Conclusion

Plurality in the distribution of political influence and authority is an essential constituent of the right to self-determination. It is the basis for indigenous inclusion in the sovereign public and for the participation of men and women in the development and evolution of cultural practices.

Mining policy provides insight into the political values motivating state resistance to substantive indigenous inclusion in public decision-making. It demonstrates an 'us' and 'them' binary that inaccurately portrays mining as always and everywhere in the public (i.e. non-indigenous) interest and always and everywhere opposed by indigenous people. This exclusive binary shows the political importance of indigenous inclusion in the sovereign whole as self-determining liberal citizens as well as the relevance of indigenous rights to human rights.

This chapter's critique of indigenous objections to the Declaration demonstrates the self-serving nature of some indigenous arguments against human rights as a contribution to discourses of self-determination, and supports the book's recurring argument in favour of a liberal theory of indigeneity requiring substantive and equal indigenous citizenship of both the state and the indigenous nation.

5

Self-Determination–the Power and the Practice

Introduction

Self-determination may, but does not usually, imply disrupting the territorial integrity of the state. However, it always presumes that the state cannot exercise singular or unilateral authority. Self-determination is a contested and complex concept. Quane (2011) has described it as 'notoriously difficult to pin down' and has argued that there is 'little if any guidance as to what it means in actual practice' (p. 69). Yet, neither of these characterisations are wholly correct nor, as this chapter will show, is Kingsbury and Grodinsky's (1992) observation that 'the right to self-determination is at present, a rather blunt ... and underinclusive instrument' (p. 393).

The Declaration does not define self-determination; however, it does provide general principles for developing the concept into policy practice. Consequently, one may think not of the right—but of the power—of self-determination. The power of self-determination includes, but is not limited to, an indigenous nation's self-government of its own affairs. It is a power that depends on political influence wherever decisions are made, which means that self-determination within the state is also fundamentally important to a meaningfully shared sovereignty.

Indigenous political authority within the state is not diminished by distinctive indigenous nationhood. The two sites of political authority are mutually reinforcing and provide opportunities for indigenous peoples to contest the coercive powers of the state. Self-determination rationalises shared political sovereignty.

Shared sovereignty affirms the indigenous citizen's political equality. It presumes that it is just for indigenous people to influence the aspirations, values and workings of the state. In this way, the state at least potentially expresses, rather than curtails, indigenous political aspirations. Shared sovereignty is a decisive statement against assimilation and coercion. It can be reflected in various ways; for example, through guaranteed representation in parliament or a voice to parliament, as is being claimed in Australia.

The Declaration helps societies to conceptualise what further capacities and powers shared sovereignty might entail and offers protections against the uncertainties of majoritarian democratic exclusion. Shared sovereignty is present when indigenous values substantively influence public policy. Shared sovereign authority reflects self-determination by presuming indigenous people's fundamental equality. It presumes that their cultural values and political aspirations rightly influence the conduct of public affairs. For example, as Justice Williams, the first Maori appointed to the New Zealand Supreme Court, argued:

> Fundamentally, there is a need for a mindset shift away from the pervasive assumption that the Crown is Pākehā (Anglo-Celtic), English-speaking and distinct from Māori rather than representative of them. Increasingly, in the 21st century, the Crown is also Māori. If the nation is to move forward, this reality must be grasped. (Waitangi Tribunal, *Te reo Māori*, 2010, p. 51)

Describing her experience as a moot court judge, Stephens (2017) explained what this remark could mean in practice:

> Of the six mooters, four of the students mooted in Māori. Each of them was able to move fluidly between an unconscious ownership of the legal system and of tikanga Māori, and a blistering critique of the same systems. Just one small symbolic and up-ending moment of something better. There are other such moments waiting to coalesce. (The Crown is also Māori, para. 5)

This illustrates the sentiment that 'we are all here to stay', or alternatively that Maori are not going to assimilate.

This chapter defines self-determination as political capacity or power, rather than simply a body of rights. It does so with reference to cross-jurisdictional examples, and examples from across policy domains, to show the political importance of indigenous peoples pursuing self-determination both within the state and within the indigenous nation. The examples also show what some indigenous policy actors imagine contributes to the self-determination of communities. Through these examples, this chapter demonstrates that there is both clarity on the meaning of self-determination and well-developed arguments to support its assertion.

Defining Self-Determination

In Canada, the right to self-government recognises an indigenous right to self-determination over matters 'internal to their communities, integral to their unique cultures, identities, traditions, languages and institutions, and with respect to their special relationship to their land and their resources' (Government of Canada, 1995, Part I – Policy framework, para. 1). The Declaration affirms this policy objective:

> Indigenous peoples, in exercising their rights to self-determination, have the right to autonomy or self-government in matters relating to their internal and local affairs, as well as ways and means for financing their autonomous functions. (UN, 2007b, art. 4)

However, self-government does not reflect self-determination's full scope. Self-government is not, for example, the same as shared sovereignty. Neglecting self-determination within the state restricts indigenous political influence—an influence that, for meaningful self-determination to occur, must be exercised wherever policy decisions are made.

Self-determination arises from geopolitical attachments. There are ways in which self-determination can only be realised with respect to those attachments. However, geopolitical rights to land, culture and independent political authority are not the sum of the right to self-determination. These rights over a defined territory do not diminish the claim to a share in national public sovereignty. As Kingsbury and Grodinsky (1992) observed, it serves no purpose to make self-determination a 'one-shot right, vindicated and exhausted by liberation from domination' (p. 393). It is self-determination—not self-government—that justifies guaranteed indigenous parliamentary representation and full participation in setting policy priorities, for example.

Self-determination within the state allows indigenous peoples to defend their independent authority against public intrusion. For example, in Canada, it allows indigenous people to defend against the effective veto that the minister of Aboriginal affairs and northern development enjoys over the decisions of a First Nations government (UN, 2014). This effective 'veto' includes reporting requirements to the federal minister that First Nations perceive as overly zealous and that perpetuate negative stereotypes. As the UN special rapporteur noted, indigenous nations are then positioned as 'inconsistent and corrupt … [which] … undermine[s] rather than promote[s] public support for self-government' (UN, 2014, p. 14).

The special rapporteur's observations parallel arguments used to discredit the Aboriginal and Torres Strait Islander Commission (ATSIC) in Australia. ATSIC was a public body exercising capacities of self-determination. The Howard Government (1996–2007) abolished it in 2005 because it 'separated' Indigenous people from the national body politic; though, in practice, Indigenous peoples had never been so included (O'Sullivan, 2017). Had Howard sought to further include Indigenous people, rather than abolish ATSIC, he would have listened to the strong political voice in favour of retaining the commission, or some other institution, to maximise Indigenous authority over their own affairs. It is for this reason that this book's central argument is that self-determination can only occur through independent indigenous nationhood if it also occurs *within* the state—that is, if indigenous peoples are included to share national sovereign authority.

Self-determination implies order and philosophical certainty. Its foundational principles insist that indigenous peoples have the capacity to decide what is morally important and to determine the political objectives they wish to pursue. Such decisions cannot be made by a guardian (in a guardian–ward relationship) or by the senior partner in a bicultural project. As Dodson has argued:

at the heart of all the violations of our human rights has been the failure to respect our integrity, and the insistence on speaking for us, defining our needs and controlling our lives. Self-determination is the river in which all other rights swim. (as cited in Scott, 1996, p. 814)

Self-determination is a state of political capacity. It is the freedom to determine one's identity and significant because 'Autonomy and self-realisation are the key concepts for a practice with an immanent purpose, namely, the production and reproduction of a life worthy of human beings' (Habermas, 1997, p. 41). The right of self-determination is important because it is preliminary to recognising and strengthening the broader human rights that indigenous people hold in common with all others. The scope of political freedom must be the same for all people.

Corntassel's (2012) understanding of self-determination is that 'By focusing on "everyday" acts of resurgence, one disrupts the colonial physical, social and political boundaries designed to impede our actions to restore our nationhood' (p. 88). However, Corntassel (2008) has also argued that self-determination is much more than political struggle. He explained that 'resurgence means having courage and imagination to envision life beyond the state' (Corntassel, 2012, p. 89) *and* having the capacity to make distinctive and substantively equal contributions to its public life. Further, it means that:

> evolving indigenous livelihoods, food security, community governance, relationships to homelands and the natural world, and ceremonial life can be practised today locally and regionally, thus enabling the transmission of these traditions and practices to future generation. (Corntassel, 2008, p. 119)

When people are self-determining, the state cannot be all powerful and singularly constraining. Self-determination limits the state's political jurisdiction by placing moral limits on the exertion of power and recognises that the state is neither a neutral entity nor one with a natural tendency towards benevolence. Self-determination cannot satisfy itself with state affirmative action policies for indigenous peoples but must advance an inherent right to participate in public affairs.

Self-determination does not threaten state sovereignty; instead, it threatens the exclusive presumptions that have traditionally positioned indigenous peoples beyond the public in whose name sovereignty is exercised and by whom its character is determined. The contemporary Indigenous

Australian claim to a voice to parliament is a claim to self-determination through a more substantive participation in state sovereignty. Just outcomes presuppose just decision-making processes.

Self-determination is not a private right; therefore, the 'project of indigenous self-determination ... [is not] a phenomenon outside of general political structures' (Kuokkanen, 2012, p. 226). The state ought not be an institution that 'consults' with indigenous peoples but an entity in which they actively and substantively participate. Sovereignty is thus shared, and political arrangements ought to allow the just and orderly distribution of that sovereignty. The Declaration provides a framework for the distribution of political authority because:

> Indigenous peoples and individuals are free and equal to all other peoples and individuals and have the right to be free from any kind of discrimination, in the exercise of their rights, in particular that based on their indigenous origin or identity. (UN, 2007b, art. 2)

The Declaration provides a framework for thinking about self-determination as not just a body of rights but also a body of capacities and powers.

Self-Determination—Beyond the Right, Towards the Power

Self-determination's translation from a right to an effective and substantive power is politically important. The point that matters is indigenous peoples' intertwining *capacities* for self-determination and citizenship. To that end, one may define self-determination with reference to Nussbaum (2008) and Sen's (2002) theory of human capabilities, which presumes that:

> Human beings live and interact in societies, and are, in fact, societal creatures. It is not surprising that they cannot fully flourish without participating in political and social affairs, and without being effectively involved in joint decision-making. (Sen, 2002, p. 79)

The right to self-determination is affirmed as one that belongs simultaneously to individuals and to peoples. According to Taylor (1994), self-determination's character and purpose 'requires that it be sought in common' (p. 59).

The right to self-determination is one of procedural justice. It flows from relational justice between the state and indigenous entities *as well as* relational justice *within* the state. It presumes a state in which indigenous people participate as free and equal citizens, not consigned to perpetual victimhood (MacDonald & Muldoon, 2006) but to substantive respect through collective and individual citizenships that are responsive to immediate political context and actively shaped by indigenous peoples. The Declaration says that:

1. Indigenous peoples have the right to maintain and develop their political, economic and social systems or institutions, to be secure in the enjoyment of their own means of subsistence and development, and to engage freely in all their traditional and other economic activities.

2. Indigenous peoples deprived of their means of subsistence and development are entitled to just and fair redress. (UN, 2007b, art. 20)

Further:

Indigenous peoples have the right to determine and develop priorities and strategies for exercising their right to development. In particular, indigenous peoples have the right to be actively involved in developing and determining health, housing and other economic and social programmes affecting them and, as far as possible, to administer such programmes through their own institutions. (UN, 2007b, art. 23)

Deliberative capacity is important. According to Anaya (2009), self-determination's:

essential idea … is that human beings, individually and as groups, are equally entitled to be in control of their own destinies, and to live within government institutional orders that are devised accordingly. (p. 187)

Rights are recognised by the state, but they are neither claimed nor provided by its benevolence. As the Organization of American States put it in 1948, 'the essential rights of man are not derived from the fact that he is a national from a certain state, but are based upon attributes of his human personality' (para. 2). Following on from this, Anaya (1993) explained:

> Self-determination is not separate from other human rights norms; rather, self-determination is a configurative principle or framework complemented by the more specific human rights norms that in their totality enjoin the governing institutional order. (p. 323)

Self-determination is the opposite of an assimilationist order in which indigenous aspirations are excluded and indigenous people are positioned beyond the political on the presumption of deliberative incapacity. Self-determination's distinctive moral quality is that it offers indigenous peoples protection in justice—if not always in practical politics—against the vagaries of majoritarian democracy.

Self-determination is diminished if one site of indigenous authority is privileged over the other. While 'the perceived size and nature of the respective spaces vary' (Broderstad, 2014, p. 72), the two spheres are mutually reinforcing of the other's authority. For example, in New Zealand, the Tuhoe iwi's desire to increase its scope of activity, influence and authority through taking responsibility for state welfare policy is intended to reduce the incidence of welfare dependence, raise educational attainment and reduce unemployment (Moore et al., 2014, p. 42). A gradual increase in the relative size of the Tuhoe middle class would be one of the outcomes that occurs over time—a further determinant of self-determination and general wellbeing.

The Crown and Tuhoe have formally acknowledged each another's mana (status and authority; Moore et al., 2014) to reflect a relationship between independent Maori authority and the state as one of 'quasi-international quality' (Gover, 2015, p. 346). This relationship is one in which state power is constrained by negotiation, the obligation to act in 'good faith', judicial intervention and Maori recourse to the moral persuasiveness of international norms of justice. The Tuhoe proposal aspires to fulfil many of the functions of the modern state. The intended relationship is also one of participatory parity, in which 'no political matter may be decided other than by the people, lest that matter (no matter how obvious or true or right) become a source of domination over the people' (Bellamy, 2007, p. 5).

A relational account of self-determination, and also of politics itself, 'encourages the view that indigenous peoples must seek influence in a variety of different political forums in which they have become integrated with non-indigenous communities and governments' (Murphy, 2008, p. 203). In contrast with the Tuhoe approach, which offers some promise as an example of differentiated citizenship (discussed in detail in Chapter 8), the right to self-government in Canada, being only concerned with the right to political authority inside the indigenous nation, is limited, especially when set apart from opportunities for indigenous people to express a distinctive citizenship of the Canadian state. The policy requires:

1. The restoration of indigenous presences on the land and the revitalization of land-based practices;

2. An increased reliance on traditional diets among Indigenous people;

3. The transmission of indigenous culture, spiritual teachings and knowledge of the land between Elders and youth;

4. The strengthening of familial activities and re-emergence of indigenous cultural and social institutions as governing authorities within First Nations; and,

5. Short-term and long-term initiatives and improvements in sustainable land-based economies as the primary economies of reserve based First Nations communities and as supplemental economies for urban indigenous communities. (Alfred, 2009, p. 56)

Self-government allows nation-to-nation relationships between indigenous groups and the Canadian state to develop. These relationships remain points of principle in Canadian politics. However, the Trudeau Government's (2015–) rhetorical support for wider self-determination is still to find policy substance. For example, in 2016, the Canadian Human Rights Tribunal found systematic discrimination against indigenous children that governments ought to have addressed. The case exemplified the absence of indigenous self-determination *within* the state as a factor contributing to disputes over the nature and quality of child welfare services. This example of Canadian self-determination's weak structural capacity highlights its inability to consider indigenous aspirations beyond territorially defined communities and shows that it 'would be careless to assume that colonialism in Canada has ended' (Richmond & Cook, 2016, p. 10).

Self-determination's concern with the large and complex task of realising indigenous authority within and over the tribe, nation or iwi is important in its own right; however, these bodies are also regulated and influenced by state policy and legislation. This, in turn, affects the lives of indigenous people as citizens of the nation-state. Conversely, indigenous people are justifiably wary of the state and its tendency to assimilate. The state is only sporadically a force for indigenous good; yet, it is also the case that political systems and values evolve with time. Liberal democracy means that people should not expect perpetual exclusion from a share in public sovereignty. Alertness for new and different opportunities is part of what it means to be a self-determining people able to influence 'the nature and levels of interactions with the non-indigenous world' (Thornberry, 2002, p. 9).

No conception of justice is fixed, and the moral persuasiveness of instruments such as the Declaration must be allowed the opportunity to influence public values. It is only in accepting self-determination's relative and relational character—in recognising the significance of one people's engagement with another—that self-determination becomes politically worthwhile. It is a matter of reasonable democratic expectation that indigenous peoples 'increase their influence through their increased ability to collaborate with the wider community through close relations with non-indigenous people' (Broderstad, 2014, p. 73). Indeed, the strength of these relationships is a principal determinant of self-determination and is also preliminary to developing relationships of 'respect and trust' (p. 73).

Self-Determination as Political Capacity

Chief Percy Guichon of the Tsilhqot'in people understood self-determination as a relative and relational capacity:

> We do live side-by-side and we need to work on a relationship to create or promote a common understanding among all our constituents ... we need to find the best way forward to consult with each other, regardless of what legal obligations might exist. I mean, that's just neighbourly, right? ... We share a lot of common interests in areas like resource development. We need to find ways to work together, to support one another on these difficult topics. (quotation is as it appears in the source, as cited in TRC, 2015, p. 301)

The capacity for self-determination is intertwined with the capacity to share sovereignty. While self-determination can constrain state sovereignty, indigenous self-determination can also be part of that sovereignty so that sovereignty is reconciled with a liberal democratic indigenous citizenship. Alternative, strictly compartmentalised views about the nature and location of political power exclude indigenous peoples from public affairs. The state is then prevented from dealing with difference. An important omission because:

> Dismissing others' norms out of hand, or refusing to engage them seriously, or giving up easily and declaring stalemate quickly all negate the cosmopolitan spirit of the proximity principle because such actions deny that one must inevitably share with others the circumstances of living … Another group's social practices are just as much 'a repository of human wisdom' as one's own, and cosmopolitan moral responsibility demands that each person try to enrich her own 'parochial' claims by entertaining these alternate sources of wisdom and modifying one's practices in light of others' persuasive standards of conduct. (Klausen, 2014, p. 37)

The question of great policy importance that self-determination asks is: how might people simultaneously 'stand in the dreaming, and in the market' (Grant, 2016)? How do they stand in the market as indigenous citizens of a plural democracy—whether it be the market for housing, education or work, or the market for culturally cognisant health care? Standing in the market as a self-determining citizen might also presume policing concerned with protection rather than victimisation, and markets for schooling that do not treat culture as foreign and troublesome.

If the right to self-determination requires authority over policy development and delivery, it is not simply an abstract claim but one that requires institutional arrangements designed specifically to give effect to that authority at all levels of the policy process. For example, Durie (2001) argued that, in New Zealand, self-determination means that Maori might 'live as Maori' or, as Bishop et al. (2010) framed it in an educational setting, *achieve* as Maori. For these reasons, the Maori Statistics Framework draws on Sen's (2002) capabilities approach to development to propose Maori wellbeing as a 'function of the capability of Maori individuals and collectives to live the kind of life that they want to live' (Wereta, 2001, p. 5).

Launched in 2010, the New Zealand social policy measure Whānau Ora develops a form of self-determination in which *whanau* (families) can:

- be self-managing
- live healthy lifestyles
- participate fully in society
- confidently participate in Te Ao Māori [the Maori world]

- enjoy economic security and successful involvement in wealth creation
- be cohesive, resilient and nurturing
- be responsible stewards of their living and natural environments. (Kukutai, Sporle & Roskruge, 2017, p. 17)

As Kukutai et al. (2017) explained, 'This whānau capacity model emphasises progressive advancement rather than the management of adversity, and focuses on functional capacities' (p. 18).

Contemporary studies of Maori wellbeing show a desire to participate in public affairs. This means that the state cannot be positioned as 'theirs' in a 'them' and 'us' relationship. The state might then acknowledge that:

> From a Māori worldview, western concepts of wellbeing that are founded on the presumption of universality and the primacy of the individual, have limited relevance for contemporary measuring and monitoring of well-being for Maori. (Kukutai et al., 2017, p. 15)

Wellbeing reflects cultural epistemology. For Maori, 'there is not a strict dividing line' (Kukutai et al., 2017, p. 15) between individual and *whanau* wellbeing.

Whānau Ora is concerned for *whanau* capacity to care for members whose wellbeing is afflicted by ill health or unemployment and presumes that the individual's wellbeing is the *whanau*'s collective moral concern. The Whānau Rangatiratanga Framework's capability dimensions are:

- Sustainability of Te Ao Māori
- Social capability
- Human resource potential
- Economic self-determination. (Social Policy Evaluation and Research Unit, 2016, p. 12)

Its *whanau rangatiratanga* principles are:

- Whakapapa/Thriving relationships
- Manaakitanga/Reciprocity & support
- Rangatiratanga/Leadership & participation
- Kotahitanga/Collective unity
- Wairuatanga/Spiritual & cultural strength (Distinctive Identity). (p. 5)

As Kukutai et al. (2017) explain, Boulton and Gifford's study of *whanau* resilience found that Maori people emphasised:

- the desire that their children experience a better life than theirs
- the importance of establishing a foundation for their children
- providing children with stability and security
- providing a 'decent' environment for them to grow up in
- instilling cultural values
- having role models and maintaining healthy attitudes and lifestyles
- having good personal health
- maintaining balance between mental, physical and spiritual wellbeing

  …

- the importance of happiness in everyday life
- having a clear sense of belonging or identity, and active participation in Te Ao Māori and mainstream contexts
- a duty of mutual care and support within each whānau
- whānau solidarity and intergenerational connectedness
- financial security
- spiritual wellbeing
- a sense of future success and potential (Boulton & Gifford, 2014). (Kukutai et al., 2017, p. 21)

Ratima et al.'s (2007) related proposal to increase the size of the Maori health workforce shows that, while self-determination can be incredibly complex, it can also be very simple. Increasing the size of the Maori health workforce does not reflect the constitutional or structural transformations that many indigenous scholars and policy actors seek; however, it does reflect political values and practices that influence people's capacity to live lives that they have reason to value. According to Ratima et al. (2007), the distinguishing characteristics of a policy to increase the Maori health workforce include:

- Māori led, focused and targeted interventions;
- consistent investment over a prolonged period;
- emphasis on the development of dual cultural and clinical competencies;
- integration of student support programs within a university environment;

- provision of comprehensive support to tertiary students, including financial assistance, access to Māori mentors and peer support, and inclusion in communities of learning;
- congruence with industry needs;
- supported transitions into and between study and work;
- attention to the broader determinants of Māori health workforce participation; and
- action across the workforce development pipeline (including secondary schools). (p. 543)

In Ratima et al.'s work, self-determination prefigures a postcolonial order despite—as Watson and Venne (2012) put it in the Australian context— 'the road back to country' being 'long and filled with colonial encounters' (p. 87). However, the point of that long road is usually remarkably clear. For Brands (2014), self-determination means that, in Australia, by 2030, there would be:

- [t]rue reconciliation—a treaty, constitutional recognition, resulting in [an] Australian society in which Aboriginal and Torres Strait Islander people and cultures have pride of place
- [r]eal community control in [the] community controlled sector
- [s]ignificant improvement in health outcomes and life expectancy
- [r]eal cultural equity, no racism
- incorporation of Aboriginal knowledge into the mainstream (i.e. 'Nunga streaming' not 'mainstreaming')
- foregrounding and privileging of Aboriginal models of health (e.g. spirituality)
- greater control of, and informed choice about, education and employment
- celebration of diversity and difference
- integration of Aboriginal values [into] the landscape
- no 'othering'
- Aboriginal representation at all levels of government and society
- Aboriginal people ... influencing decisions, across all dimensions of society
- a return to values and ethics (individual and community), meaning less focus on consumerism and capitalism, and [more on] sustainable and ecological ways of living. (p. 12)

Anderson (2014) imagined displacing Australia's neo-colonial order with a post- or even noncolonial one. Accordingly, by 2030, a representative 29-year-old Indigenous Australian woman would:

- [have] higher education qualifications [and be] ... technically, socially and culturally savvy
- [be m]entally and socially in touch with community and family
- [be a n]on-smoker, [and have a] good BMI [Body Mass Index] [and] no drinking problem
- [be in a s]table relationship
- [have] choice and control over fertility, childcare and employment
- [be w]orld-aware but with a sense of individual purpose
- [be w]ell-travelled [and have] global visions
- [be e]conomically independent
- [be g]rounded in mixed cultures
- [build] on family history for positive outcomes. (Brands, 2014, p. 13)

Alternatively, 'we can imagine an Australia [that] turns its back on diversity, [that] increases the divide between rich and poor, and [that] sees little or no real improvement in the health and wellbeing of its First Peoples' (Anderson, 2014, pp. 4–5). The representative 29-year-old woman's life would then be distinguished by:

- [f]amily breakdown/violence
- [a]busive relationship[s]
- [s]chool dropout
- [s]ubstance abuse
- [i]mprisonment
- [h]ousing crisis
- [having c]hildren at risk/social service involvement
- [s]tress/mental illness
- [c]hronic disease
- [p]remature death
- [having a] family and community deeply affected by her loss. (Brands, 2014, p. 13)

Anderson's view of self-determination defines the conditions of equality. Since equality is not a neutral concept, it is not understood by all people in the same ways and for the same purposes. Rather than an abstract state, equality is a political value whose functions and proper distributions are culturally contextualised.

There are examples of Indigenous Australians exercising self-determination in policy development and implementation. Indigenous-led peak bodies have influence across policy domains. However, 'the Government could achieve significant progress in realising the rights of indigenous people if it consulted and worked much more closely with these organisations' (UN, 2017b, para. 5). In this context, it is significant that the National Congress of Australia's First Peoples 'has been dismally disregarded by the Government' (para. 6). Conversely, Aboriginal community–controlled health organisations (ACCHOs) show that people think about the right to health as a right that is realised through citizenship-as-capacity—that is, through self-determination.

The first Aboriginal medical service was established in Sydney in 1971. Its purpose was to support 'self-determination through community control … initiated, designed and controlled by Aboriginal people' (Foley, 1991, p. 4). Almost 50 years later, '[ACCHOs] are leading the way in our community, in translating what [the Declaration] means, in practice, through community control' (Davis, 2013, p. 12). ACCHOs give the Declaration practical application. As Davis has observed, they pursue 'self-determination through the right to health' (p. 11) and, in doing so, provide a model that the UN Permanent Forum on Indigenous Issues has advanced as a model of international best practice.

Australian self-determination is not the 'failed experiment' of the Howard Government's (1996–2007) rationale for abolishing ATSIC in 2005. Instead, it is a contemporary aspiration that Australian Indigenous peoples actively pursue as far as prevailing policy paradigms will allow. Among the constraints that ACCHOs face is that, like New Zealand's various tribal bodies, they may influence public policy but are not usually able to make it. In 2016, the National Health and Medical Research Council's (NHMRC) Translating Research into Policy and Practice Forum facilitated significant and substantive Indigenous contributions to policy debate. However, it had no formal capacity to develop these ideas to give them official sanction. The forum showed that, while there were mechanisms for Indigenous voices to be heard, they were unable to hold influence. Its recommendations and priorities emphasised citizenship as an underlying political theme that must be considered as part of the policy process.

The capacity to influence depends on the strength of one's citizenship. The remedial nature of contemporary policy priorities reflects citizenship's historic weaknesses. The forum's overarching aim was to 'identify evidence gaps … and policy gaps, informed by … systematic reviews' (NHMRC, 2016, p. 1). The forum stressed 'Community grounded responses to social and emotional well-being' (p. 2). Its principled recommendation for pregnancy and childbirth was a plea for the opportunity to make personal choices equivalent to that which urban dwelling women take for granted: 'policies should reflect and respect women's choice to stay in community and to decide who can be present at the birth' (p. 2).

The forum's report of proceedings is a claim for citizenship. It is not a claim for privilege or additional rights, nor is it a claim for differentiated citizenship. It is simply a plea for public policy to work effectively for Indigenous members of the Australian nation. As a further example, in terms of access to data and bureaucracy, the report stressed that the focus was on 'better sharing of data, particularly across portfolios, and its use by bureaucrats' (NHMRC, 2016, p. 4). Acutely aware of what had eluded the bureaucracy in the past, the forum identified a connection between broad principles, aspirations and data 'to prioritise needs and policy, and identify research gaps and needs' (p. 4).

The inadequate collection of population data weakens the relationship between policy and self-determination. According to the forum, it is important to know how 'existing data can be better used to improve understanding of, and provide insight into, the health and wellbeing (and the health care needs) of young Aboriginal and Torres Strait Islander Australians' (NHMRC, 2016, p. 3). The forum identified housing, criminal justice and education as determinants of health and proposed better policy integration. The absence of a specific 'Aboriginal community controlled education sector' (p. 3) was also noted.

Education is the only Council of Australian Governments Closing the Gap target in which progress is consistently made (Commonwealth of Australia, Department of the Prime Minister and Cabinet, 2018b). Its importance as an underlying determinant of self-determination means that education warrants constant policy attention. Education is also the underlying determinant of indigenous access to the middle class, which is itself a determinant of better health, housing and general wellbeing (O'Sullivan, 2017). Much is known about success in indigenous education, yet there are also many instances of policy failure. Just as Indigenous peoples in Australia have clear expectations of the health system, there is clarity of thought among Indigenous actors on what they expect education to provide to them as Indigenous citizens of the state.

The National Congress of Australia's First Peoples (2018) argued that the Declaration and the right to self-determination should inform education policy. However, it also noted that 'Our children continue to be denied access to culturally appropriate and effective education, which prevents them from flourishing later on in life' (p. 2). Earlier, the congress summarised the principles that informed its expectations of schooling: 'The maintenance and advancement of our cultures and full participation of our Peoples in national economic, political and social life' (National Congress of Australia's First Peoples, 2013, p. 7). It argued that schools that help to achieve these objectives will:

- Foster a genuine shared sense of responsibility with the communities they serve, and a respectful and committed sense of partnership;
- Recognise and value the diversity of Aboriginal and Torres Strait Islander cultures and languages;
- Value and foster the maintenance of Aboriginal and Torres Strait Islander cultures by incorporating Indigenous knowledge in their curriculum;
- Are free from discrimination and hold institutionally-supported high expectations for students;
- Have a high quality, experienced, skilled and stable workforce. (National Congress of Australia's First Peoples, 2013, p.7)

In New Zealand, the Waikato-Tainui people has a well-developed strategy to inform its people's education (see Waikato-Tainui, 2015). Its influence is important but ultimately constrained by its lack of capacity to operate schools and determine what and how they will teach. The Key (2008–2016) and English (2016–2017) governments' charter schools policy was intended to facilitate such capacity. Charter schools were established in New Zealand in 2011; however, the model was heavily criticised for failing to meet the stated policy expectations (Thrupp, 2016) and was abolished by the Ardern Government in 2017. The educational quality of charter schools was potentially compromised, as they were not required to employ registered teachers nor to follow the national curriculum (Jenkins, 2018). Yet, according to some Maori commentators, neither of these things—teacher registration and national curriculum—routinely supported Maori achievement. They claimed that charter schools, unlike public schools, provided opportunities for Maori to exercise authority over their education. An ethnic divide on the policy was noticeable within the government's senior coalition partner, the Labour Party. Its decision to abolish charter schools was not supported by Maori members attracted to their self-determining potential (Paterson, 2017).

Charter schools were intended to improve student achievement, with a particular focus on children who had not succeeded in the state system. Maori featured disproportionately among the policy's target group— namely, those who had:

1. Low academic baselines and lack of core skills for learning
2. Histories of disengagement from education
3. Complex socio-economic and health needs that create barriers to education
4. Lack of education role models to support economic and educational success. (Jenkins, 2016, p. 9)

The flexibility that charter schools enjoyed was intended to promote innovation. However, their focus on Maori children with histories of underachievement in mainstream schooling meant that there was no scope for teaching according to Maori pedagogies and epistemologies for the benefit of any Maori citizen who wished to be educated in that way. Charter schools were an admission of state failure and a haphazard and incomplete response that did not obviously add to the provisions for schooling in the Maori language and culture that were already well established within the state system.

Indigenous education systems are important expressions of the right to self-determination; however, so too is mainstream education's cultural responsiveness and ability to serve indigenous aspirations. For example, Te Kotahitanga, a successful project to improve Maori achievement in secondary schools, was developed on the presumption that it is important for education systems to understand indigenous peoples and their cultures. Its philosophy of Maori policy leadership presumed that the solution to entrenched Maori educational failure lay not with the system itself but with the people the system determined as lacking in the capacity to define and pursue success, and their capacity for self-determination (Bishop et al., 2010). Te Kotahitanga shows the importance of Maori policy and professional leadership inside the state because, in the case of Maori education, non-Maori state schools are the places where most Maori receive their early formal education. It is through schooling that people develop many of their capacities for citizenship and the relationships and skills to work out the terms of their membership of the political community.

Conclusion

The capacity to engage with others is an essential constituent of the right to self-determination. Indigenous peoples must contribute equally to working out the terms of their membership of the nation-state and must also have the capacity to exercise self-determination within their own political structures. Self-determination is not absolute autonomy. As Kuokkanen (2012) explained:

> The aboriginal political discourse regarding self-determination would be more useful to communities if it incorporated an understanding of the individual as relational, autonomous and self-determining. That is, they developed a perspective of individual self-determination as necessary to move collective self-determination beyond rhetoric to a meaningful and practical political project that engages aboriginal peoples, and is deliberately inclusive of indigenous women. (p. 237)

Self-determination recognises that 'real power' lies in 'inherent *responsibilities*' (emphasis in original, Corntassel, 2012, p. 91). It does not constitute reconciliation as a 'politics of distraction' (p. 91) but as a politics of possibility. One knows that self-determination is occurring when indigenous peoples find that there is a reconfiguration of state power opening new and meaningful spaces of political opportunity. Those spaces are opened when public sovereignty is truly the people's authority and when all people—not just some—share that authority and have a meaningful say in determining what it means to be a citizen—what it means to be one who deliberates.

Possibilities are opened further when indigenous peoples work out for themselves what it means to be an indigenous citizen; in particular, when they work out the institutional values and arrangements that are needed for indigenous people to deliberate in ways that make sense to them and that recognise their distinctive aspirations. Chapter 7 uses sovereignty as a theoretical framework for discussing these questions and examining what it means to argue that greater self-determination requires a different kind of sovereignty. It follows Chapter 6, which examines self-determination in selected jurisdictions that were not opposed to the Declaration when it was adopted in 2007 but have not necessarily committed to its comprehensive implementation in their own jurisdictions.

6

The Declaration in Comparative Context

Introduction

Self-determination is universally important as a relative and relational political authority. It is also important as a body of political capacities. This chapter examines the ways in which the right to self-determination has been interpreted in various jurisdictions that voted in favour of the Declaration or, in the Russian Federation's case, abstained from the vote. The comparison is instructive both in respect of the scope of the right to self-determination (including the matter of defining what constitutes an indigenous people) and in understanding the effect that prevailing political values and broader conceptions of human rights may have on self-determination's substantive form.

Unlike Australia, Canada, New Zealand and the US, Bolivia and Ecuador incorporated the Declaration into their constitutions, which, for Gussen (2016), makes them 'technically postcolonial' (p. 871). However, like Belize and the Scandinavian states—especially Sweden and Finland—they display an inconsistent practical regard for the Declaration. In none of these jurisdictions are indigenous peoples satisfied that it is being implemented. Their view is supported by UN special rapporteurs on the rights of indigenous peoples and by independent civil commentators, as discussed in this chapter. In these jurisdictions, indigenous rights to culture are generally accepted along with sometimes significant pluralism in public affairs. However, the extent of such rights is variable, and plurality can be limited and conditional. As in the four dissenting states, the most significant point of contention is over the scope of the principle of free, prior and informed consent.

The question of whether self-determination belongs to indigenous peoples only in relation to their own institutions, or whether it also belongs to indigenous peoples within the state as part of a substantive differentiated citizenship, is also contested, though not to the extent of there being no examples of effective indigenous voice as part of an inclusive national polity. In this respect, this chapter's comparative focus draws out lessons that expand or limit the bounds of political possibility.

This chapter's discussion of authoritarian states—the Russian Federation, Fiji and Malaysia—demonstrates the importance of prevailing political values in terms of self-determination and shows that disagreements over the meanings of self-determination and indigeneity occur amid wider uncertainty about the concept of human rights itself. The chapter discusses definitional problems in working out the rights of indigeneity and notes the limits of conflating indigenous and minority rights; such conflation sets geopolitical and cultural relationships aside as the foundational point in indigenous peoples' identity. For the same reason, this chapter contests the notion of indigenous peoples as necessarily subjugated or dominated, as this conception makes indigeneity a temporary political status rather than a permanent cultural one.

The distinction between indigenous and minority ethnic status is an important feature of Ainu politics in Japan. The chapter uses Ainu experience to show the importance of international cooperation among indigenous peoples in asserting the claim to self-determination. It discusses the importance of an indigenous people's self-recognition as indigenous, as well as the importance of mutual recognition by the state to indigenous people's capacity for full and meaningful participation in public affairs.

Participation, Inclusion and Self-Determination

'Sovereign' indigenous peoples share public authority in the Plurinational State of Bolivia. They coexist as many nations under one state and under a new and inclusive constitution. The Constitution of Bolivia was approved at a public referendum in 2009 and attracted 60 per cent support. Coincidentally, Bolivia's constitutional review, which occurred as the Declaration was being developed, was proposed under the leadership of an indigenous state-president (Rice, 2014).

Bolivia's Constitution recognises 36 indigenous languages. It guarantees proportionate indigenous representation in the parliament and provides for indigenous 'autonomies' as units of local government (*Constitución Política del Estado* [Political Constitution of the State] 2009 [Bolivia]). Rice (2014) described these local government arrangements as 'plurinational constitutionalism' (p. 59).

Bolivia's Constitution includes clauses that closely parallel articles in the Declaration. For example, its second article, which corresponds with the Declaration's fourth, asserts that the right to self-determination '[consists in the indigenous] right to autonomy, self-government, their culture, recognition of their institutions, and the consolidation of their territorial entities' (*Constitución Política del Estado*, art. 2). Meanwhile, the Declaration affirms that:

> Indigenous peoples, in exercising their right to self-determination, have the right to autonomy or self-government in matters relating to their internal and local affairs, as well as ways and means for financing their autonomous functions. (UN, 2007b, art. 4)

Bolivia has the world's most developed public recognition of the Declaration and its principles, yet its full application remains constrained and contested.

Indigenous peoples in Bolivia used the Declaration for the first time in 2011 to resist a highway development that was ultimately approved in 2017. This result notwithstanding, the objection was 'an important test of the state's internalization of indigenous rights norms'; according to Rice (2014), 'by framing their claims in the Declaration's terms, indigenous groups' went some way towards 'narrowing the gap between legislation and practices' (p. 59).

Conversely, however, Bolivia does not protect non-renewable resources on indigenous lands. The state accepts no obligation to acquire indigenous consent before resource extraction occurs. Therefore, the Bolivian Constitution does not 'fully change power relations between the state and indigenous peoples' (Rice, 2014, p. 61). Similarly, autonomies are unable to operate according to indigenous decision-making processes.

These restrictions do not support Rice's further contention that, in taking 'the rights and responsibilities of municipalities', these units of government are 'in essence subverting indigenous governance to the logic of the state' (p. 60).

An alternative explanation is that this kind of independence, which works to undermine notions of an exclusive settler state in binary conflict with indigenous institutions, is a step towards an inclusive plurinational polity in which public institutions are arranged to support independent indigenous participation in decision-making. From this perspective, a more important constraint is that autonomies can only be established in rural areas with majority indigenous populations. Although it is a model available to just half the indigenous population (Rice, 2014), it is one with potential for expansion in respect of geographic coverage, domains of responsibility and culturally cognisant modes of operation. It is also the case that countries such as Ecuador, which has an indigenous population comprising 25 to 30 per cent of the total population, voted for the Declaration because it creates no new rights.

Ecuador saw the Declaration as ensuring the extension of existing human rights norms to indigenous peoples. The country claims to recognise indigenous rights especially in relation to language and land (UN, 2013). The 2008 Constitution of the Republic of Ecuador (*Constitución de la República del Ecuador*) recognises indigenous rights to culture, land and language, and allows legal pluralism in public affairs. Therefore, in contrast to Rice's (2014) objection in relation to Bolivia, Gussen (2016) argued that, in Ecuador, autonomous indigenous local governments establish the principle of subsidiarity that provides self-determination with an important philosophical foundation.

Subsidiarity complements indigenous participation in national state affairs. It is the idea that decision-making authority is best located as close as possible to the point of policy impact. It informed devolution policies in New Zealand during the 1980s and rationalised the creation of iwi authorities to contract with government to deliver public services with at least some reference to cultural preferences in policy delivery (O'Sullivan, 2007). The principle was imperfectly implemented as contracts were often burdened by excessive reporting requirements and insufficient funding for the work required (Boston, 1996). Nevertheless, the idea that indigenous people should, as far as possible, have the capacity to take responsibility for their own affairs is essential to self-determination.

Subsidiarity is a logical expression of the right to self-determination in Ecuador. As Gussen (2016) noted:

> The fact that there were already international instruments that provided guidance on Indigenous rights meant that the most efficient way forward (as far as obtaining consensus is concerned) was to import these instruments into municipal law, and give a constitutional weight to ensure their implementation. (p. 898)

However, as in other jurisdictions that claimed an advanced commitment to the Declaration, there were broader domestic values that shaped its translation into substantive political practice. In 2013, Ecuador introduced restrictions on freedom of expression and freedom of association. These restrictions contravene Articles 16 and 19 of the Declaration. There are also examples of the harassment of indigenous political actors and of the right to free, prior and informed consent being overridden (Cultural Survival, 2016). Rather than recognising a right to offer or withhold consent, Gussen (2016) explained that Ecuador recognises the right to 'free, prior and informed consultation' (p. 897). Consent and consultation are different concepts. Gussen's example does not unequivocally establish that what is elsewhere regarded as an aspirational goal has 'actually become part of the enforceable domestic law in Ecuador' (p. 898).

Ecuador attempted to justify its use of consultation (as opposed to consent) in response to a UN Human Rights Council Universal Periodic Review (UPR) recommendation from Germany. However, Ecuador's explanation only served to highlight the political inadequacy of consultation in terms of substantive and meaningful participation as part of the state:

> The Constitution of the Ecuadorian State establishes consultation as a right of all Ecuadorians, but particularly for communities, peoples and nationalities, a previous, free and informed consultation, but not their consent. Additionally, it is necessary to indicate that Ecuador recognizes the existence of Indigenous Peoples living in voluntary isolation, with the consequent obligation of guaranteeing their lives, of respecting and making others respect their self-determination and will to remain in isolation, and defend the validity of their rights, which turns unviable obtaining their consent. (as cited in Cultural Survival, 2016, p. 5)

Ecuador's argument was that indigenous rights are qualified and belong only to groups who choose to live in isolation. Such rights are not full and comprehensive rights to self-determination. The country's position demonstrates the importance of the distinction between self-government and self-determination as discussed in Chapter 5.

An alternative approach, and one that is more significant in terms of the breadth of possibilities it creates for interpreting the right to self-determination, is to read the Declaration in conjunction with other instruments including the Universal Declaration of Human Rights (UN, 1948). This foundational document shows the scope of the rights that indigenous peoples share with other citizens *within* the state:

1. Everyone has the right to take part in the government of his country, directly or through freely chosen representatives.
2. Everyone has the right of equal access to public service in his country.
3. The will of the people shall be the basis of the authority of government; this will shall be expressed in periodic and genuine elections which shall be by universal and equal suffrage and shall be held by secret vote or equivalent free voting procedures. (UN, 1948, art. 21)

These points are not diminished by the greater—though not exclusive—attention that the Declaration on the Rights of Indigenous Peoples places on rights *beyond* the state. Nor are they diminished by the Declaration's primary focus on state responsibility rather than indigenous capacity, though it is in this respect that the UPR's recommendations to Ecuador did not reflect the breadth of the Declaration's possibilities.

Focusing on states 'doing justice' to indigenous peoples is important, but it is not the same as creating space for indigenous peoples to do justice to themselves. The following illustrative recommendations were supported by Ecuador (parentheses indicate the recommending state in the UPR; UN, 2012b):

> Take targeted measures to address the situation of girls and the challenge of ensuring the accessibility to registration for indigenous peoples and people of African descent as well as for migrant families. The right of every child to a name and nationality should be guaranteed (Finland). (s. 135.33)

Ensure that community activists and indigenous leaders can exercise their right to peaceful assembly and protest and that anti-terrorist legislation is not misused to inappropriately censure such activities (Canada). (s. 135.37)

Develop a mechanism to gather statistics on education of indigenous groups. (s. 135.55)

Adopt special measures for the realisation of collective rights of indigenous peoples and the adoption of mechanisms to ensure their right to be consulted (Hungary); Undertake effective measures to further strengthen the existing mechanisms for consultation with the indigenous population on issues which have an impact on the economic and social aspects of the indigenous population (Malaysia); Continue to improve the promotion and protection of the rights of indigenous peoples, in particular the respect of their cultural and linguistic diversity, and further think about programmes and policies for indigenous peoples, particularly focusing on women and children (Morocco); Institutionalize the right to consultation of the indigenous population and involve civil society and indigenous groups in the elaboration of a functioning consultation mechanism in line with Ecuador's commitments under ILO [International Labor Organization]-Convention 169 (Norway). (s. 135.57).

Adopt legislation to guarantee the fulfilment of the collective rights of the indigenous population and Afro-Ecuadoreans, so as to increase affirmative actions in favours of racial and gender equality (Paraguay). (s. 135.58)

The following illustrative recommendation was not supported by Ecuador:

Establish clear consultation procedures in order to implement the right to free, prior and informed consent of indigenous peoples as contained in the Constitution (Germany). (UN, 2012b, s. 136.3)

Belize is another example of a state that supports the Declaration but habitually contravenes its provisions. It does this even though its own Supreme Court found that:

This Declaration, embodying as it does general principles of international law relating to indigenous peoples and their lands and resources of such force that the defendants, representing the Government of Belize, will not disregard it. Belize, it should be remembered voted for it. (as cited in Boyer, 2014, p. 13)

In its 13-page report to the Human Rights Committee of the International Covenant on Civil and Political Rights, the Maya Leaders Alliance (2018) of Belize argued that:

> Despite orders from its own Supreme Court and the Caribbean Court of Justice to do so, the government of Belize has failed to delimit, differentiate, and title the Maya territory, or to meaningfully consult with Maya peoples to protect Maya land rights. The government's failures have resulted in the violation of the Maya peoples' rights to be free from discrimination, rights to self-determination, and rights to property. (p. 1)

The report recommended solutions that were consistent with the Declaration and did not threaten the integrity of the state. They included recognition of a representative body to engage in state policy formation and the full implementation of court orders affirming indigenous claims that are consistent with the Declaration (Maya Leaders Alliance, 2018).

The Maya Leaders Alliance (2018) also argued for the recognition of customary rights, customary systems of government, repair of environmental damage due to logging and other non-Maya commercial activity on Maya lands. In line with the Declaration, it called on the state to:

> refrain from acting, or permitting or tolerating third parties to act, in ways that might affect the existence, value, use, or enjoyment of the property located within the geographic area occupied and used by the Maya peoples, until such time as it has developed a mechanism to delineate, demarcate, or otherwise protect Maya lands. (Maya Leaders Alliance, 2018, p. 13)

In Scandinavia, Sami peoples, cultures and traditional livelihoods are constitutionally protected. There are structured opportunities for Sami participation in the public affairs of Denmark, Norway and Sweden, all of which voted for the Declaration. In 2017, together with Finland and Iceland, these states reaffirmed their support for the Declaration: 'The Nordic countries strongly support the Declaration, including its emphasis on the right to self-government and participation. These are central to ensure that the rights of indigenous peoples are respected' (Hattrem, 2017, para. 2).

The Norwegian Government established the Sami Rights Commission in 1980. Its 'positive rights' interpretation of Article 27 of the International Covenant on Civil and Political Rights (UN, 1966a) contributed to the establishment of the Sami Parliament (*Sámediggi*), which has become an important institution and distinctively indigenous part of the state (Broderstad, 2014). Sami self-determination in Norway is best understood from a relational perspective. Broderstad (2014) argued that, while contemporary arrangements are an improvement on the benign interpretations of the International Covenant on Civil and Political Rights that undermined Norwegian assimilationist policies, they do not embody the active protection of distinctive indigenous rights that the covenant imagined, namely:

> In those States in which ethnic, religious or linguistic minorities exist, persons belonging to such minorities shall not be denied the right, in community with the other members of their group, to enjoy their own culture, to profess and practise their own religion, or to use their own language. (UN, 1966a, art. 27)

A 'consultation agreement' establishes the terms of the relationship between the Sami and Norwegian parliaments. The agreement proceeds with reference to Convention 169 of the International Labor Organization on indigenous and tribal peoples and its principles of relational justice: 'the rights of indigenous people to consultation, negotiation and real participation in decision-making processes' (Broderstad, 2014, p. 84). According to Broderstad (2014), the 'enhanced recognition of rights expresses both a principle of autonomy and close relations between the Sami and wider political community' (p. 84).

The right to autonomy is an expression of subsidiarity, and the emphasis on relationships with the wider community reflects principles of differentiated citizenship. However, the Norwegian model is limited in the sense that the right to autonomy is restricted to Sami homelands. If the right to self-determination belongs to all peoples, it ought not be restricted in this way.

Broderstad (2014) is careful not to position the agreement as one that guarantees justice. Even in these Nordic jurisdictions, the UN Special Rapporteur on the Rights of Indigenous Peoples argued that it is necessary:

> To explore ways to ensure that there is policy coherence between the positions they take in international human rights forums and those they take at home … the standards of the final [policy] outcome should not be lower than those to which all three states have committed in endorsing the Declaration. (UN, 2016b, p. 6)

The special rapporteur recommended that the Norwegian Sami Parliament be granted a role in the 'oversight and evaluation of Sami education programs and their quality' (UN, 2016b, p. 20). The rapporteur also recommended better support for Sami languages of which there are nine—each of them 'threatened' or 'extremely threatened' (p. 6).

The special rapporteur made similar recommendations to the Swedish state. Critical of that country's Sami language policy, she was blunt in her 'encouragement' of Sweden 'to introduce reforms to ensure that the Sami Parliament has greater independence from State institutions and authorities' (UN, 2016b, p. 20). She urged Sweden to review the Sami Parliament's statutory status and function in relation to government institutions and to ensure that adequate funding was allocated for the parliament to carry out its work as a popularly elected body (UN, 2016b).

The special rapporteur had earlier recommended that Norway strengthen mechanisms for assessing land and resource claims, and had proposed more effective consultative measures and arrangements for the settlement of these claims. She also proposed stronger measures to protect indigenous interests in relation to commercial mining licences, arguing that Sami interests ought to be managed consistently with contemporary human rights values (UN, 2016b). Norway is yet to adopt the recommendations (UN, 2016b). Nevertheless, it is an important measure of relational justice that, under the Norwegian consultation agreement, most of the 40–50 consultations that occur each year lead to concurrence on legislation. The agreement makes consensus possible in ways not achievable in Australia, for example, because, as objections to the idea of a guaranteed indigenous voice to parliament show, there is no political agreement that an entrenched procedure for meaningful participation should in fact exist.

The Norwegian and Swedish Sami parliaments are popularly elected; however, they differ in their broader structures and capacities to influence national public policy. The Norwegian *Sámediggi* was established to 'enable the Sami people in Norway to safeguard and develop their language, culture and way of life'; by contrast, the Swedish *Sámediggi* was established as a 'special government agency' (Josefsen, Mörkenstam & Saglie, 2015, p. 37). In Norway, the *Sámediggi* may consider 'any matter that in the view of the Sami parliament particularly affects the Sami people'; in Sweden, the *Sámediggi*'s authority is to 'monitor issues related to Sami culture' in that country (Josefsen et al., 2015, pp. 37–38). The parliaments provide voices *to* government—not voices *in* government.

In relation to Australia, this distinction may be instructive as the country works out the functions of its proposed Indigenous voice to parliament (see Chapter 7).

The UN special rapporteur found that, relative to Norway, Sami opportunities for self-determination in Finland were severely restricted. The rapporteur's recommendations to the Finnish Government were comprehensive and concerned elementary breaches of the right to self-determination. There were unresolved differences between the state and Sami people on the functions that the Sami Parliament ought to enjoy, and Sami interests in relation to mining were inadequately protected. According to the special rapporteur, Sami people in Finland were not properly included in decision-making over the use of forestry lands, which has significant implications for the right to culture. It also has significant implications for the provision of education. The special rapporteur argued that Finnish public education did not adequately contribute to the linguistic and cultural aspects of the right to self-determination (UN, 2016b).

The special rapporteur stressed the importance of people being able to make decisions about the distribution of *adequate* resources. The importance of this capacity for self-determination appeared in the observation that the 'solution' to cultural and linguistic revitalisation lies in further strengthening indigenous peoples' ability to develop and implement their own programs for economic development and job creation, education, preservation and development of cultural expression and knowledge, and public order, including the protection of women and children (UN, 2016b).

In January 2017, Sami peoples and Finland, Norway and Sweden concluded negotiations on a common framework for the implementation of the right to self-determination. However, the resulting Sami Convention was contested and, by December that year, had been returned to the Sami parliaments for further negotiations. The Norwegian National Human Rights Institution was not convinced that the convention, which privileges the right to consultation over the right to full democratic participation complied with the Declaration.

According to the Sami parliaments, the states' consultative efforts reflect the limits of consultation as a pathway to self-determination. Nevertheless, as a reflection of the inconsistencies and uncertainties that universally distinguish indigenous public policy, all three states are working to strengthen consultation's legal basis (International Work Group for Indigenous Affairs, 2018). Also, in marked contrast with Australia, the Sami Convention recognises free, prior and informed consent as an essential constituent of the right to self-determination. Like Canada, the Norwegian Parliament has established a Truth Commission to consider the effect of state assimilation policies. Sweden and Finland are contemplating similar measures. Broderstad (2014) argued that 'by making use of the political rights of citizenship', Sami people in Norway have 'had significant breakthroughs in terms of their political influence and ability to self-govern' (p. 74). Subsequent chapters of this book develop theoretical arguments on the relationship between self-determination and public sovereignty, exploring possibilities for noncolonial expressions of citizenship, sovereignty and democracy, and concluding that the Declaration provides important moral and political guidance on the strengthening of these relationships.

The Right to Self-Determination and the Politics of Definition

The Russian Federation is the only nonliberal state that exists over Sami territory. Significantly, it did not participate in discussions on the Sami Convention and abstained from the vote to adopt the Declaration. It does not routinely acknowledge indigenous fishing and other natural resource rights or the principle of free, prior and informed consent (International Work Group for Indigenous Affairs, 2018). The state's general restrictions on political expression further compromise the right to self-determination. The UN Committee on the Elimination of Racial Discrimination observed that:

> Russia had again failed to provide disaggregated data on the socio-economic status of indigenous peoples and other vulnerable groups, something that had been explicitly requested by the committee in the previous concluding observation. It also noted with concern the broad application of the term 'extremism' to silence indigenous and other organisations ... Further concerns and recommendations were noted regarding indigenous land rights, specifically Russia's failure to create federally protected Territories of Traditional Nature Resource Use, irreparable harm

caused to indigenous land by extractive industries and denial of hunting and fishing rights. (International Work Group for Indigenous Affairs, 2018, p. 47)

In 2013, the Russian Federation informed the UN special rapporteur of the politically significant fact that indigenous peoples in that country had not been colonised. The special rapporteur agreed that this was true but argued that they shared with indigenous peoples elsewhere 'marginalisation and other struggles arising from their minority status' (UN, 2013, Interactive dialogue, para. 4). This argument understated the significance of geopolitical associations, and also of indigeneity itself, as geopolitical associations are inescapably determinants of what it means to be indigenous.

Newcomb (2011) similarly understated the meaning of indigenous by adopting 'dominated peoples' (p. 578) as his definition of indigeneity. The indigenous experience in Fiji, for example, shows this definition's inherent and far-reaching limits. Indigenous Fijians comprise more than 50 per cent of their country's population and are not dominated by another ethnic group. However, their contemporary politics is shaped by colonial experience, state rejection of many of the claims that they make by virtue of prior occupancy, and conflict over land and natural resource use. These claims of indigeneity are usefully evaluated with reference to the Declaration (O'Sullivan, 2017), which will not 'overturn' domination as Newcomb (2011) observes, but may, over time, influence the ways people think about the configuration of the state and the place that indigenous peoples occupy within it. Certainly, it is a gross overstatement to argue that 'not one of the [Declaration's] 46 Articles … addresses the issue of domination' (Newcomb, 2011, p. 579).

Fiji's vote in favour of the Declaration was conditional. It noted that the Declaration may not have been adopted if the UN General Assembly had insisted on consensus on the full scope of the right to self-determination (UN, 2013). It did not accept that an indigenous right to self-determination was applicable in its own jurisdiction. For Fiji, demography (i.e. the indigenous population's majority status) trumped culture and geopolitical attachment in its definition of indigenous. Nor could Fiji accept a definition of self-determination if it threatened the territorial integrity of any state and rejected the idea that prior occupancy could justify ethnic privilege for indigenous people (UN, 2013).

Ethnic privilege is an argument often raised to discredit indigenous claims. It has some justification in Fiji where there is a history of interpreting indigenous 'paramount' political authority as creating political rights depending on others' exclusion by, for example, limiting appointment to the offices of president and prime minister to indigenous Fijians (O'Sullivan, 2017). Similarly, while the three coups and putsch that have overthrown governments since 1987 were vastly more complex than a politics of ethnic struggle, all but the most recent were expressed by the perpetrators as claims to the rights of indigeneity (O'Sullivan, 2017).

Conversely, ethnic privilege is raised to discredit land rights claims in Australia. In 2018, member of the Australian Parliament and leader of the One Nation Party Senator Pauline Hanson said that she 'gets really upset when people say this is Aboriginal land' (Khalil, 2018, para. 2). Ethnic privilege is also used to justify the narrow and exclusive liberalism of people like the former Australian prime minister John Howard (see Chapter 3).

The Declaration's ultimate concern is the codification of rights, not the codification of privilege. The distinction between rights and privileges would nevertheless be especially helpful to Fijian indigeneity's conceptualisation of a just and robust body of political capacities and responsibilities. It would also help to conceptualise and express just claims against the state (O'Sullivan, 2017). The Declaration shows that indigenous claims to distinctiveness—to live and participate in public life as indigenous—need not be claims to privilege.

Doubts about the Declaration's applicability to Fiji deprive that country of a moral and legal framework likely to contribute to a more just and stable political order (O'Sullivan, 2017). The Declaration would assist the Fijian politics of indigeneity to develop theoretical consistency and cohesion as well as a pragmatic account of the self-determination that Fijian people seek, which neither majority population status nor the ethnicity of the prime minister or president can achieve.

To take the argument further, Bowen (2000), in questioning whether 'a reversal in political fortunes could create newly "indigenous" peoples out of formerly dominant ones' (p. 13), exposed the problem with defining indigenous with reference to domination. The politics of indigeneity's defining purpose is to achieve substantive and enduring self-determination; in other words, nondomination. A people does not cease to be indigenous when it ceases to be dominated. From this perspective, Martinez Cobo's (1981) widely accepted working definition of an indigenous people is limited and limiting:

> Indigenous communities, peoples and nations are those [that], having a historical continuity with pre-invasion and pre-colonial societies that developed on their territories, consider themselves distinct from other sectors of the societies now prevailing in those territories, or parts of them. They form at present non-dominant sectors of society and are determined to preserve, develop and transmit to future generations their ancestral territories, and their ethnic identity, as the basis of their continued existence as peoples, in accordance with their own cultural patterns, social institutions and legal systems. (p. 379)

The question of domination or nondomination is shrouded in greater complexity than Martinez Cobo's definition can address. Peoples' perceptions of rights are culturally conditioned. Fiji's majority indigenous population, for example, views indigeneity as a source of political rights for much the same reasons as the minority indigenous populations of Australia and New Zealand (O'Sullivan, 2017).

Domination and subjugation can only describe a contemporary circumstance, yet the Declaration's point is to establish an enduring politics of nondomination. The Fijian case shows the contested nature of the meaning of domination and the different perspectives that indigenous people hold of the relationship between domination and substantive self-determination. Nor does an indigenous group dominating others, as has occurred in Fiji, guarantee its self-determination (O'Sullivan, 2017). Power relationships are not so simple; their complexities need to be understood and the limits of— as well as the possibilities for—self-determination worked out. As the Fijian case shows, the desire to lose the status of nondominance does not suggest losing the status of indigeneity because indigeneity describes a political status only after it describes a cultural one.

The indigenous chief executive of Fiji's Citizens' Constitutional Forum, Akuila Yabaki, argued that the Declaration would contribute to indigenous Fijians' self-determination by recognising:

> our right to be different, and to act as an individual or as part of a community as we choose. It encourages participation in matters [that] affect us all such as education, social welfare, health, environment and governance without discrimination.

> From it we should learn that multiculturalism is what makes us all part of the common heritage of mankind. We are all entitled to exercise and practice our beliefs, cultures and religions, and should not interfere in the rights of other people to do the same. (Yabaki, 2011, para. 10)

This account of political authority allows corporate indigenous membership of a single national polity alongside the rights and responsibilities of indigenous citizenship. A further distinction with Canada and New Zealand is that, in those jurisdictions, the rights of citizenship are liberal political rights. While institutional racism impedes their realisation, political rights are not constitutionally limited as they are in Fiji. Indeed, the Declaration indicates that the relationship between individual liberty and group rights is circuitous and interdependent, with each being equally important missing constituents of the Fijian right to self-determination (O'Sullivan, 2018a).

There should be no question of the Declaration's applicability to Fiji. As UN special rapporteur James Anaya (2008) explained:

> The basic normative justification of the Declaration is stated in the sixth preambular paragraph, which acknowledges that 'indigenous peoples have suffered from historic injustices as a result of, inter alia, their colonization and dispossession of their lands, territories and resources, thus preventing them all from exercising, in particular, the right to development in accordance with their own needs and interests'. (p. 16)

Indigenous Fijians fit Watson and Venne's (2012) description of peoples who 'have not been able to decolonize' (p. 93). Although they have recovered their majority population status and have been able to dominate national political institutions, they have not been able to translate power into meaningful opportunities. The reasons are complex and multifaceted (O'Sullivan, 2017, 2018a). They show that indigenous politics is not distinguished by what Carroll (2012) described as the 'imperial binaries' of 'assimilation or secession' (p. 156).

The extension of the Declaration's terms and provisions to Fiji is legitimate and efficacious. The withdrawal of colonial power has not removed the constraints placed on postcolonial indigenous self-determination (O'Sullivan, 2017, 2018a). The native Fijian experience as a people excluded from normative definitions of 'indigenous', and thus from the Declaration's provisions, provides a point of contrast.

Durie (1998) explained why, from a Maori perspective, one cannot accept indigeneity as a temporary status belonging to a people while they are 'oppressed' but not once they have successfully contested that oppression:

> A firm Māori identity … [requires] access to whānau, hapū, and iwi and confirmation that future generations of Māori will be able to enjoy their lands and forests, rivers and lakes, harbours and the sea and the air. These goals underlie the significance of Māori self-determination. (p. 239)

Ainu experiences in Japan also show indigenous peoples making geopolitics—rather than just politics—fundamental to their identity and ensuing political claims. Ainu attach great significance to public recognition of their status as indigenous people as distinct from an ethnic minority.

Rights and Recognition

Although Japan voted for the Declaration, its recognition of the distinction between Ainu as an indigenous population and Ainu as an ethnic minority has been mixed and conditional. Its vote for the Declaration occurred in a climate of philosophical inconsistency, and, by 2007, it had not ratified the International Labor Organization's convention (Convention 169) on indigenous and tribal peoples (International Work Group for Indigenous Affairs, 2018).

From 1899 until 1997, Ainu policy was managed under the *Hokkaido Former Aborigines Protection Act*. In 1997, a proposed 'New Ainu Law' became a point of contention between Ainu people and the state. The UN Special Rapporteur on Contemporary Forms of Racism, Racial Discrimination, Xenophobia and Related Intolerance was concerned that the proposed law focused only on narrowly defined conceptions of culture, and argued that:

> The Ainu want to see included in this law the recognition of their status as indigenous peoples, the promotion of their indigenous rights in conformity with international law, and the fight against the discrimination they face. However, the Government has not acceded to this request … They are among the few indigenous peoples in the world who have no land recognized as their indigenous land. (UN, 2006a, para. 49)

Indigenous claims against the state are supported by an international indigenous politics that predates cooperation on the Declaration. The Ainu claim to self-determination benefited from the globalisation of indigenous political thought and practice that occurred during the 1970s. International cooperation propelled Ainu political activity 'into large-scale social movements' (Tsutsui, 2018, p. 42). Most importantly, it created a political focus 'beyond dependence on the government toward a more full-throated assertion of their rights as indigenous people' (p. 42). For a people whose indigeneity was denied by the state, the evolution of new internationally sanctioned norms of justice was especially significant. Recalling a visit to a Canadian First Nation in 1978, an Ainu observed:

> To my complete amazement, when I stepped out of the gate at the Vancouver airport, I was greeted by a group of indigenous people performing their traditional dance in their traditional costume. It was shocking to me that an indigenous people could exhibit its traditional culture with such pride in a highly modernised setting of an international airport ... The leader of the indigenous people told us that they are trying to organise a conference on indigenous peoples and the UN and encouraged us to be a part of it. To us, the UN was like a different world and it just didn't seem realistic that we could be part of such a conference. (as cited in Tsutsui, 2018, p. 47)

This story of the normalisation of indigenous culture in the public space, and of indigenous political expression, documents a step towards indigeneity's mainstreaming—a contested and tortuous, but nevertheless important, process.

Mainstreaming indigeneity is important because it contributes to recasting 'otherness' from political marginalisation to the positive assertion of distinctive presence (O'Sullivan, 2017). It is a statement that we are among the 'all' who 'are here to stay'. Its intent is to bring the human rights of indigenous peoples into the mainstream of political thought. The Declaration contributes by providing indigenous peoples with nonstate benchmarks and value systems against which to define their claims in language that, in liberal societies at least, makes sense to the state. At the same time, domestic indigenous politics is exposed to new ideas about what is just and how justice might be pursued.

Human rights are not conditional on conforming to externally imposed values and modes of behaviour; yet it is indigenous peoples' reluctance to conform to the values and expectations of majority populations that leads to social isolation and political exclusion. The tension between group rights and individual rights is a significant demonstration of this reluctance. The indigenous desire to privilege collective rights to land as a source of material sustenance and spiritual meaning contrasts with views of land as an exploitable commodity.

In 1980, Japan told the UN Human Rights Committee that ethnic, religious and linguistic minorities do not exist in that country. However, by 1987, international and domestic pressure led Japan to change its position. The government told the UN Working Group on Indigenous Populations that it 'does not claim that Japan is "a mono-ethnic state" nor does it deny the existence of Ainu people' (Tsutsui, 2018, p. 58). Its vote for the Declaration was followed by parliamentary recognition of Ainu indigeneity in 2008.

However, recognition does not always lead to meaningful political influence. The broader political context in which indigenous claims are made are also important. Just as the Russian Federation's authoritarian political culture limits all people's fundamental freedoms, Malaysia's recognition of 13.8 per cent of its population as indigenous does not set aside state hegemony. Malaysia voted for the Declaration, and its constitution protects native customary rights, yet the provisions of both are routinely violated (Cultural Survival, 2018). In its 2018 submission to the UN Human Rights Council UPR, the international nongovernment organisation Cultural Survival (2018) argued that Malaysia continues to 'initiate' contraventions of land rights; disregard the right to free, prior and informed consent; and not take adequate measures to confront violence against women.

In Sarawak, indigenous peoples faced (and continue to face) displacement due to dam construction. Though a number of dams forming part of a proposed 12-dam project were discontinued, partly due to indigenous resistance, others were planned that would add to human displacement (Cultural Survival, 2018). Conversely, in 2015, the federal Cabinet established a committee for the land rights of indigenous peoples, which prioritised improvements to land administration, infrastructural development, education and training for young people, increasing sustainable economic activity, assistance for people in the bottom two income quintiles and improvements in public service delivery (Human Rights Commission of Malaysia, 2017).

Such tensions between the general authoritarianism of states like Malaysia and the Declaration's human rights principles are important. The Special Rapporteur on the Rights of Indigenous Peoples told a committee of the UN General Assembly in 2013 that 'Without greater awareness of the human rights values and concerns encompassed in [the Declaration], its implementation would be "difficult, if not impossible"' (UN, 2013, para. 1).

Different perspectives on what ought to comprise the minimum rights of indigenous peoples reflect different perspectives on the source of those rights. Are rights the state's to confer as an expression of its sovereignty or do they belong inherently by virtue of humanity? Are they contextualised by virtue of one's indigeneity? If human rights belong inherently and are not the gift of state benevolence, one strengthens the capacity for self-determination to develop as a worthwhile relative and relational politics. However, authoritarian states carefully safeguard sovereignty, not just against external interference but also against the claims of people living under their rule. They can rationalise voting for the Declaration to satisfy the interests of international diplomacy while giving it minimal domestic recognition on the basis that it is simply aspirational.

The Indigenous Peoples Network of Malaysia (2013) represents 62 indigenous communities and organisations. Its simple but profoundly important opening argument to the UPR in 2013 was that:

> Collectively our peoples count as among the most poor in Malaysia, due to marginalisation from the mainstream society on account of the non-recognition of our rights as contained in both national and international customary law. ('Context', para. 1)

The submission identified violations of the Declaration in respect of land; free, prior and informed consent; self-governance; intimidation and harassment by public authorities; and violations of the right to citizenship. Interestingly in terms of this book's arguments for indigenous political authority inside the state, the submission also requested UN advocacy and capacity-building assistance that would 'contribute to expanding opportunities for indigenous peoples to participate meaningfully in the development of Malaysia, while maintaining our laws, customs, and identity' (Indigenous Peoples Network of Malaysia, 2013, Needs of Malaysia and role of UN, para. 3).

China is another authoritarian Asian state that voted for the Declaration. In contrast to its prevailing approach to human rights, it 'stressed' in 2013 to a committee of the UN General Assembly that the international community has a duty to ensure that indigenous peoples share the 'fruits of socioeconomic development, to protect their basic human rights and fundamental freedoms, and to preserve their natural environment and the traditional cultures essential for their survival' (UN, 2013, Statements, para. 12). In 2016, Taiwan apologised to indigenous peoples for previous policy positions and, in 2017, passed legislation giving indigenous languages official status. Taiwan's formal recognition of 14 other indigenous groups, who are guaranteed representation in parliament (International Work Group for Indigenous Affairs, 2018), casts as politically extreme the Australian suggestion that a guaranteed indigenous voice to parliament would threaten national political cohesion (Belot & Laurence, 2017).

The office of the Taiwanese president had also established a broadly representative committee:

> to check into violations against indigenous peoples throughout history; to formulate measures to provide compensation for deprivation of indigenous rights; to implement [the Declaration] and the relevant international rights convention; [and] to collect and review information regarding indigenous historical justice and transitional justice. (International Work Group for Indigenous Affairs, 2018, p. 276)

According to Conway-Long (2016), indigeneity poses the same fundamental questions to all states, whether liberal or illiberal:

> Can international law [and politics] be utilized to free indigenous people both politically and culturally, now that the UN has declared its interest? … Can indigenous issues bring pressure upon the system of international law to help transform it from the Eurocentric vision of states' rights rooted in the Westphalian Peace it now has? (p. 116)

This transformation is precisely the politics of indigeneity's point. The comparison between liberal and illiberal states is also instructive in moving beyond a theoretical to a practical understanding of self-determination that is ultimately concerned with a people's capacity 'to live well and humanly in their own ways' (Conway-Long, 2016, p. 116).

Liberal states constrain indigenous aspirations to protect both their own integrity and what majority populations hold in common. However, as Corntassel (2012) explained, this does not foreclose opportunities for self-recognition, which is an essential condition of self-determination. The Ainu experience illustrates this point: it shows self-recognition as a form of political expression that does not exist in nonliberal states that view protecting their own authority as an overriding state political objective. Self-recognition precedes liberal mutual recognition, which, though usually unequal for indigenous peoples in postsettler liberal states, still assures indigenous peoples of at least some capacity for political influence. For example, as Chapter 9 shows, the Canadian state requires at least some cooperation with indigenous citizens to pursue its economic aspirations.

In jurisdictions like Ecuador, Taiwan, Malaysia and the Russian Federation, state recognition is essential. Structural limits on an indigenous people's political capacity to claim their indigeneity by and for themselves limits the Declaration's transformative potential. In spite of the examples of Taiwanese respect for the Declaration noted in this chapter, there remain indigenous peoples in Taiwan—the Pingpu population of 400,000—who have not received state recognition of their indigeneity even though 'recognition is fundamental ... to the enjoyment of a number of specific rights under Taiwanese and international law' and is viewed as safeguarding 'the cultural identity of aboriginal tribes and individuals' (van Bekhoven, 2016, p. 202).

Although liberal societies share the practice by which the 'law determines the indigenous status of communities and individuals that claim this status' (van Bekhoven, 2016, p. 202), indigenous peoples in those jurisdictions have recourse to a political framework more conducive to resistance, and they use it to assert their self-determination. In contrast, the limited capacity for self-recognition in a jurisdiction like Taiwan allows the state to be more successful in assuming an 'exclusive concept of being "indigenous"' (p. 202). The ensuing 'artificial indigenous identity ... results in a persisting colonial dominance of the State over the aborigines' (p. 202). In contrast, human rights are the capacities of citizenship. They are intended to raise political agency. As human rights are vested in people, they make people prior to the state with the capacity to contest state authority.

There is no normative internationally accepted conception of the balance between human rights and state rights; therefore, the minimum standards reflected in the Declaration represent an extraordinary political achievement and comprehensive blueprint for thinking about political relationships and reasonable policy outcomes. However, the Declaration is still more heavily focused on the obligations of states rather than the capacities of people. A conception of rights that is truly grounded in the inherent dignity of the human person would reverse this order.

Conclusion

The Declaration is inconsistently interpreted by states that voted for its adoption. Those states also contest the scope of the right to self-determination. The incorporation of principles that correspond with the Declaration into national constitutions does not necessarily mean that the rights of indigenous peoples are better respected than in other jurisdictions. Nor does a generally authoritarian political culture mean that indigenous rights are completely set aside.

In general, states are inclined to accept rights to culture; however, most view the principle of free, prior and informed consent as too much of a constraint on state sovereignty. The impasse between states and indigenous peoples on this point is resolvable only within the broader conceptions of sovereignty, citizenship and democracy that this book advances. These conceptual discussions are also important to questions of whether the right to self-determination is confined to indigenous institutions that exist in isolation from the state or whether it is also a right reasonably exercised within the state. The nature of indigenous participation in public affairs varies widely across jurisdictions.

The definition of indigenous, which is important in establishing the source and purpose of indigenous claims, is also contested. This book's argument that minority status and political domination are not essential criteria for recognition as indigenous informs its conception of the rights of indigeneity. It also informs its evaluation of the Declaration's usefulness to contemporary indigenous politics. The book's further argument is that accepting a majority indigenous people—like that in Fiji—as indigenous is also essential to a consistent account of indigeneity as first and foremost a cultural status.

In short, self-determination's possibilities are shaped by domestic practices of sovereignty. As the next chapter argues, the right to self-determination means that all people are entitled to share in the public authority of the communities in which they live. Sovereignty is not an absolute, inflexible and unchanging site of political authority. It is widely dispersed among individual and institutional actors—the following chapter shows how and why. It also shows how rethinking the nature of sovereignty in liberal societies broadens self-determination's scope and value to indigenous peoples.

7

Sovereignty

Introduction

Self-determination flows from sovereignty's character, shape and form. It comes from the political values and institutional structures that determine where power lies: the values that influence the nature of one's belonging to the state and one's opportunities for distinctive indigenous citizenship, deliberating according to values and processes that make cultural sense.

Sovereignty was originally a defence against outside interference in one's affairs, yet, for indigenous peoples, it can be an instrument of colonial subjugation. As an instrument, it is commonly confused or overstated. Sovereignty is not simply a body of rights once exclusively exercised by indigenous peoples, taken by settlers and reclaimed through indigenous resistance. Politics is more complex. The Declaration helps to make sense of sovereignty's character, limits and potential.

The meaning of Maori vis-a-vis Crown sovereignty has been a point of contention in New Zealand politics since the signing of the Treaty of Waitangi in 1840. This chapter introduces what it means for New Zealand's Waitangi Tribunal to find that the treaty did not signal the cession of Maori sovereignty. This finding invites the exploration of new theoretical possibilities, including the proposition that, if sovereignty is the people's collective authority, indigenous ethnicity can never be grounds for democratic exclusion.

Discourses of sovereignty open and close different political and theoretical spaces for thinking about who belongs to the political community, the terms of belonging and how and by whom those terms are set. Examples from Australia and the US are also used to show how and why, and to contribute to the chapter's argument that sovereignty is not a static concept; it is not always interpreted in the same ways nor for the same reasons. People's changing values and the shifting nature of what is and is not possible change people's ideas about sovereignty—in particular, about the ways in which they think about conflicts between sovereignty as it is and as they would like it to be. The Declaration proposes new spaces of inclusion for indigenous peoples—a different kind of liberal sovereignty that makes the concept a potential instrument of self-determination through differentiated liberal citizenship.

Differentiated citizenship means that, in New Zealand for example, Maori are both part of the Crown and separate from it. The Crown and iwi and hapu (subtribes) exercise relative and relational political powers, which means that Maori are not junior partners in a bicultural project (O'Sullivan, 2007) but equal participants and shareholders in public sovereignty. Equal participation in public affairs provides the foundation for the development of noncolonial political relationships.

The powers of state sovereignty are diminishing. However, power imbalances remain a defining characteristic of indigenous politics. Sovereignty still provides a political and theoretical framework for responding to those imbalances. This is because sovereignty is part of the language that both states and indigenous peoples use to explain the powers that they think they justifiably hold and through which each makes its claims and counterclaims against the other. However, if one sees sovereignty as a relative and relational power—not absolute and incontestable—then one can think more broadly about the political significance of difference. 'Otherness' need not be a way of framing people negatively and outside the political system but a way of indigenous peoples asserting their differences positively and for their own purposes. Difference can be asserted as legitimate in the formation of public values and institutions, and the logic of participatory parity can be established. Not only indigenous people, but also indigenous epistemologies, may then contribute to public affairs with substantive authority.

With sovereignty thus reconfigured, when the Declaration gives the state priority over indigenous peoples in the event of conflict, the power of settler populations is mediated by indigenous people being able to participate in the development of the state's position on every political issue that requires deliberation. This is an essential part of the substance of shared sovereignty. This chapter provides examples of the ways in which different indigenous peoples conceptualise sovereignty. While such conceptions contest settler hegemony, they nevertheless provide a foundation from which settlers and indigenous peoples can acknowledge that 'we are all here to stay' and that indigenous peoples are here to stay *as* indigenous. This chapter's consideration of sovereignty foreshadows the next chapter's discussion of a political order in which public decisions are made with reference to public reason and participatory parity, where the indigenous citizen is one who deliberates with substantive equality.

Contemporary Discourses of Sovereignty: New Zealand

In 2014, New Zealand's Waitangi Tribunal found that the Treaty of Waitangi was not a Maori agreement to transfer sovereignty to the British Crown. The finding did not fundamentally change the claim to self-determination, but it did lend moral and political urgency to the question of contemporary sovereignty's attributes. It also contextualised discussion of what sovereignty meant for the nature of indigenous nations' belonging to the postsettler state.

Further conceptual clarity on the meanings of sovereignty is still required, focusing on meanings that are just, pragmatic and politically valuable to self-determination and to indigenous peoples being 'sovereign in their own right yet sharing sovereignty with society at large' (Maaka & Fleras, 2005, p. 5). It was, in fact, the same search for shared sovereignties that has distinguished New Zealand politics since the treaty's signing in 1840.

The treaty provides context to that search, although not always in ways that contribute coherently to public discourse. As Apirana Ngata, a government minister, noted in 1923, the Treaty of Waitangi 'is on the lips of the humble and the great, of the ignorant and of the thoughtful' (as cited in Hill, 2004, p. 129). In 2004, another government minister, Trevor Mallard, remarked that the treaty is 'both bigger and smaller than many people think' (Mallard, 2004, para. 22). Public debate on the treaty's meanings and utility reflect evolutions in political and jurisprudential thought from it being a 'simple nullity' (*Wi Parata v Bishop of Wellington*, 1877, p. 78) to an instrument of important policy significance in contemporary times (Tawhai & Gray-Sharp, 2011).

The 2014 tribunal finding reinforced sovereignty as a site of critical inquiry concerned with fundamental questions of who belongs to the national polity, on whose terms and on what terms. Drawing sovereignty meaningfully and purposefully into contemporary politics is more complex than understanding the concept as a body of authority that Maori once held and that the Crown usurped and retains exclusively. Yet, as Chapter 9 shows, it is from this (over)simplified account that contemporary debates about sovereignty tend to occur.

The Waitangi Tribunal ('He Whakaputanga me te Tiriti', 2014) found that:

- The rangatira who signed te Tiriti o Waitangi in February 1840 did not cede their sovereignty to Britain. That is, they did not cede authority to make and enforce law over their people or their territories.
- The rangatira agreed to share power and authority with Britain. They agreed to the Governor having authority to control British subjects in New Zealand, and thereby keep the peace and protect Māori interests.
- The rangatira consented to the treaty on the basis that they and the Governor were to be equals, though they were to have different roles and different spheres of influence. The detail of how this relationship would work in practice, especially where the Māori and European populations intermingled, remained to be negotiated over time on a case-by-case basis.
- The rangatira agreed to enter land transactions with the Crown, and the Crown promised to investigate pre-treaty land transactions and to return any land that had not been properly acquired from Māori.
- The rangatira appear to have agreed that the Crown would protect them from foreign threats and represent them in international affairs, where that was necessary. (p. 529)

The New Zealand Government did not accept this finding; however, for Ngapuhi—who took the claim to the tribunal—and other Maori iwi, it vindicated their long-held position that the treaty was not a cession of sovereignty (Waitangi Tribunal, 'He Whakaputanga me te Tiriti', 2014).

The minister for Treaty of Waitangi negotiations, Chris Finlayson, argued that:

> There is no question that the Crown has sovereignty in New Zealand. This report doesn't change that fact ... The Tribunal doesn't reach any conclusion regarding the sovereignty the Crown

exercises in New Zealand. Nor does it address the other events considered part of the Crown's acquisition of sovereignty, or how the Treaty relationship should operate today. (as cited in Kenny, 2014, paras. 5–6)

This claim to exclusive Crown sovereignty may be interpreted as a statement of appeal to non-Maori reactionary sensitivities rather than wider political possibilities. However, the finding raises the important political question of whether sovereignty must belong to Maori or the Crown alone, or whether it is a fluid and evolving descriptor of political authority widely dispersed and exercised.

Sovereignty is complex, complicated and contested. It is challenged as public attitudes to power and authority change. These attitudes evolve with time and context, with people's values, and with political and economic constraints and opportunities. A more flexible interpretation than Finlayson's may position the state and indigenous nations as repositories of a relative and relational power that is not fixed in time, context or capacity.

Contemporary Maori politics and economic development strategies reflect the state's diminishing importance. As Habermas (1997) argued, 'the integrative capabilities of the state continue to diminish under the presence of regional movements, on the one hand, and worldwide corporations and transnational organisations on the other' (p. 37).

The state and the indigenous nation are fluid entities. They evolve, sometimes in ways that strengthen their political capacities and sometimes in ways that do not; sovereignty's strength and character is thus also fluid. Claiming a share in national sovereignty alongside an independent indigenous sovereignty is politically worthwhile because of what sovereignty is (as opposed to what it is not).

Britain entered into treaty negotiations in 1840 intending to acquire sovereignty and therefore the power to make and enforce laws over both Maori and Pakeha; however, it did not explain this intention to the *rangatira* (chiefs). Instead, it was proposed that Britain be given the right to exercise authority over its own settlers. In the Maori-language version of the treaty, this authority was described as *kāwanatanga* (governorship). *Rangatiratanga*, or chieftainship over their own affairs, was to remain as the chiefs 'full exclusive and undisturbed possession of their Lands and Estates, Forests, Fisheries and other properties' (New Zealand History, n.d.,

Article the Second, para. 1). Cession of sovereignty cannot be read into this translation of the Maori version of the Treaty of Waitangi. Its reading into the translation is contested (Orange, 1987), and while the British governor, William Hobson, proclaimed sovereignty over the North Island by virtue of the treaty, his claim to the remaining islands was by 'right of discovery'. It was some time after the treaty's signing that the Crown acquired 'substantive sovereignty' (Orange, 1987, p. 13).

Sovereignty's capacity to recognise distinctive Maori claims, not as junior partners in a bicultural treaty 'partnership' (O'Sullivan, 2007) but as equal participants in a commonwealth, is important. It means that political thought need not be constrained by the bicultural presumption that sovereignty rests with the Crown acting as the Pakeha polity, conditioned by an obligation, read into the Treaty of Waitangi, that sovereignty be exercised in partnership with a homogenous Maori polity (O'Sullivan, 2007). In New Zealand, self-determination is not 'granted' by biculturalism's 'Pakeha state'; it is not the gift of a benevolent 'partner' but an inherent and extant right of prior occupancy that the Declaration affirms. The distinction is important, for a partner is not a substantively equal member of the sovereign polity (see Chapter 9).

This limited and limiting account of political authority diminishes self-determination's transformative potential. The underlying distinction is whether one understands sovereignty as a power that belongs independently to the state or whether it is exercised by the state as the agent of the people's shared political authority. Is sovereignty 'exercised from the people' or 'over them' (McCue, 2007, p. 22)? Are indigenous peoples part of the state or are they excluded as the 'other'—a people outside the state who are not entitled to a democratic voice?

If sovereignty was neither ceded nor pragmatically returnable to Maori as an absolute and incontestable embodiment of political authority, one must reframe debates about where political power belongs, and why, to include the possibility that it might be shared and to consider what recourses there might be 'for thinking about the possibilities of a non-colonial relation between indigenous and non-indigenous peoples' (Tully, 2000, p. 50). Rethinking the Crown as a commonwealth, rather than as a binary opponent, would significantly transform political possibilities. Recognising the Crown as not simply the Pakeha polity allows a shared liberal sovereignty in which the Crown is *also* Maori, as Justice Williams proposed (see the introduction to Chapter 5). In relation to this, Gover (2015) asked:

whether the right of self-determination can operate as a *chapeau* for the self-governance provisions of the Declaration and so serve as a justificatory basis for those corporate rights, even if they are not supported by any equality-based justifications. (p. 366)

However, the possibilities of shared liberal sovereignty are broader than this legal framing suggests. The politics of indigeneity are 'an attempt to come to terms with how discourses and practices of sovereignty ... set the conditions under which indigenous and other forms of "marginal" politics occur at all' (Shaw, 2008, p. 8).

Sovereignty and Power

Sovereignty's positioning as either an absolute and unconditional indigenous authority, or as an absolute and exclusive Crown authority, contrasts with Palmer's (1995) argument that:

Notions of sovereignty are collapsing all over the world ... Far from being the indivisible omnipresent concept that Hobbes made it in *Leviathan*, sovereignty is more like a piece of chewing gum. It can be stretched and pulled in many directions to do almost anything. Sovereignty is not a word that is useful and it should be banished from political debate. (pp. 153–154)

However, sovereignty is real and powerful when one does not share it and when it is used as an obstructive force, though its dispersed location sometimes means that it is like the New Zealand constitution—one 'can't find it' (Palmer, as cited in Espiner, 2017). However, this makes sovereignty no less worth finding and reconfiguring. Otherwise, Alfred (1999) was correct to propose that 'Native communities will occupy a dependent and reactionary position relative to the state' (p. 59). If, instead, sovereignty is a way of describing power and authority (and where they are vested vis-a-vis where they might alternatively be vested), it is a very useful analytical tool.

Removing sovereignty from political discourse does not remove the centrality of power to relationships among peoples. Nor does it remove the unequal relationships that exist between coloniser and colonised, although it may diminish the language one has to think about these concepts and experiences. Shaw (2008) used Hobbes's account of sovereignty to explain liberal democracy's capacity for exclusion:

> The structure of sovereignty that Hobbes produces is enabled and authorized through the production of a shared ontological ground, and identity. This identity, in turn, rests upon the necessary exclusion of Indigenous peoples at several different levels, not least through the explicit marking of Indigenous peoples as 'different' as 'Other'. What is more crucial in determining the character of contemporary Indigenous politics, however, is that Hobbes renders the construction of this exclusionary identity, the process through which authority is produced and guaranteed, as pre-political, as necessary and natural rather than contingent and violent. (p. 9)

Sovereignty reflects a society's ideas about the origins, nature and proper location of political power within a political system. It can be used to position indigenous peoples as a political 'other'—beyond the state and beyond the political. These powerful constraints on political capacity may devalue humanity as the basis for membership of the political community and belonging. Such accounts of public authority make difference a political problem—they do not acknowledge liberalism's capacity to manage differences in human expectations of the good life.

Sovereignty, then, describes the location of public power and authority, the source of that authority and the manner of its exercise. A liberal theory of indigeneity may instead broaden liberal democratic practice to allow indigenous peoples to frame 'otherness' in their own ways and for their own purposes (O'Sullivan, 2014). 'Otherness' is not necessarily problematic as long as indigenous people are free to define the ways in which they will differ from the assimilationist paradigm's homogenous ideal. They might frame 'otherness' in ways that allow them to work out for themselves the terms of their inclusion in the postsettler liberal state. Difference then ceases to be the basis of political disadvantage. It becomes the basis on which indigenous peoples retain their identities and political structures to manage their own affairs.

Difference also becomes the basis on which indigenous peoples contribute to the formation of the values and systems that inform public policy decisions. It becomes a legitimate basis from which to enjoy influence over policy debate through asserting a substantive participatory parity (Fraser & Honneth, 2003).

Participatory parity presumes that the citizen is a person who deliberates (Aristotle, 1988). It supports differentiated citizenship as an alternative to an isolationist interpretation of indigenous self-determination and recognises King's (2012) view that 'The fact of Native existence is that we live modern lives informed by traditional values and contemporary realities and that we wish to lead lives on our terms' (p. 302). Participatory parity is important because indigenous claims:

> are not only about compensation or reparations, but also about the terms of association between them and the colonial state. The injustice of expropriation of Aboriginal lands, for example, is not only about the dispossession of property ... but the violation or denial of just terms of association. (Ivison, 2002, p. 100)

As Bohman and Rehg (1997) argued, 'deliberative democracy evokes ideals of rational legislation, participatory politics and civic self-governance' (p. ix). However, people participate with culturally framed conceptions of what is rational. If all are to deliberate, political systems need ways of admitting plural perspectives and rationalities.

Equal capacity to influence depends on a desirable but not always attainable condition: 'that each citizen be able to advance arguments that others might find persuasive' (Knight & Johnson, 2011, p. 295). Indeed, Rawls (1997) argued for the 'fact of reasonable pluralism' rather than the 'fact of pluralism' per se (p. 765). Cohen (1997) maintained that, rather than pursuing 'ideal fairness', one should pursue 'ideal deliberation' in public institutions (p. 70). This is because nobody 'is required to defer to the expert authority of another' (Estlund, 1997, p. 173) in conceptualising what is just nor in determining what weight should be given to justice in arriving at a decision.

Participation as a deliberator (Aristotle, 1988) with equal capacity implies opportunities for culturally grounded influence. Its precondition for equality is that 'first, *citizens* must be equal and, second, their *reasons* must be given equal consideration' (Bohman, 1997, p. 321). Participatory democracy is fundamentally different from exclusive majoritarian democracy. Therefore, it is not democracy per se that excludes indigenous people and their distinctive perspectives, but its structure.

Public reason guarantees voice in ways that other democratic forms do not require. Benhabib (1996) argued that deliberative democracy is theoretically well equipped to admit cultural claims alongside 'democratic inclusiveness and legitimacy' (Williams, 2004, p. 338). However, public reason presumes that all of the claims to be prioritised are morally just. Public reason is not equipped to manage unjust claims because these are, by definition, 'unreasonable'.

Participation through differentiated liberal citizenship—not distinctive nationhood alone—is preliminary to realising the Declaration's full potential as an instrument of self-determination. Nevertheless, there remain structural barriers to indigenous peoples' inclusion in policy development, including insufficient human capacity within both indigenous and state agencies (Quitian & Rodríguez, 2016). Policymakers need to know how indigenous people and institutions think about effective public policy. It is reasonable for indigenous people to expect this knowledge through their own presence and participation in the policy process. Indigenous workforce development strategies are important across all sectors of the economy. However, they are especially important in the public sector where they help to secure indigenous policy participation, contribute to indigenising bureaucratic policymaking (Maaka & Fleras, 2009) and the mainstreaming of indigenous thought. Indigenous research also contributes to the mainstreaming of indigenous policy by contributing to the politics of presence (Phillips, 1995)—that is, the presence of indigenous ideas in the national cultural and economic realms. Brayboy, Fann, Castagno and Solyom (2012) observed that:

> Native [university] faculty serve as activists, advocates, and change
> agents ... by challenging dominant, racist, and discriminatory
> scholarship, practices and perceptions; by stimulating research in
> Indigenous issues; by developing and improving curriculum that
> is inclusive of Native perspectives and scholarship. (p. 93)

Indigenous intellectual presence means that, just as governments ought not focus on 'doing' justice 'to' indigenous peoples, policy ought not focus on doing things 'for' (or even 'with') them, as has become fashionable in Australia. Instead, as Cook (2017) explained in the New Zealand context, one might aspire to policy grounded 'on the richness of the Māori "way of thinking"' (We cannot forget the past, para. 1). Indigenous presence is an expression of shared sovereignty, a condition that helps liberal democracy to demonstrate its value to the aims and expectations of indigenous self-determination.

Shared Sovereignty

The Declaration helps to align shared sovereignty with the liberal presumption that government should occur by the people's consent. It allows discourses of sovereignty to contribute to capacities for citizenship that allow people to enjoy lives that they have reason to value (Sen, 1999a).

The first section of Article 46 of the Declaration (cited in Chapter 3) confirms the power of the nation-state. Its second section qualifies that power:

> In the exercise of the rights enunciated in the present Declaration, the human rights and fundamental freedoms of all shall be respected. The exercise of the rights set forth in this Declaration shall be subject only to such limitations as are determined by law, and in accordance with international human rights obligations. Any such limitations shall be non-discriminatory and strictly necessary solely for the purpose of securing due recognition and respect for the rights and freedoms of others and for meeting the just and most compelling requirements of a democratic society. (UN, 2007b, art. 46[2])

The nation-state's interests will prevail in the event of conflict. However, Article 46 must be read in conjunction with the full Declaration, which explicitly presumes that indigenous peoples are part of the nation-state and shareholders in its sovereignty.

Indigeneity may conceptualise 'general forms of authority in competition with states' (Picq, 2014, p. 24) or it may reconfigure the meaning of the term 'state' itself. Rather than plural forms of authority in 'competition with states', a liberal theory of differentiated citizenship might imagine plurality within the state as an essential complement to the extant indigenous authority that exists beyond the state. Differentiated citizenship may then address what Picq called an 'inadequacy of the state' (p. 24). It may be that indigeneity 'disrupts state sovereignty' (p. 23). However, this raises questions about what or who is sovereign, where the sovereign power lies and how it might reasonably be distributed.

Shared sovereignty is concerned with the processes that are used to make decisions. It does not guarantee that policy outcomes will be just, but it does guarantee that, when injustice occurs, there is a mechanism for all people to contribute to a reconsideration of the offending policy position. For example, it is an ambitious but worthy ideal for public institutions to recognise Habermas' (1997) argument that:

> when someone prescribes for another, it is always possible that he thereby does the other an injustice, but this is never possible with respect to what he decides for himself (for *volenti non fit injuria*—'he who consents cannot receive an injury'). Hence, only the united and consenting will of all—that is, a general and united will of the people by which each decides the same for all and all decide the same for each—can legislate. (p. 45)

Although an assimilationist rationale can potentially be read into this aspiration, an intellectual alignment with the politics of indigeneity ensures that one does not have unmediated majoritarian democracy such that the same people are always and necessarily on the losing side.

Indigenous conceptions of sovereignty are culturally located; they do not exactly parallel the concept as it is used at international law. However, the juxtaposition of international and indigenous perspectives to develop a liberal theory of differentiated citizenship may be possible and may hold considerable political value in helping to advance and give meaning to the right to self-determination.

While indigenous peoples can ordinarily identify a common territory, the capacity to utilise and govern it independently remains diminished for most indigenous populations. However, this does not mean that their sovereignty is, as a matter of course, overridden. It is certainly a weaker sovereignty than that which existed before colonial settlement, yet so too is state sovereignty a continuously less strong and secure construct that, in turn, creates new and different opportunities for indigenous peoples. Although these are not opportunities of absolute power, many indigenous peoples find purpose in their pursuit. Sovereignty 'depends on conditions that operate above the level of the individual states themselves' (Hindess, 2000, p. 31).

Modern sovereignty evolved in response to 'capitalist production requir[ing] a normative code with legal force to reorganize resources and space so they can be turned into commodities' (Forman, 2016, p. 285). The extent to which indigenous peoples influence that normative code is largely the product of their relative importance to the national economy. State sovereignty's relative importance as either a constituent of (when inclusively structured) or constraint on (when exclusively structured) indigenous self-determination depends on the size of the state's incursions into indigenous affairs. However, state capacity is subject to increasing global economic constraints. At the same time, indigenous economic and political capacity to trade and engage with nonstate actors is increasing. Economic independence challenges subservience to the state. The international economic opportunities that Maori pursue are illustrative. Treaty settlements strengthen Maori contributions to the national economy. For example, between 2001 and 2010, the Maori economic asset base increased from NZ$9.4 billion to NZ$36.9 billion due in part to these settlements (Westpac New Zealand, 2014).

Treaty settlements strengthen democratic capacity by creating further avenues for independence. They show that Altamirano-Jiménez (2004) was wrong to dismiss economic entrepreneurship as the 'yoke of internal colonialism' (p. 354). Economic independence is preliminary to self-determination and essential to reducing subservience to the state. Economic factors show that sovereignty is more complicated than just indigenous authority over their own affairs. In Canada, substantive participation within the state is a pragmatic imperative when one considers that economic marginalisation costs the country C$28 billion a year (Public Policy Forum, 2017). Basic infrastructural investment in indigenous communities would reduce the financial cost of poverty by $2.2 billion each year (Public Policy Forum, 2017).

Sovereignty determines people's political location vis-a-vis the state. However, locations change, and, therefore, it is conceptually useful to find a language for discussing where one thinks power ought to lie and why. According to Wiessner (2008), sovereignty inheres in its bearer: 'it grows or it dies from within' (p. 1176). It can be summarised as an indigenous peoples' right to 'recapture their identity' (p. 1176) and to enjoy the political rights and responsibilities that such capacity requires. Sovereignty is concerned with the political capacity *for* citizenship to share in the construction of the public interest because:

> In the absence of a Philosopher King who reads transcendent normative verities, the only ground for a claim that a policy or decision is just is that it has been arrived at by a public [that] has truly promoted the free expression of all. (Young, 1989, p. 263)

Sovereign authority is best distributed to allow people to lead flourishing lives as politics' ultimate purpose (Aristotle, 1988). It ought to be distributed with reference to principles of 'objectiveness, reasonableness, necessity and proportionality' (Xanthaki, 2008, p. 282). Indigeneity means that sovereignty is inclusive and 'grounded in the right of all citizens to shape the society in which they live' (Clarke, 2006, p. 119). The concept of indigenous peoples as shareholders in public sovereignty assumes an active citizenship quite different from assimilation into a single homogenous entity. It is thus a form of citizenship of inherent political value—without it, self-determination's potential is curtailed.

Sovereignty as Ideology

Traditionally, political discourses of sovereignty are neither natural nor neutral (Shaw, 2008). They are not always attentive to diverse ways of thinking about public authority and what it could mean for indigenous peoples. One needs a responsive political theory to refute arguments that sovereignty is an absolute and coercive force with which indigenous people cannot compete. One needs to be able to set aside Alfred's (1999) argument that, for indigenous peoples to seek sovereignty, they must imitate all that it implies as a negative force inconsistent with indigenous political values. Alfred (2005) argued that one ought to 'de-think' sovereignty, which he labelled a 'social creation' reflecting non-indigenous political values. He wrote of the 'reification of sovereignty in politics' (Alfred, 2005, p. 33)—of a system that states use against indigenous political authority. However, Carroll (2012) objected that Alfred's (1999) 'intellectual battle is constructed around monoliths: the state versus indigenous peoples' (p. 157). Public sovereignty can instead be shared to advance indigenous interests.

A share in public sovereignty is not a right to be 'consulted' in policy development simply because the state cannot find the political will to ensure participation. Even the all-powerful sovereign of Hobbes's *Leviathan* exercises an authority for the people's collective benefit. It is an authority that can be withdrawn if it is not exercised for that purpose. The *Leviathan*'s sovereignty is indivisible and, for the time being, absolute, but it is not forever unconditional (Hobbes, 1946). Hobbes allowed sovereignty to reside in an assembly and for the individual to retain liberty over things that cannot be transferred to the commonwealth. The sovereign rules for all, not for itself. When 'our refusal to obey frustrates the End for which the Sovereign was ordained; then there is no liberty to refuse: otherwise there is' (Hobbes, 1946, p. 142). Sovereignty is only valid when it is given freely by the commonwealth and exercises 'protection' as its specific purpose. Thus, a commonwealth is not simply a vesting of sovereignty in a person or assembly but a forging of unity (Hobbes, 1946).

Sovereignty's 'dynamism' appears when it is juxtaposed with a more substantive account of an indigenous right to self-determination. This book's principal intent is to show how the Declaration allows one to think broadly of power; that is, to accept Shaw's (2008) argument that sovereignty is not 'apolitical and uncontestable' (p. 9) but an expression of how people understand the just distribution and expression of political authority. Sovereignty ought also reflect the ways in which people wish to belong to a national political community.

McCue (2007) described her people's (Ned'u'ten) power as 'rooted in our creation stories, our spirituality and our organic and peaceful institutions. Sovereignty requires the energy of the land and the people and is distinct about locality' (pp. 24–25). In McCue's conceptualisation, sovereignty is not concerned with the power of domination but with balanced political relationships.

Shared sovereignty need not presume the 'parallel law-making system' that the Federal Court of Australia dismissed in *Yorta Yorta v The State of Victoria* (1998, para. 44) because, wherever sovereignty resides, it is shared and distributed in ways more complex than a simple binary can describe. The Uluru Statement from the Heart described enduring indigenous sovereignty as:

> *a spiritual notion: the ancestral tie between the land, or 'mother nature', and the Aboriginal and Torres Strait Islander peoples who were born therefrom, remain attached thereto, and must one day return thither to be reunited with our ancestors. This link is the basis of the ownership of the soil, or better, of sovereignty.* It has never been ceded or extinguished, and co-exists with the sovereignty of the Crown.
>
> …
>
> With substantive constitutional change and structural reform, we believe this ancient sovereignty can shine through as a fuller expression of Australia's nationhood. (Referendum Council, 2017, paras. 3–5, emphasis in original)

The Referendum Council (2017) sought 'constitutional reforms to empower our people and take *a rightful place* in our own country' (para. 8, emphasis in original). Arguing that 'When we have power over our destiny our children will flourish' (para. 8), the council called 'for the establishment of a First Nations Voice enshrined in the Constitution' (para. 9). It was maintained that a guaranteed voice would structure public reason into Australia's constitutional framework. Having such a voice implies changing political relationships to alter what it means to be an indigenous citizen. Constitutions are statements about who belongs and who does not. The *Australian Constitution* is clear—citizens do not belong on equal terms and race is a criterion for exclusion:

> If by the law of any State all persons of any race are disqualified from voting at elections for the more numerous House of the Parliament of the State, then, in reckoning the number of the people of the State or of the Commonwealth, persons of that race resident in that State shall not be counted. (s. 25)

Liberal societies exclude to protect the interests of the more powerful and for fear that another's claim to a share in political authority might diminish their own. 'They exclude through the denial of history to make another's claim seem unreasonable' (O'Sullivan, 2018b, para. 7) and often in the language they use to describe democracy. For former Australian prime minister Malcolm Turnbull, the proposed voice was 'contrary to equality and citizenship' (Belot & Laurence, 2017, para. 1), as it gave indigenous people rights beyond those held in common with other citizens. There was to be no space for political participation from distinctive cultural or sociohistorical perspectives. 'One person, one vote' satisfied liberal democracy, whereas the Referendum Council seemed to propose one voice of equal value, reflecting a more expansive and inclusive conception of equality.

McCue's (2007) account of sovereignty provides a further perspective. In exercising their sovereignty, Ned'u'ten:

> Clan members and hereditary chiefs are guided by the attributes of peace, respect, generosity, balance, harmony, compassion, sharing, gifting and discipline in their relations with all that is alive, all that has gone before, and all that has yet to come. These attributes are inalienable, inherent and sacred. (p. 25)

However, as McCue (2007) remarked, it remains difficult to examine sovereignty as a term that describes 'inherent' indigenous power. This is because the 'meaning of "sovereignty" is yet to undergo significant Indigenous and political treatment, definition and elaboration, especially with respect to its coordinate relationships to the right to self-determination and Indigenous worldviews' (pp. 19–20). This book goes some ways towards filling that gap in both liberal and indigenous political thought, confirming that, at the very least, sovereignty presumes protection from external interference.

McCue (2007) explained that, for the Ned'u'ten people, 'the exercise of sovereign jurisdiction' occurs:

- within our potlatch system, our clan and house structures as units of politics/territories;
- when our hereditary leaders fulfil their responsibilities and obligations; and
- when there is a transmission of oral histories and traditions, principal customs, and ceremonies from one generation to the next. (pp. 24–25)

According to Coates and Newman (2014), the Supreme Court of Canada's decision in *Tsilhqot'in Nation v British Columbia* highlights that:

> at a fundamental level … Aboriginal communities have a right to an equitable place at the table in relation to natural resource development in Canada. Their empowerment through *Tsilhqot'in* and earlier decisions has the potential to be immensely exciting as a means of further economic development in Aboriginal communities and prosperity for all.
>
> …
>
> the time is now for governments, Aboriginal communities, and resource sector companies to work together to build partnerships for the future … We need to keep building a national consensus that responsible resource development that takes account of sustainability issues and that respects Indigenous communities contributes positively – very positively – to Canada and its future. (p. 21)

From another Native American perspective, sovereignty is:

> more of a continued cultural integrity than of political powers … to the degree that a nation loses its sense of cultural identity, to that degree it suffers a loss of sovereignty. (Deloria, 1999, p. 113)

In the US, the Circuit Court of Appeals for the District of Columbia held that:

> The principle of tribal sovereignty in American law exists as a matter of respect for Indian communities. It recognizes the independence of these communities as regards internal affairs, thereby giving them latitude to maintain traditional customs and practices. But tribal sovereignty is not absolute autonomy, permitting a tribe to operate in a commercial capacity without legal constraint. (as cited in Wiessner, 2008, p. 1168)

Wiessner (2008) explained that the Court 'also observed that tribal sovereignty is strongest when based on a treaty or when the tribal government acts within the borders of the reservation in matters concerning only tribal members' (p. 1168). Tribal sovereignty is then restrained and conditional.

Independent Indigenous Nations

In 1831, in *Cherokee Nation v Georgia*, Supreme Court Chief Justice Marshall described indigenous nations as 'domestic dependent nations' (p. 2). According to Carroll (2012), the concept, which resembles 'that of a ward to his guardian', continues to influence 'a large part of the present definition of tribal sovereignty' (p. 145). An alternative perspective is that indigenous nationhood implies equality. Justices Thompson and Story's dissenting opinion, in the same case, sets out principles of sovereignty that are capable of plural interpretation and are not conditioned by ward like dependence:

> The terms *state* and *nation* are used in the law of nations ... as importing the same thing; and imply a body of men, united together, to procure their mutual safety and advantage by means of their union.... We ought, therefore, to reckon in the number of sovereigns those states that have bound themselves to another more powerful, although by an unequal alliance. The conditions of these unequal alliances may be infinitely varied; but whatever they are, provided the inferior ally reserves to itself the sovereignty of the right to govern its own body, it ought to be considered an independent state [...] to be placed among sovereigns who acknowledge no other power. (as cited in Duthu, 2013, p. 13)

In 2016, in *United States v Bryant*, the Supreme Court considered tribal courts' capacity to ensure fair trials and safe verdicts. The case, which became a test of tribal sovereignty, recognised that 'no liberal sovereign can be absolved of the imperative to protect the rights of the accused in its criminal proceedings' (Cutler, 2016, p. 1752).

Significantly, in her analysis of the case, Cutler (2016) did not use the state courts' standards as the necessary point of comparison. This is because tribal sovereignty is not simply a replication of the state's. Tribes predate the US itself, being 'both preconstitutional and extraconstitutional' (Cutler, 2016, p. 1755), which entails that their sovereign powers do not proceed from the national constitution. Therefore:

> Procedural protections for tribal court defendants should be measured not by replication of state and federal public defense systems, but rather by analyzing tribal courts under international principles of comity to determine if a verdict is fundamentally fair. (Cutler, 2016, p. 1752)

Affirming tribal sovereignty's independence makes it clear that it is not a subset of the colonial authority of the state. People have the right to a fair trial—not as the colonial state defines it, but as international law protects it (Cutler, 2016). The Declaration provides guidance on procedural fairness:

> Indigenous peoples have the right to promote, develop and maintain their institutional structures and their distinctive customs, spirituality, traditions, procedures, practices and, in the cases where they exist, juridical systems or customs, in accordance with international human rights standards. (UN, 2007b, art. 34)

The difficult question for contemporary politics to resolve is that the 'inherent' sovereignty recognised in *United States v Bryant* conflicts with Chief Justice Marshall's earlier insistence that tribal sovereignty belongs to indigenous nations as 'domestic dependent nations'.

Dependency undermines sovereign political authority, leaving much of the scope for indigenous wellbeing vulnerable to the goodwill of the state. '[T]he rights-affirming strain of [Chief Justice Marshall's] doctrine' is important, while its 'rights-limiting strain ... is out of step with contemporary human rights values' (UN, 2012a, p. 7). The politics of indigeneity must resolve the philosophical contradiction between recognising indigenous rights so that states may honour international standards of justice, supported by economic and social imperatives to maximise indigenous capacity, and, conversely, the state's wish to retain political authority over indigenous peoples.

Five hundred and sixty-six American Indian and Alaskan Native tribes enjoy nation-to-nation relationships with the US. However, there are many other groups, including Native Hawaiians, that do not receive equivalent recognition (Independent Sovereign State of Hawai'i, 2017) even though they have long sought it. For example, the Nation of Hawaii, the oldest Hawaiian independence organisation, wishes to restore the 'National Sovereignty of the Hawaiian people' as a meaningful and practical path to self-determination (Independent Sovereign State of Hawai'i, 2017, p. 1).

Indigenous Hawaiians do not enjoy any legal arrangements for self-government to support the apology that the US offered in 1995 for 'the overthrow of the Kingdom of Hawaii' in 1893 and the suppression of the people's 'inherent sovereignty' (UN, 2012a, p. 11). While the US acknowledged that reconciliation logically follows apology, it remains an elusive aspiration.

H-K Trask (1999) demonstrated sovereignty's simplicity and reasonableness for Hawaii:

> Because of the overthrow and annexation, Hawaiian control and Hawaiian citizenship were replaced with American control and American citizenship. We suffered a unilateral redefinition of our homeland and our people, a displacement and a dispossession in our own country … orphaned in our own land. Such brutal changes in a people's identity—their legal status, their government, their sense of belonging to a nation—are considered among the most serious human rights violations by the international community today. (p. 16)

An alternative Hawaiian perspective is that, for 'Kanaka Maoli, our struggle has always been about nationhood, an essential foundation for the practice and perpetuation of our culture' (Trask, 2012, p. 285).

Land and education are essential to culture. Ho'omanawanui (2012) argued that the Declaration validates indigenous claims to recover lands from military jurisdiction. For example:

1. Military activities shall not take place in the lands or territories of indigenous peoples, unless justified by a relevant public interest or otherwise freely agreed with or requested by the indigenous peoples concerned.

2. States shall undertake effective consultations with the indigenous peoples concerned, through appropriate procedures and in particular through their representative institutions, prior to using their lands or territories for military activities. (UN, 2007b, art. 30)

Hoʻomanawanui (2012) also argued that the implementation of the right to education, at Articles 13 and 14 of the Declaration could have 'dramatic' and 'positive' (p. 291) effects on measures such as teaching in the Hawaiian language:

1. Indigenous peoples have the right to revitalize, use, develop and transmit to future generations their histories, languages, oral traditions, philosophies, writing systems and literatures, and to designate and retain their own names for communities, places and persons.

2. States shall take effective measures to ensure this right is protected and also to ensure that indigenous peoples can understand and be understood in political, legal and administrative proceedings, where necessary through the provision of interpretation or by other appropriate means. (UN, 2007b, art. 13)

Further:

1. Indigenous peoples have the right to establish and control their educational systems and institutions providing education in their own languages, in a manner appropriate to their cultural methods of teaching and learning.

2. Indigenous individuals, particularly children, have the right to all levels and forms of education of the State without discrimination.

3. States shall, in conjunction with indigenous peoples, take effective measures, in order for indigenous individuals, particularly children, including those living outside their communities, to have access, when possible, to an education in their own culture and provided in their own language. (UN, 2007b, art. 14)

The cultural validation that public support for indigenous education provides is an important measure of political recognition. It is a statement that indigenous people belong to the nation-state as citizens.

The Inuit Circumpolar Council (2009) asserted its sovereignty with reference to the Declaration and earlier UN instruments, insisting that 'Central to our rights as a people is the right to self-determination' (art. 1.4). The council's declaration on sovereignty is an assertion of a transnational Inuit right to share political authority with the Arctic states. It challenges sovereignty as the preserve of single nation-states in whose formation Inuit people had no say. The right to self-determination transcends state boundaries to once again show that indigenous sovereignty is not a simple parallel to the sovereignty claimed by the postsettler state. From one Haudenosaunee perspective:

> We were and are not citizens of the United States, Britain, or Canada and as it was agreed when the US–Canadian border was drawn it ought to remain 'ten feet above our heads'. (Garrow, 2012, p. 172)

Sovereignty is a treaty right compromised by interference with indigenous people's free passage across traditional territories divided by an imposed international border. The Declaration states that:

1. Indigenous peoples, in particular those divided by international borders, have the right to maintain and develop contacts, relations and cooperation, including activities for spiritual, cultural, political, economic and social purposes, with their own members as well as other peoples across borders.
2. States, in consultation and cooperation with indigenous peoples, shall take effective measures to facilitate the exercise and ensure the implementation of this right. (UN, 2007b, art. 36)

The Declaration may lend moral persuasiveness to a treaty right that neither Canada nor the US have respected, for it maintains that:

1. Indigenous peoples have the right to the recognition, observance and enforcement of treaties, agreements and other constructive arrangements concluded with States or their successors and to have States honour and respect such treaties, agreements and other constructive arrangements.
2. Nothing in this Declaration may be interpreted as to diminish or eliminate the rights of indigenous peoples contained in treaties, agreements and constructive arrangements. (UN, 2007b, art. 37)

The Distribution of Sovereignty

The Declaration is ultimately concerned with plurality in the distribution of public sovereignty to uphold diversity. Ivison, Patton and Sanders (2000) claimed that:

> one of the interesting consequences of the encounter between liberalism and its colonial past and present might be a more context-sensitive and multilayered approach to questions of justice, identity, democracy and sovereignty. The result would be a political theory open to new modes of cultural and political belonging. (p. 21)

A series of polarising questions concern how political authority is distributed, how people belong and how and why they might consent to state authority. Indigenous demands for an inclusive public authority occur because people are entitled to 'safe spaces' (Wiessner, 2008, p. 1174) to construct lives that they have reason to value (Sen, 1999a). Indigenous peoples are not going to go away; sovereignty is their insistence on the right to be present and 'to stay' *as* indigenous. Yet states resist the reconfiguration of sovereignty, not recognising that one community's need for relationships with others makes sovereignty relative and relational. Sovereignty ought not be conditional on indigenous peoples sacrificing their cultural values or adopting institutional arrangements at odds with those values.

Sovereignty can be understood as the authority to realise self-determination's potential, which in turn presumes substantive recognition of property and governance rights. From this foundation, broader consideration of the distribution of political authority and the precise terms on which sovereignty is shared might occur—that is, the terms on which peoples might belong together differently (Maaka & Fleras, 2005). The nation-state is not necessarily the only place in which sovereignty lies. When the nation-state exercises sovereignty, it only does so on the people's behalf. In this context, distinctions between the people who are included and the people who are excluded assume great political importance.

The idea that indigenous people constitute distinct groups disturbs the presumption that consent to government might be given through culturally homogenous majoritarian democracy. Majoritarian democracy is routinely used to challenge indigenous claims and to restrict distinctive and guaranteed indigenous participation in public affairs—as Australian prime ministers Turnbull's and Morrison's rejection of an Indigenous Australian voice to parliament showed. The presumption that a majority is always morally prior to a minority and more likely to be virtuous in its policy objectives means that the arguments for particular and distinctive indigenous contributions to policymaking are not always admitted. However, sovereignty ought not be used as a 'shield' to protect the state from indigenous objections to its abuse of power (Wiessner, 2008). It is significant that, as early as the 1830s, the Native American William Apess sought recognition of the 'rights of indigenous peoples as liberal subjects' (Dahl, 2016, p. 3).

Liberalism's inability to give theoretical justification to 'conquest' does not mean that it needs to understand indigenous peoples 'as paternalistic wards of the state unable to make political claims of their own' (Dahl, 2016, p. 3). Liberal political rights presume personal agency, not the patient anticipation that the benevolent state will one day 'do justice' to indigenous claims, as Waldron (2004, p. 253) expected. Instead, the Declaration is both the outcome and expression of indigenous agency as liberal citizens sharing national sovereignty, just as sovereignty is shared by other citizens.

Contemporary postsettler states struggle to manage political pressures for inclusion and exclusion; likewise, they struggle to acquire legitimacy, at least symbolically, in the eyes of indigenous citizens. Legitimacy would mean that indigenous peoples would find it unnecessary to think exclusively outside a liberal framework to acquire political voice and influence—that is, a share in national sovereignty. They would find their experiences aligned with Rousseau's understanding of popular sovereignty as the mechanism through which individuals become citizens concerned with the common good (Habermas, 1997). Maximum authority over their own affairs would occur alongside a distinctive space in public sovereignty as one of the Declaration's central presumptions. Indeed, if 'sovereignty ... is a social creation' as Alfred (2005, p. 46) proposed, it is logically a continually evolving phenomenon. The very fact that it is not an 'objective or natural phenomenon, but the result of choices made by men and women, indicative of a mindset ... rather than a natural force creative of a social and political order' (p. 471) means that it is a phenomenon over which people can reasonably expect to enjoy agency.

Conclusion

As a concept, state sovereignty is both constrained and variable (i.e. not static). Public attitudes to power and how it should be shared evolve with time and context and in response to changing political and economic constraints and opportunities. Politics occurs from assumptions about what makes power legitimate and what makes it illegitimate. It is the political spaces that sovereignty creates, and those that it limits, that are important. An expansive politics of potential cannot be defined or limited by these theoretical descriptions of political possibility but nor can it develop without reference to them. Colonial political theory gave states power over people (e.g. the power to dominate was the essential message that the colonial order took from Locke's theory of labour, as discussed in Chapter 3). However, indigeneity's juxtaposition with liberalism proposes the state as the *agent* of the people's sovereignty (as opposed to the *force* that exercises coercive and destructive power over some—but not necessarily all—people).

The juxtaposition provides ways of thinking about the political values and expectations that would moderate the dominance of the majority. Ultimately, indigenous sovereignty over their own affairs, and through equal membership of a liberal state, is possible, and the Declaration shows how. To this end, the politics of indigeneity's theoretical engagement with liberal democracy requires a form of differentiated citizenship to check unbridled majoritarian rule.

Differentiated citizenship promotes a cohesive and inclusive liberal political community, for indigeneity is a politics of 'shared sovereignties' (Maaka & Fleras, 2005, p. 187). Its substantive character and relationship with self-determination and sovereignty is the following chapter's concern. Differentiated citizenship's opposite is an exclusionary politics in which a settler cultural identity, rather than citizenship, is the criteria for democratic participation. A New Zealand proposal of this kind is then discussed in Chapter 9 and contrasted with models of indigenous inclusion in the sovereign public, including New Zealand's guaranteed Maori parliamentary representation.

8

Difference, Deliberation and Reason

Introduction

Liberalism is concerned with freedom, autonomy and the development of human capacity. Therefore, if one presumes that freedom and autonomy should belong equally to everybody, then political systems and processes need to be arranged for inclusivity and equal democratic participation. Substantive indigenous voice is important because political systems and political decisions reflect the values of those who have designed or made them. Democratic inclusivity means that it is fair and reasonable for indigenous values and epistemologies to influence decision-making. However, indigenous policy is often made without reference to indigenous people's evidence of what works or to their views of the values that ought to inform policy, which makes exclusion one of the causes of the unfair distribution of power.

Public reason and participatory parity may help to create political systems in which indigenous people can see their own values and priorities reflected. However, public reason requires an informed public, the lack of which was a particular concern to the TRC. The commission showed that reason means that public policy is informed by truth and evidence, not prejudice. This chapter argues that all people should have equivalent opportunity to contribute to public debate and thus to the 'formation of [public] values and priorities' (Sen, 1999b, p. 153). This is because politics is concerned not just with abstract or theoretical rights but also with helping to bring people 'as close to good functioning as their natural circumstances permit' (Nussbaum, 1987, p. 5).

Self-Determination as Inclusive Citizenship

The Declaration shows that, for all its negative consequences, colonial settlement has not reduced indigenous peoples to a 'state of absolute disempowerment' (Collingwood-Whittick, 2012, p. 125). Instead, and as a politics of possibility (O'Sullivan, 2017), indigeneity is concerned with human potential—with the right to self-determination through inclusive and differentiated citizenship and with self-determination's transformative capacity to contribute to people's enjoyment of lives that they have reason to value (Sen, 1999a). From this perspective, decolonisation may include assimilating 'the colonizer into Aboriginal processes of power-sharing' (Watson & Venne, 2012, pp. 88–89) in which indigenous agency is taken for granted. Indigenous peoples might then consider the ways in which postsettler states may be reconfigured for inclusivity. A liberal theory of indigeneity's distinctiveness is its focus on group rights and cultural context as essential constituents of individual liberty.

Differentiated citizenship can be structured to promote democratic participation in which all people enjoy the full rights of liberal democratic citizenship, and indigenous people enjoy guaranteed authority over their own affairs. From this perspective, an inclusive liberal polity can be structured in congruence with self-determination and in association with the Declaration. This conceptualisation of differentiated citizenship is consistent with Ivison's (2002) postcolonial liberalism, which argues for:

> a space within liberal democracies and liberal thought in which ... Aboriginal perspectives and philosophies can not only be heard, but [also] given equal opportunity to shape (and reshape) the forms of power and government acting on them. (p. 1)

Differentiated citizenship is politically valuable to indigenous self-determination. It acknowledges the expression of political rights in language that is amenable to international sympathy and the liberal insistence that 'individuals or groups cannot simply assert that they want something; they must say that justice requires or allows that they have it' (Horscroft, 2002, p. 263).

Colonialism brings a distinctive context to people's experiences of citizenship. That context in turn requires distinct processes for agreeing on public values to provide people with meaningful political voice. Politics is not concerned only with who holds which public office but with the exercise of political authority for the common good. The politics of indigeneity that the Declaration may support is not concerned with superior rights but with giving expression to liberal rights in a meaningful context. Liberalism cannot find difference repugnant to the integrity of the state, for as Young (1989) argued:

> The responsible citizen is concerned not merely with interests but with justice, with acknowledging that each other person's interest and point of view is as good as his or her own, and that the needs and interests of everyone must be voiced and be heard by others. (p. 262)

Patton (2005) identified three elements of a just noncolonial politics 'derived … from the requirements of reparative, distributive and relational justice' (p. 256). The first requires states to repair, as far as they can, the consequences of historical injustice. The second requires non-discrimination in public policy such that any lingering 'views about the hierarchy of peoples and cultures' (p. 257) are dismissed. The third, which is concerned with the nature of political relationships (Patton, 2005), is potentially the most important and far-reaching in giving effect to the Declaration.

Relational justice addresses the limits of distributive justice. On its own, distributive justice can have assimilationist tendencies. It is not necessarily attentive to the historical, political and cultural contexts of material need and does not consider that greater need in the distribution of material resources can be the outcome of the colonial experience itself. While indigenous political claims often have distributive implications, their foundation is in a broader moral argument for the recognition of prior occupancy. However, liberal societies are most responsive to those with the greater political voice. A strong relationship between indigenous peoples' relative population size and political influence is to be expected. Conversely, the broader liberal theory that the Declaration embraces ought to give moral reasoning greater influence, including, especially, indigenous moral reasoning in the determination of just policy objectives. Moreover, it ought to allow the claims of indigeneity to carry political authority in ways and for reasons that are independent of relative population size.

Mansbridge (1996) argued that liberal theory need not assume that a majority is always more likely to be objectively correct in its claims, nor must liberal theory insist that majority interests necessarily exist at the expense or exclusion of all others. Under liberal democratic arrangements, a group's relative population size ought not be the determinant of its capacity for self-determination, nor should size explain its relative wellbeing. Indigeneity is a political theory that makes no such presumption. Instead, it shows liberal democracy's theoretical capacity to frame the possibilities of indigenous citizenship to promote substantive political participation and to make self-determination an attainable human right.

Limited indigenous voice means that indigenous preferences are unlikely to be reflected in policy outcomes. Therefore, it is inadequate to characterise geocultural attachments as a choice 'not conducive to the kinds of full participation in Australian society that everyone should have', as former Australian prime minister Tony Abbott did, for example (as cited in Dorfmann, 2015, p. 13). Abbott made the argument in support of the Western Australian Government's proposal to cease providing municipal services to indigenous communities it deemed unviable (Dorfmann, 2015).

The underlying argument was that self-determination should not be available to all indigenous peoples and that such people's material wellbeing ought to be conditional on surrendering historical connections to country. Yet the Declaration holds that:

> Indigenous peoples shall not be forcibly removed from their lands or territories. No relocation shall take place without the free, prior and informed consent of the indigenous peoples concerned and after agreement on just and fair compensation and, where possible, with the option of return. (UN, 2007b, art. 10)

Abbott styled himself the 'Prime Minister for Indigenous Affairs'; however, by his actions, he showed himself to be mainly interested in those indigenous people who were willing and able to exercise a choice to assimilate. The Declaration, however, maintains that 'Indigenous peoples and individuals have the right not to be subjected to forced assimilation or destruction of their culture' (UN, 2007b, art. 8[1]). Further:

> Indigenous peoples and individuals have the right to belong to an indigenous community or nation, in accordance with the traditions and customs of the community or nation concerned. No discrimination of any kind may arise from the exercise of such a right. (UN, 2007b, art. 9)

It can be difficult to rank a series of proposals as more or less just when justice itself is contested and not neutral. Indigenous policy is often made on the basis of assumptions, not evidence. The collection of data on what works in Australian Indigenous policy is a newly accepted priority, and the notion that the role of public policy is to improve Indigenous people's lives is a recent development, as the earlier discussion of the Australian National Audit Office's (2017) report on the government's Indigenous Advancement Strategy showed (see Chapter 1). Conversely, prejudice is self-justificatory: it removes the need for evidence-based policy (O'Sullivan, 2015, 2017).

The test of liberal democracy's capacity to facilitate indigenous citizenship is not simply its mediation of difference but also its establishment of common ground that is not threatened by indigenous peoples' unique identities. 'Deliberative democracy requires the most expansive possible conditions of entry to formal or official political arenas' (Knight & Johnson, 2011, p. 283); yet liberal societies commonly exclude 'others' to protect what their majority populations hold in common, which is why institutional structures are determined according to a particular set of cultural values that are not neutral.

Institutional values stem from the cultural expectations of those who have designed them and reflect the values of those who determine the purposes that public institutions should serve. Institutional designers may have predetermined expectations about who is to be included and who is not. By contrast, institutional cultures might create the expectation that people will engage with each other to settle national policy priorities. Although deliberative democracy is 'a complex ideal' (Bohman, 1997, p. 321), it assumes ordered and inclusive terms of political association precisely because it has an essential liberal concern for the less powerful.

Liberal democracy is reasonably concerned with *all* and not just *some* citizens' deliberative capacity. In this way, politics may counter the market failure that would occur if public life were the sum of uncoordinated individual choices (Elster, 1997). However, politics does not always and necessarily admit that people live in subnational communities. Nor does it always acknowledge that intergroup relationships need to be managed towards fair distributive outcomes. As Bohman (1997) asked, 'What sorts of social inequalities are relevant to democratic deliberation? How large can actual inequalities be before they undermine the democratic ideal?' (p. 321). Inequality in terms of who loses, and why, explains the weakness in Waldron's (2004) argument that fair and reasonable political arrangements could supersede injustice. The idea is that just terms of association allow a polity to treat the past as though it never occurred.

Self-determination finds an inevitable and irremovable contradiction in the argument that:

> Claims about historical injustice predicated on the *status quo ante* may be superseded by a determination to distribute the resources of the world in a way that is fair to all of its existing inhabitants. (Waldron, 2003, p. 71)

Self-determination's concern for relational justice, or just terms of association, means that it is not simply a state that is reached and secured as a single event. Just terms of association require that the causes of unequal distributions of power are admitted.

Bohman (1997) argued that democratic systems can manage unequal distributions of power as long as these 'fall within the limits of the rule of law' (p. 322). However, this holds only if the rule of law is itself just; that is, if the burdens and possibilities of the law are distributed fairly and impose no structural discrimination on particular groups of people. Political equality means equal capacity to influence and to acknowledge that, even if one's preferences do not always prevail, they have the opportunity to carry influence and that the decision-making process is fair and reasonable in considering all perspectives.

None but the most routine political decisions can be equally acceptable to everyone. Democracy does not work in the absence of philosophical disagreement. Conflicting perspectives and aspirations are not always and necessarily undesirable, nor must conflicting perspectives and aspirations preclude finding sufficient commonality for social cohesion and political community to occur. Ideas must be exposed to contest. However, the question of who loses and whether that is because of unfair decision-making processes is important. Liberal societies ought to be guided by the values implicit in Rousseau's (1984) social contract—that 'no citizen should be rich enough to be able to buy another, and none so poor that he has to sell himself' (p. 75)—from which deliberative democracy is developed. Inequality of power means that some people cannot meet the conditions of deliberation as peers.

In a remark to a TRC hearing, the then Minister of Indian Affairs and Northern Development, Chuck Strahl, explained the procedural significance of indigenous deliberative exclusion:

> Governments like to write ... policy, and they like to write legislation, and they like to codify things and so on. And Aboriginal people want to talk about restoration, reconciliation, forgiveness, about healing ... about truth. And those things are all things of the heart and of relationships and not of government policy. Governments do a bad job of that. (quotation is as it appears in the source, as cited in TRC, 2015, p. 20)

In Australia, the UN special rapporteur noted that:

> While [Australia] has adopted numerous policies aiming to address Aboriginal and Torres Strait socio-economic disadvantage, the failure to respect the right to self-determination and the right to full and effective participation ... is alarming. The compounded effect ... has contributed to the failure to deliver on the targets of the areas of health, education and employment in the Closing the Gap strategy and has contributed to aggravating the escalating incarceration and child removal rates of Aboriginal and Torres Strait Islanders. (UN, 2017b, Self-determination and participation, para. 15)

Self-Determination, Democracy and Reasoned Public Decision-Making

Democracy requires competing philosophical ideas for its effectiveness (Benhabib, 1996), but it needs to manage these in ways that recognise the distinctiveness of the indigenous position vis-a-vis the postsettler state. The form that democracy takes influences policy outcomes. Indigenous peoples must have reason to acknowledge that there is, in fact, a national common good and that they can benefit from contributing to it. Questions must be asked. For example: Can the common good be understood in ways that are not homogenising? Are conflict and the common good points on a continuum or are they mutually exclusive possibilities? Is conflict inevitable and public reason impossible because, as Schumpeter asserted in his elitist theory of democracy, 'citizens in modern democracies [are] politically uninformed, apathetic, and manipulable' (Bohman & Rehg, 1997, p. x)?

An ill-informed public with a news media that does not accept a mission of public education is an obstacle to deliberative democracy. Public ignorance of the historical conflicts that arise between indigenous peoples and the state undermines reasoned public debate. According to Miller (2016), in the assessment of conflict, it is often true that:

> Politicians, journalists and ordinary citizens understood neither how nor why the crisis of the moment had arisen, much less how its deep historical roots made it resistant to solutions ... [This] does not bode well for effective public debate or sensible policy-making. (p. ii)

Deliberative democracy works best when elitist democracy's underlying presumptions are wrong and when the determinants of political authority are distributed equally so that all people may share the deliberative capacities of citizenship. This is because, as Aristotle (1988) put it, deliberation is citizenship's defining characteristic.

Deliberation through the public reason that participatory parity allows is essential 'to the formation of [the] values and priorities' (Sen, 1999b, p. 153) that a society wishes to privilege. At the same time, political agreement is not always necessary: people must be free to express their own conceptions of justice and be confident that these will be considered and have the capacity to influence public deliberation. As Bohman (1997) argued, 'the achievement of consensus in public deliberation depends on the discussion being guided by an ideal of impartiality' (p. 266). It also depends on equal access to education because, as Rawls (1993) argued, the capacity to deliberate requires that citizens 'have, at least to the essential minimum degree, the moral, intellectual and philosophical capacities that enable them to be fully cooperating members of society over a complete life' (p. 183). Schooling plays an important role in developing skills of critical reasoning and 'public reasonableness'. Education helps to create the public expectation that a well-functioning liberal democracy depends on deliberation grounded in these attributes (Gutmann, 1993). However, the attributes that participation assumes may not be culturally neutral and may be unequally available to different citizens. For example, the TRC (2015) found discrepancies in education funding for indigenous children educated on reserves vis-a-vis all others and recommended focused strategies to remove educational disparities between indigenous and other Canadians.

From the TRC's perspective, reconciliation requires that all citizens are well informed about colonial conflict and the particular aspects of political relationships and deliberative opportunities that indigenous politics seek to change. Its recommendation for museums and archives brings public memory into reconciliation in an overt and structured way. Public memory cements indigenous experiences into the national story. For example, indigenous people's 'inalienable right to know the truth about what happened and why' (TRC, 2015, p. 332) in residential schools is complemented by the wider community's duty to know that same truth so that they can reasonably deliberate and understand the claims that indigenous people make as members of the sovereign citizenry. The TRC also emphasised journalism's role in developing an informed public equipped with the knowledge to deliberate reasonably, which is not, in fact, a simple process. As one witness to the TRC (2015) explained:

> Journalism's first obligation is to the truth. … Journalism does not pursue truth in an absolute or philosophical sense, but it can—and must—pursue it in a practical sense. … Even in a world of expanding voices, accuracy is the foundation upon which everything else is built—context, interpretation, comment, criticism, analysis and debate. The truth, over time, emerges from this forum. …
>
> Its practitioners must be allowed to exercise their personal conscience. Every journalist must have a personal sense of ethics and responsibility—a moral compass. Each of us must be willing, if fairness and accuracy require, to voice differences with our colleagues. … This stimulates the intellectual diversity necessary to understand and accurately cover an increasingly diverse society. It is this diversity of minds and voices, not just numbers, that matters. (quotation is as it appears in the source, p. 296)

However, journalist Duncan McCue argued that editorial positions 'are often rooted in century-old stereotypes rather than reality' (as cited in TRC, 2015, p. 295) and that:

> Yes, protests often meet the test of whether a story is 'newsworthy,' because they're unusual, dramatic, or involve conflict. Yes, Aboriginal activists, who understand the media's hunger for drama, also play a role by tailoring protests in ways that guarantee prominent headlines and lead stories. But, does today's front-page news of some traffic disruption in the name of Aboriginal land rights actually have its roots in a much older narrative—

of violent and 'uncivilized' Indians who represent a threat to 'progress' in Canada? Are attitudes of distrust and fear underlying our decisions to dispatch a crew to the latest Aboriginal blockade? Is there no iconic photo of reconciliation, because no one from the newsrooms believes harmony between Aboriginal peoples and settlers is 'newsworthy'? (as cited in TRC, 2015, p. 295)

Reconciliation requires reasoned deliberation by a public whose positions may differ but who are at least accurately informed.

Deliberative democracy is grounded in reason; its relationships are necessarily respectful. Each party is required to be attentive to the other and to consider another's perspectives as legitimate because they are reasoned, even if one disagrees with their substance.

Reasonableness is subjective and emotive, especially when prejudice is presented as reasonable or—as Pauline Hanson, leader of the overtly racist One Nation Party put it—as the views of 'mainstream Australia' (Jackman, 1998, p. 167). If some people are free to promote policies grounded in prejudice, then indigenous peoples must be free to find platforms of resistance within the democratic system itself. Public reasonableness removes presumptions of 'self- or group-interest, prejudice or bias, and of such deeply entrenched errors as ideological blindness and delusion' (Rawls, 1999, p. 478). Public reasonableness is theoretically attractive for its insistence on inclusion and presumption that liberal politics would, as a matter of course, consider different culturally framed perceptions of the good life.

Christiano (1997) explained the contribution that public reasonableness would make to policy outcomes and showed how it would differ from prevailing indigenous experience:

When I submit my views and my arguments to you for your consideration and response and I listen to your ideas and arguments with an eye to learning something from you, I express a kind of respect for you, I am treating you as a kind of rational and intelligent being who has something to offer. (p. 251)

The converse is a common indigenous democratic experience:

If I am discussing some topic with you or someone else and you say something germane to the discussion [that] I simply ignore, I express a kind of contempt for you. (Christiano, 1997, pp. 251–252)

The idea that 'the force of the better argument' (Habermas, 1997, p. 24) determines the prevailing position does not account for the marked philosophical differences that can reasonably exist among peoples. It is only the reasonableness of one position that can test the unreasonableness of another. However, 'Imposing substantive criteria of reasonableness as an *ex ante* filter on admissibility would prevent that very process of reasonable argument' (Knight & Johnson, 2011, p. 286). Reasonableness 'is defined … in terms of a willingness to entertain and respond to objections' (Cohen, 1994, pp. 1537). Alternatively, unreasonableness is to advance 'institutions and policies that cannot be justified to others' (p. 1538). Public reasonableness may require some people to accept that their relative advantage over others is unjust:

> Political equality requires that when the time comes to make one's final decision on a question, the asymmetries in the social distribution of power and resources should not play a role in that decision. (Knight & Johnson, 2011, p. 294)

Plural perspectives will have been admitted into the conversation. No perspective is given greater or lesser status simply because of whose perspective it is, or to whom its underlying cultural values belong. There has been an obviously fair process for dealing with difference. Prejudice has been illegitimised because 'equal opportunity of influence requires that asymmetries not give unfair advantage' (Knight & Johnson, 2011, p. 293). However, indigenous experience shows that it is difficult to reach a point at which each participant has 'equal opportunity to influence others' (p. 295). Indeed, Knight and Johnson argued that 'real opportunity of influence is unachievable under democratic procedures because the very nature of the process makes the outcome uncertain and subject to the exigencies of political debate and deliberation' (pp. 295–296).

Rawls (1999) likened justice to procedural fairness, so that even if one does not accept a particular decision, one can still accept the process by which it was made. Social cohesion requires that people are able to see that procedural fairness occurs, which means that public reason is only achievable through participatory parity. Conversely, as Knight and Johnson (2011) put it, liberal societies are distinguished by party political systems developed because people are, in fact, routinely motivated by 'self-interest, blinded by prejudice, or deluded by ideology' (p. 284). However, the presumption that self-interest and ideology are objectively wrong, rather than simply reflective of difference, is problematic. If plurality is objectionable, colonialism's inherent inequality is reinforced.

Everybody ought to contribute to the development of the values by which state institutions operate. It is unjust to exclude some people from the definition of collective values if the values that are ultimately adopted then become determinants of people's access to public services. There is a relationship between indigeneity and participatory parity that aspires to 'institutionalised patterns of cultural value [that] express equal respect for all participants and ensure equal opportunity to achieve social esteem' (Fraser & Honneth, 2003, p. 36). People must have had the opportunity to contribute to a policy's development if they are to accept its legitimacy. Participation, then, is a necessary precondition for just and efficacious policy outcomes. Participatory parity presumes two conditions:

> First, the distribution of material resources must be such as to ensure participants' independence and 'voice.' ... the second condition requires that institutionalized patterns of cultural value express equal respect for all participants and ensure equal opportunity for achieving social parity. (Fraser & Honneth, 2003, p. 36)

Understood in this way, difference becomes a normative liberal presumption and a point against which justice can be measured. Sharing a dispersed sovereignty is no longer problematic.

Politics Is 'Not Simply the Allotment of Commodities'[1]

Linguistic, cultural, resource and participatory rights are 'external protections' (Kymlicka, 1995, p. 126) against domination. They are important liberal concerns even though they belong to groups before they can belong to individuals. Their deprivation constitutes 'a morally arbitrary disadvantage compared to those who can live and work in their own language and culture' (p. 126).

Indigeneity is a theory of the indigenous right to exist as distinct peoples. It is a political strategy of self-determination that makes wellbeing a concept that is political as much as it is material. It gives expression to Aristotle's (1988) argument that human flourishing is the point of political activity, which Nussbaum (1987) understands as 'the capability to function well if one so chooses' (p. 20).

---

1   Quotation from Nussbaum (1987, p. 1).

Political arrangements are most worthy when they maximise human capacity (Aristotle, 1988). From this perspective, one can deduce a political aspiration consistent with the politics of indigeneity and supported by the Declaration. According to Nussbaum (1987):

> The aim of political planning is the distribution to the city's individual people of the conditions in which a good human life can be chosen and lived. This distributive task aims at producing capabilities. That is, it aims not simply at the allotment of commodities, but at making people able to function in certain human ways ... The task of the city is, then, to effect the transition from one level of capability to another. (pp. 1–2)

There are innumerable conceptions of the good life. A 'deliberator would seem to inquire and analyze' these culturally framed and expressed conceptions 'as though analyzing a diagram' (Aristotle, 1995, p. 383). One analyses through a sociocultural and political lens. Analysis is necessary because a certain and constant 'right way to act is undefined' and each must deliberate by 'grasping [for] the truth, involving reason, and concerned with action about human goods' (Aristotle, 1995, p. 403).

Indigeneity's capabilities include the capacity to deliberate, which is not simply an abstract right but one that is present to varying degrees—a function of the obstacles and possibilities that are structured into a political community. In thinking of equality, it is only with reference to cultural and political contexts that one can answer Sen's (1979) question: 'equality of what?' (p. 1).

Equality is not neutral. It is culturally contextualised and defined with reference to one's ideological disposition. For example, personal conceptions of equality may influence the professional practice of those whose work affects others' access to equality as they themselves define it. Bureaucratic discretion means that teachers, nurses, doctors, police officers and others in frontline public employment have the capacity to distort policy intent to make it conform to their own values: to their own conceptions of equality and to the weight that equality should carry as a policy objective (Lipsky, 2010; O'Sullivan, 2015). This is why, for example, the TRC (2015):

> Call[ed] upon medical and nursing schools in Canada to require all students to take a course dealing with Aboriginal health issues, including the history and legacy of residential schools, [the Declaration], Treaties and Aboriginal rights, and Indigenous

teachings and practices. This will require skills-based training in intercultural competency, conflict resolution, human rights, and anti-racism. (p. 323)

Decisions about whose health care to privilege, whose learning to prioritise and who to prosecute have a significant influence on people's experience of public policy. These are not merely administrative decisions; they are deeply political in their rationale and in their consequences (O'Sullivan, 2015). However, in examining street-level bureaucracies as the places where people experience government that 'they have implicitly constructed', Lipsky (2010, p. xi) excluded the particular experience of indigenous peoples who have rarely implicitly constructed those bureaucracies (i.e. schools, hospitals, universities and police stations). This omission illustrates the democratic significance of indigenous participation at every level of the policy process, not only the legislative. The bureaucracy that the indigenous legislator may have helped to construct is more likely to use its bureaucratic discretion against indigenous interests if indigenous people are not present to influence its operations. Therefore, it is significant that, in 2018, Australia accepted that there ought to be periodic indigenous-led evaluations of its Closing the Gap policy (see Chapter 2).

Politics is 'not simply the allotment of commodities, but [is concerned with] making people able to function in certain human ways' (Nussbaum, 1987, p. 1). Equal capacity for democratic inclusion requires plurality in how, by whom and for whom public policy is developed. Equal opportunity requires that individuals and some groups of individuals are differently treated, even though it is wrong to suggest that this must involve privileged consideration in the distribution of political authority and public resources.

Deliberative democracy is 'a (broadly speaking) procedural ideal correlative to a bottom-line demand for political self-government by the people—where "by the people" is taken to mean "by everyone"'(Michelman, 1997, p. 149). However, indigenous peoples may be politically vulnerable in situations in which their distinctive interests are not easily explained according to the expectations of 'public reasonableness'. Distinctive arrangements may be required to satisfy procedural justice. A political system's sustainability depends on sufficient numbers of the polity's citizens having reason to support it or simply the incapacity to resist. Its objective of autonomy:

is realized by citizens when they act from principles of justice that specify the fair terms of cooperation they would give themselves when fairly represented as free and equal persons. (Rawls, 1993, p. 77)

Differentiated liberal citizenship, which is discussed in detail in the next chapter, occurs only if sovereignty belongs to the people and the people accept plurality in the distribution of political power and authority.

Plurality recognises that indigenous social units and political structures may develop to serve an indigenous public. Just as sovereign political authority might rest in many locations, so too does policy capacity. For example, Martinez Cobo (1981) argued that self-definition is preliminary to indigenous control over indigenous nationhood: 'There must be no attempt to define them according to the perceptions of others through the values of foreign societies or the dominant sections in such societies' (p. 92).

The capacity to manage relationships with the state and others is among sovereignty's most important characteristics. Indigenous political institutions must be equipped for this task, which is difficult, as colonialism's very purpose has been to undermine these bodies as institutions of resistance.

The state can make space for indigenous agency, but it cannot create that agency. The Declaration shows that there is scope for what Maaka and Fleras (2000) called 'sovereignty without secession' (p. 92). It will not achieve what Watson and Venne (2012) and Carroll (2012) view as just, but it does propose transformational possibilities. Many indigenous peoples find these possibilities important and worth pursuing, even though they conflict with Champagne's (2013) argument that the choice to participate in state institutions is a choice to assimilate. Champagne contrasts assimilation with the restoration of indigenous political structures as a choice to exclude oneself from the politics of the state. However, the contrast is a false dichotomy in that it represents an unnecessary choice that indigenous peoples often reject in favour of some form of differentiated citizenship.

Conclusion

The right to self-determination is the 'right to effective, democratic governance within States, making it possible for the population as a whole to determine their political status and pursue their development' (Solano, 2002, pp. 17–18). These principles are foundational to a liberal theory of indigeneity grounded in the extant rights of prior occupancy and developed for the reclamation of political authority in both proportionate and distinctive ways 'to confront prevailing prejudices and create opportunities to contextualise the meaning of indigenous liberty' (O'Sullivan, 2014, p. 66). Public sensitivity to others' needs and aspirations is important, especially when these are framed by conceptions of the common good that differ from one's own.

Deliberative democracy presumes recognition, including in the distribution of political capacity. It presumes that peoples can understand one another better if there is respect for the legitimacy of difference. Consequently, democracy's structure and form matter enormously. It is to illuminate differentiated liberal citizenship's value that the following chapter contests the illiberal foundation of the New Zealand Independent Working Group on Constitutional Transformation's *He whakairo here whakaumu mō Aotearoa* report and recommendations for a rigid bicultural polity. Examples of differentiated citizenship's practice and potential are provided, not as a panacea for the realisation of self-determination, but as alternatives to isolated indigenous nationhood.

9

Differentiated Citizenship: A Liberal Politics of Potential

Introduction

This chapter discusses differentiated liberal citizenship. It shows the constraints on power that arise when an indigenous people reject differentiated liberal citizenship, as occurred in New Zealand when the Iwi Chairs Forum's Independent Working Group on Constitutional Transformation, Matike Mai Aotearoa (2016), recommended a constitutional order based on rigid distinctions between Maori and Crown authority. The working group's report, *He whakairo here whakaumu mō Aotearoa*, made the distinction by positioning the New Zealand Crown as an exclusively Pakeha entity, thereby making it the site of just *some* citizen's political authority (O'Sullivan, 2007).

This chapter presents the case for a more inclusive commonwealth to allow Maori to exercise liberal citizenship of the state as an essential complement to the political authority that iwi may exercise. Through a series of examples in which differentiated liberal citizenship has in fact been applied in New Zealand and other jurisdictions, this chapter highlights its potential as a path to self-determination. It also shows how measures such as guaranteed parliamentary representation, a 'voice to parliament' in Australia and democratic participatory parity at all levels of the state political system are important constituents of the right to self-determination. As the Declaration affirms:

> Indigenous peoples have the right to determine their own identity
> or membership in accordance with their customs and traditions.
> This does not impair the right of indigenous individuals to obtain
> citizenship of the States in which they live. (UN, 2007b, art. 32)

It is important to attend to not only the constitutional or legal aspects of
the right to self-determination but also the political. Constitutions may
set the rules, but politics is the process through which self-determination's
practical meanings are worked out with others. Consequently, this chapter
is especially concerned with political transformation; in particular,
the ways in which political systems might work to include indigenous
people, epistemologies and values in the policy process. This requires an
indigenised bureaucracy and policy processes—that is, an indigenous
voice and presence wherever policy is made.

In these ways, the idea of an indivisible and absolute Crown sovereignty
is challenged. Public authority becomes the property of the sovereign
citizenry of which indigenous peoples are a part, just as much as they
are a part of their own nations or iwi. In New Zealand, as this chapter
explains, this means that the Crown cannot be presented as the repository
of Pakeha authority alone.

The chapter shows that departing from a bicultural binary in favour of
differentiated liberal citizenship creates more expansive opportunities
for political influence and greater opportunities for self-determination as
a meaningful practice that may improve people's lives. The connection
between citizenship and self-determination is especially strong when there
is public policy space for indigenous peoples to manage public services
for themselves and in their own ways. The chapter presents ACCHOs,
introduced in Chapter 5, as an example and proposes ways of strengthening
this model of self-determination—not so much through the redistribution
of resources but through the redistribution of power. Inequitable health
outcomes reflect more than just the failings of egalitarian justice. This is
because health outcomes, like outcomes in education and employment
for example, are reflections of people's capacities of citizenship.

The political will to change the nature of citizenship by allowing it to be
exercised differentially is weak across most jurisdictions, many of which
are struggling to come to terms with the politics of indigeneity that the
Declaration imagines and strengthens. As this chapter discusses, with
reference to Canada, strengthening capacities for self-determination may
also call for a deliberate focus on the reconciliation of interests and not

simply the reconciliation of conflict. Recognising difference is important, but difference ought not blind the policy process to overlapping interests that may become more obvious in political systems in which decisions are made according to processes of reasoned deliberation. In other words, equal political capacity means active citizenship, which in turn is the practice of self-determination.

He Whakairo Here Whakaumu mō Aotearoa

In 2016, the New Zealand Iwi Chairs Forum's Independent Working Group on Constitutional Transformation, Matike Mai Aotearoa, published a report on how New Zealand's constitutional arrangements might be transformed to entrench a bicultural form of government. The report sought stronger political relationships between iwi and the Crown, and restoration of the sovereignty that was, according to the Waitangi Tribunal ('He Whakaputanga me te Tiriti', 2014), usurped, not ceded. The report's purpose was to foster 'constitutional transformation'.

According to Jones (2014), Maori constitutionalism proceeds from:

1. Whanaungatanga – 'the centrality of relationships to Maori life';
2. Manaakitanga (and kaitiakitanga) – 'nurturing relationships, looking after people, and being very careful how others are treated …;
3. Mana – 'the importance of spiritually sanctioned authority and the limits on Māori leadership';
4. Tapu/Noa – 'respect for the spiritual character of all things';
5. Utu – 'the principle of balance and reciprocity'. (p. 191)

Importantly, these precepts do not require the Crown and Maori to be treated as rigidly distinct entities, with the Crown's affairs a matter for 'them' not 'us' in an unproblematic bicultural binary. Instead, they can be understood as examples of the values that Maori citizens might bring to their participation in public affairs that might 'indigenise' the policy process, as discussed later in this chapter.

Extensive consultations preceded *He whakairo here whakaumu*. These were among the most comprehensive and considered constitutional discussions in recent New Zealand history. However, constitutions are restraining just as they are emancipatory. The goals of Maori self-determination are realisable only through political transformation. Constitutional transformation may support political goals, but it does not guarantee them. An agreeable constitution, especially in a state that does not have a single written instrument, is not an end in itself. To provide scope for political transformation beyond that which already exists, a constitution would need to have greater force than the combined influence of the Treaty of Waitangi, common law and international legal instruments such as the Declaration. Ultimately, and simply, political transformations require political voice wherever power is exercised, not only within the Maori sphere of *He whakairo here whakaumu*'s bicultural world.

Biculturalism views Maori and non-Maori populations 'as if they [run] on separate parallel train tracks' (Chapple, 2000, p. 7). The distinct non-Maori ethnicity that it ascribes to the Crown leaves the Crown to make decisions for 'its people' (Matike Mai Aotearoa, 2016, p. 9)—a distinct, easily identifiable and homogenous people in whose affairs Maori have no business.

Maori may enjoy the right, in principle, to distinct separation from biculturalism's Pakeha Crown. However, self-determination embodies greater political authority when sovereignty is recognised as the concern of relative and relational distributions of power. The proposition that some authority belongs to 'us' (i.e. Maori) and some to 'them' (i.e. Pakeha) is a common theme in Maori political rhetoric. However, the theme is inconsistent with Maori political practice, especially the considered Maori pursuit of parliamentary membership from general and party list seats as well as from the guaranteed Maori constituencies.

Maori unapologetically and systemically pursue participation in the executive. Since the 1970s, it has been extremely rare for Cabinets not to include Maori ministers. *He whakairo here whakaumu* understated the essential role that Maori members of parliament play in advancing opportunities for self-determination. Rather than acknowledge this inclusive model of Maori participation in the executive and legislature, the report proposed six alternative structural models to distinguish Maori political authority from that of the Crown-in-Parliament:

1. A tricameral or three sphere model consisting of an Iwi/Hapū assembly (the rangatiratanga sphere), the Crown in Parliament (the kāwanatanga sphere) and a joint deliberative body (the relational sphere).

2. A different three sphere model consisting of an assembly made up of Iwi, Hapū and other representation including Urban Māori Authorities (the rangatiratanga sphere), the Crown in Parliament (the kāwanatanga sphere), and a joint deliberative body (the relational sphere).

3. A further three sphere model consisting of an Iwi/Hapū assembly (the rangatiratanga sphere), the Crown in Parliament (the kāwanatanga sphere), and regional assemblies made up of Iwi, Hapū and Crown representatives (the relational sphere).

4. A multi-sphere model consisting of an assembly of Iwi/Hapū and other Māori representation (the rangatiratanga sphere) and the Crown in Parliament (the kāwanatanga sphere). It also includes a relational sphere which would have two parts – a constitutionally mandated set of direct Iwi/Hapū/Crown relationships to enable direct Iwi/Hapu-Crown decision-making plus a unitary perhaps annual assembly of broader Māori and Crown representation.

5. A unicameral or one sphere model consisting of Iwi/Hapū and the Crown making decisions together in a constitutionally mandated assembly. This model does not have rangatiratanga or kāwanatanga spheres. It only has the relational sphere.

6. A Bicameral Model made up of an Iwi/Hapū assembly and the Crown in Parliament. This model has distinct rangatiratanga and kāwanatanga spheres but has no provision for a relational sphere. (Matike Mai Aotearoa, 2016, p. 10)

The first four of these models, and the sixth, diminish Maori political authority in ways that prevent self-determination *within* the state. The fifth is essentially the current national parliament with some strengthening of Maori representation. However, in making no provision for *rangatiratanga* (chiefly authority), it became the first serious Maori proposal since 1840 to set aside the Treaty of Waitangi. Were it amended to include *rangatiratanga,* it would be the only model consistent with differentiated liberal citizenship and the meaningful sharing of sovereignty.

He whakairo here whakaumu's models were intended to constrain Crown sovereignty. However, and by contrast, self-determination contests Crown sovereignty's exclusive form; it contests the very idea that public sovereignty is not shared by Maori. The report does not consider what it means for a Maori person to be a citizen of a liberal democratic state. It makes passing references to citizenship's limits but does not consider its possibilities. For Maori to separate themselves from the 'Crown's people' is a radical political and constitutional proposal that would logically exclude Maori from membership of the New Zealand Parliament and from the right to vote for members of parliament.

A more productive approach would be for the 'relational sphere'—in which Maori and other citizens 'make decisions together'—to remain the national parliament, accompanied by the strengthening of Maori participation in other spheres of influence in which sovereign power is dispersed. Guaranteed participation at every level of the political system allows indigenous people to pursue their distinctive aspirations and to engage in public affairs as members of the sovereign citizenry rather than as subjects waiting for others to conceptualise the justice that ought to be 'done' to them.

He whakairo here whakaumu sought the restoration of mana, which:

> as a political and constitutional power ... denotes an absolute authority. It was absolute because it was absolutely the prerogative of every polity, but it was also absolute in the sense that it was commensurate with independence and an exercise of authority that could not be tampered with by any other polity. (Matike Mai Aotearoa, 2016, p. 34)

This perspective of mana positions sovereignty in absolute and indivisible terms, yet modern sovereignty is undeniably dispersed. Sovereign political authority does not reside with one being or institution alone; it is relative, relational and shared. This is because the sovereign citizenry is not a singular being. Mana is shaped by external influences, with colonialism a transgression of mana. Moral objection alone cannot prevent that transgression. Mana's protection through constitutional arrangements is possible only through politics, which is why full attention to political context is preliminary to self-determination. As one participant in the *He whakairo here whakaumu* discussions observed:

> Although times have changed those old tikanga remain ... we never lost or ceded our mana and never forgot what was tika [right] about how we should exercise it. The challenge now is to adapt those things in the 21st century. (Matike Mai Aotearoa, 2016, p. 36)

The idea that the body of authority that is not exclusively Maori belongs to a *Leviathan*-like Crown prevents Maori from fully exploring political possibilities and makes substantive justice unachievable. Power is continuously rebalanced by demographic changes and by changes in people's perceptions of what is just and pragmatic. Indeed, as a *He whakairo here whakaumu* participant remarked:

> Sometimes we get caught in the trap of just accepting what colonisation has done, like setting up its own government, and saying that it's right or it can't be changed because it's too hard … we should try because that's what the treaty talked about. (Matike Mai Aotearoa, 2016, p. 37)

Maori make claims against the Crown for breaches of the Treaty of Waitangi. In this sense, they are binary opponents. However, to see Maori and Pakeha persons as apart in the politics of citizenship is limiting.

If people do not simply wish 'to talk about structures but rather the ideals that might transform how their right to make their own decisions is perceived' (Matike Mai Aotearoa, 2016, p. 38), it may be useful to consider how their right to citizenship is perceived, protected and advanced. While *He whakairo here whakaumu* rightly distinguishes *rangatiratanga* from *kāwanatanga* (governorship) as spheres of political influence, Maori need not surrender one for the other. Participation in *rangatiratanga* is an ancestral right. Participation in citizenship is a treaty right and a liberal right and the Declaration upholds both forms of political authority.

The notion of 'subjecthood' as it was understood in 1840 and extended to Maori under Article 3 of the Treaty of Waitangi has evolved into a more far-reaching and politically meaningful citizenship. *He whakairo here whakaumu* provides a clear account of *rangatiratanga*, but *kāwanatanga* is left as something belonging to others. However, if Maori are not active participants in *kāwanatanga*—the domain of the liberal citizen—they are confined to subjecthood.

The ascription of a non-Maori ethnic character to the Crown prevents consideration of the relationship between *rangatiratanga* and *kāwanatanga* in a liberal democratic state—a political structure that is very different from a Crown reigning over its subjects. Liberal democratic citizenship may constrain self-determination but not in the same ways or for the same reasons as subjecthood. The constitutional and political context of 1840 does not provide a lens through which the limits and possibilities for Maori autonomy can presently be considered. It does not explain how *kāwanatanga*, especially, might support self-determination.

He whakairo here whakaumu makes no comment on how or by what authority the state bureaucracy ought to function. Nor does it provide any path for Maori appointments to the executive. The report reflects a significant dissonance between constitutional thought and political practice. Contemporary politics is pragmatic rather than theoretical and influenced by immediate political possibilities, economic imperatives and treaty settlements. Contemporary Maori politics reflect differentiated liberal citizenship's possibilities. Moreover, it provides a foundation for extending Maori influence both within and beyond the state, and for recognising that opportunities for self-determination are greatest when *rangatiratanga* and *kāwanatanga* are accepted as sites of legitimate Maori political authority.

Given *He whakairo here whakaumu*'s perspective on the validity of an absolute and easily distinguishable Maori–Pakeha binary, it might be assumed that workshop participants were people of singular Maori identity. If so, their perspectives are likely to be more fixed than the 53.5 per cent of Maori who claim two or more ethnic identities (Statistics New Zealand, 2013). The report's models require people of Maori descent to take a singular identity: Maori or Pakeha. Imposing a choice of this kind would be culturally and socially problematic for a people inclined to place significant value on *whakapapa* (ancestry) from wherever it comes. The views of Maori who claim additional non-Maori, non-Pakeha ancestries may further complicate the report's simple view of the relationship between ethnicity and political arrangements.

Although *He whakairo here whakaumu* represents a significant body of Maori political thought, it is difficult to imagine Maori being satisfied with structural separation from the state. Maori have always wanted to sit in the executive, parliament and judiciary. They surely want equal capacity to influence public sector policymaking, and those who participate in public life in these ways are not the state's junior bicultural partners but active participants in its structure, character and purpose. The Declaration does not imagine junior and senior partners because:

> Indigenous peoples have the right to maintain and strengthen their distinct political, legal, economic, social and cultural institutions, while retaining their right to participate fully, if they so choose, in the political, economic, social and cultural life of the State. (UN, 2007b, art. 5)

He whakairo here whakaumu presumes 'public reasonableness' (introduced in the previous chapter). For example, it requires a suspicious public to accept that legislation should be assessed for consistency with the Treaty of Waitangi in the first place. If public reasonableness establishes that consistency with the treaty is a shared value, there would still need to be public agreement that consistency be assessed through an especially established parliamentary chamber. As Bohman and Rehg (1997) explained:

> a democracy based on public deliberation presupposes that citizens or their representatives can take counsel together about what laws and policies they ought to pursue as a commonwealth. And this in turn means that the plurality of competing interests is not the last word, or sole perspective, in deciding matters of public importance. The problem, to use Kant's terms is to bring about 'the public use of reason'. (p. x)

The Treaty of Waitangi means that the Crown will always remain integral to political discourse; however, the Crown is a concept that, in its current ordinary usage, raises significant obstacles to Maori capacity for self-determination through differentiated citizenship. Current ordinary usage means that the Crown is inevitably an instrument of bicultural exclusion rather than the expression of a political authority that all are entitled to share.

Beyond Bicultural Exclusion

The theoretical tension between the Crown as treaty partner and transgressor, and the Crown as the repository of *all* citizens' collective sovereignty, is an important one, yet its significance is not widely recognised in treaty scholarship nor in public discourse. *He whakairo here whakaumu*'s conceptual weakness is its failure to consider this tension between the Maori citizen's dual membership of a *hapu* that signed the treaty and a sovereign national public from which the Crown derives its authority.

Beyond biculturalism, there may lie a commonwealth with distinct parts and united by equal moral capacities to determine how those parts are ruled. Commonwealth means sharing individual authority with a collective power from which protection is obtained. Commonwealths are based on trust, as Hobbes (1998) declared: 'Justice and Propriety

Begin with the Constitution of Commonwealth. But … Covenants of mutual trust, where there is a fear of non-performance on either part … are invalid' (p. 424). For Hobbes:

> The Essence of the Common-wealth is One person [or assembly]… by mutual Covenants one with another that made themselves every one the Author, to the end he may use the strengths and means of them all, as he shall think expedient, for their Peace and Common Defence. (p. 515)

Accepting membership of the common citizenry is preliminary to holding public institutions accountable for what they do and for the values that inform their actions. All people ought to take their place within the commonwealth—a body in which authority is always contested and never exclusive.

To bring indigenous politics from the margins to the mainstream, citizenship requires a commonwealth alongside a liberal theory of indigeneity. This means reconfiguring the ways in which Hobbes's understanding of sovereignty prevails as a justification for exclusion. For example, in New Zealand, the idea that *rangatiratanga* constrains sovereignty is important: it implies a distinction between the two. However, it may be that reconceptualising *rangatiratanga* as a legitimate part of the sovereign whole better reflects the political status that Maori are entitled to claim. *Rangatiratanga* then contributes to self-determination within the state; rather than constraining sovereignty, *rangatiratanga* helps to define it. In helping to define national sovereignty and sever biculturalism's exclusive association of the sovereign Crown with the Pakeha polity, *rangatiratanga* strengthens the possibilities for the Maori exercise of authority in and over their own affairs.

Rangatiratanga is diminished if it is not accepted into the sovereign whole. Its absence means that it is only from beyond the state (as bicultural partner) that scope exists for Maori to contribute to public policy. Separating *rangatiratanga* from sovereignty imposes a structural limit on self-determination and depends on a fiduciary obligation to Maori in place of the participatory parity of Maori citizens as equal shareholders in Crown sovereignty.

Self-determination cannot occur if the complementary relationship between differentiated citizenship's two spheres—the indigenous nation and the state—does not enjoy the space to develop. Indeed, as the Canadian Public Policy Forum (2017) argued:

The outcome of true reconciliation must be to ensure that Indigenous peoples are fully accorded the opportunity to fully participate in the economic and social fabric of our country … of the broader society—on corporate boards in business-school case studies, in executive roles, and union leadership, in associations, in government and in regulatory and environmental assessment bodies. (pp. 6–7)

First Nations people need to be part of the national middle class because that is where a disproportionate share of national sovereignty resides and where national wealth and decision-making capacity are found. They also need to be part of the 'sovereign' public. Poor education and low incomes compromise indigenous people's capacity as citizens, whereas increasing the size of the indigenous middle class raises capacity to engage as equals in the affairs of the nation-state.

Notwithstanding this book's objections to *He whakairo here whakaumu*, the report did identify 'a very real desire for a more open constitutionalism and what we describe as a conciliatory and consensual democracy rather than an adversarial and majoritarian one' (Matike Mai Aotearoa, 2016, p. 9). In this sense, the report is a most important and instructive document, as it shows the values that people wish to inform political engagement. These values are consistent with differentiated liberal citizenship and may, in fact, enjoy greater influential possibilities under liberal (as opposed to bicultural) political arrangements:

1. *The value of tikanga* [cultural values] – that is the need for a constitution to relate to or incorporate the core ideals and the 'ought to be' of living in Aotearoa.

2. *The value of community* – that is the need for a constitution to facilitate the fair representation and good relationships between all peoples.

3. *The value of belonging* – that is the need for a constitution to foster a sense of belonging for everyone in the community.

4. *The value of place* – that is the need for a constitution to promote relationships with, and ensure the protection of Papatūānuku [the Earth].

5. *The value of balance* – that is the need for a constitution to ensure respect for the authority of rangatiratanga and kāwanatanga within the different and relational spheres of influence.

6. *The value of conciliation* – that is the need for a constitution to have an underlying jurisdictional base and a means of resolution to guarantee a conciliatory and consensual democracy.

7. *The value of structure* – that is the need for a constitution to have structural conventions that promote basic democratic ideals of fair representation, openness and transparency. (Matike Mai Aotearoa, 2016, p. 69)

He whakairo here whakaumu also showed the importance of relational justice:

> Contest and debate were regarded [at the consultation meetings that informed the report] as essential to good decision-making but there was concern that unless it was placed upon some tikanga about how conflict or difference could be managed then any rangatiratanga and kawanatanga spheres of influence would have difficulty working together. (Matike Mai Aotearoa, 2016, p. 71)

The following points were considered important:

- Recognising and acknowledging the kawa and tikanga [culture and cultural practices] of each marae, hapū and iwi [meeting house, sub-tribe and tribe];
- Restoring, reclaiming and re-practicing our tikanga and kawa;
- Learning, teaching and transmission of Te Reo Māori [the Maori language];
- Retelling our own histories in our own ways;
- Learning and understanding how our tipuna [ancestors] lived before us;
- Understanding the roles of men and women, tuakana and teina [older and younger relatives of the same generation], and their importance in our societies;
- Ensuring that Te Ao Māori becomes a living reality for us as tangata whenua [people of the land]. (Matike Mai Aotearoa, 2016, p. 119)

These values could reasonably inform Maori citizenship and political voice.

Guaranteed Maori representation in parliament is an effective illustration of deliberative democracy's capacity to include an indigenous voice. It means that Maori contribute to the parliamentary check on the executive while also enjoying a greater likelihood of ministerial appointment and shows that New Zealand politics is distinguished by a differentiated liberal citizenship of significant potential. It is of much greater potential than contemporary Maori discussions about 'constitutional transformation' care to admit. Indeed, the indigenous right to participate fully 'if they so choose … [in the] life of the state' (UN, 2007b, art. 5) is a right that biculturalism understates, and that *He whakairo here whakaumu* does not properly consider.

Guaranteed representation in parliaments is one of the ways in which political systems recognise difference. Such recognition allows for inclusion: when different people sit in the one parliament, their commonalities emerge from the respect that is implicit in the recognition of difference.

Guaranteed Maori representation in the New Zealand Parliament has occurred since 1867. Initially, the number of Maori seats was fixed at four. Since 1993, the number has been set in proportion to the number of Maori voters who choose to register on the Maori electoral roll. In 2019, there were seven Maori parliamentary seats. The social-democratic Labour Party won all seven of those seats at the 2017 general election. Maori citizens were also elected from general constituencies and party lists, providing additional Maori members of parliament from the Labour, National, New Zealand First, ACT and Green parties.

In Maori constituencies, Maori candidates are free to use their own culturally reasoned arguments to elicit support. Voters are free to evaluate alternative positions through a meaningful self-defined cultural prism, yet the UN special rapporteur's endorsement of New Zealand's liberal inclusivity has been conditional. While he welcomed 'New Zealand's efforts to secure Maori political participation at the national level' (UN, 2011, p. 20), he observed that:

> these efforts should be strengthened, and the State should focus special attention on increasing Maori participation in local governance. The Government should consider reversing its decision to reject the findings of the Royal Commission on Auckland Governance and guarantee Maori seats on the Auckland City Council. (p. 20)

Local governments do not have to assure Maori representation, but they are required to 'establish and maintain processes to provide opportunities for Maori to contribute to the decision-making processes of the local authority' (*Local Government Act 2002* [NZ], s. 81) 81). Vulnerability of this kind shows the importance of indigenous peoples asserting their positions as members of the nation-state. It is only in this way that the rights that indigenous peoples might enjoy in and over their own affairs can be protected.

'Constitutional Recognition Must Make Indigenous Lives Better. Otherwise What's the Point?'[1]

In 1996, the Canadian Royal Commission on Aboriginal Peoples recommended the creation of an aboriginal parliament. The recommendation followed the Native Council of Canada's proposal that a House of First Peoples should 'have the power to veto certain legislation put before it, or that passing such legislation require a double majority of the House of Commons and the House of First Peoples' (as cited in Boutilier, 2017, p. 14). The Canadian royal commission's remarks on the purpose of an aboriginal parliament is equally relevant to New Zealand:

> The creation of an Aboriginal parliament would not be a substitute for self-government by Aboriginal nations. Rather it is an additional institution for enhancing the representation of Aboriginal peoples within Canadian federalism. (*Royal Commission on Aboriginal Peoples*, 1996 [Canada], p. 363)

In Australia, Axelby and Wanganeen (2017) proposed a number of political and institutional values to assure indigenous people's meaningful decision-making authority. They argued that political power can only come, in a substantive way, from the *Australian Constitution* (Axelby & Wanganeen, 2017). Yet, as they acknowledged, and as this chapter has also argued, there is no absolute connection between the citizenship rights that constitutions recognise and the *capacity* for citizenship. Constitutions are grounded in law, but *capacity* is also grounded in politics, leading Axelby and Wanganeen to declare, in the title of their opinion piece, 'Constitutional recognition must make indigenous lives better. Otherwise what's the point?'.

Constitutional recognition must lead to political recognition—to assessing political questions of transformative potential and dealing with questions of how and on whose terms indigenous peoples belong to the modern state,

---

1   The title of Axelby and Wanganeen's (2017) opinion piece in *The Guardian*.

such as: What political capacities ought to proceed from one's position as an indigenous citizen of the Commonwealth of Australia? What does 'the Commonwealth' mean for an indigenous person? While citizenship is the embodiment of the rights one holds by virtue of one's membership of a political community, it is the capacity to make something of those rights that creates the connection between citizenship and self-determination. Watson and Venne (2012) argued that the Declaration cannot contribute to establishing that connection. In their view, it is inadequate as an instrument of indigenous rights because its provisions do not counter the state's assimilationist tendencies. However, an alternative question for a transformative politics of indigeneity is whether the Declaration can assist with the reconfiguration of the state and its internal distributions of power.

Effective policy requires that the right questions are asked and the right problems identified. Policy paradigms that are successful for indigenous peoples (in Australia and elsewhere) are ones in which people may exercise the capacity for self-determination—that is, where they may enjoy the capacity to harness the powers and opportunities of citizenship for their own purposes. For example, Davis (2013) argued that, as the Australian Indigenous community–controlled health sector can reach 'individuals and families that no government could ever possibly reach' (p. 13), 'we cannot leave it to the state' (p. 13). Further:

> The next phase does not require us to agonise over how the state is or is not implementing [the Declaration]; we need to take ownership of the text and we need to put meat on the bones of [the Declaration]. (p. 13)

Around 50 per cent of the Indigenous Australian population use Indigenous health services (Mazel, 2016). As discussed in Chapter 5, ACCHOs were established in response to the systematic exclusion of Indigenous peoples from health policymaking and the health system's sustained failure to provide Indigenous peoples with services of equivalent quality to those provided to other citizens (O'Sullivan, 2015). Their use by Indigenous people suggests the importance attached to cultural context in the provision of health services. ACCHOs give communities (as opposed to governments) the power to determine how health services are provided. However, self-determination requires stronger institutional arrangements for supporting community priorities in the allocation of resources. This suggests that there is a case, both morally and pragmatically, for an Indigenous entity to make funding decisions based on contestable bids from ACCHOs. An Indigenous-health purchasing agency was recommended to the government by the Health and Hospitals Reform Commission in 2009. It was thought that such an agency would provide strong institutional support to self-determination in health by giving Indigenous people self-determination over funding decisions and removing from debate the proposition that health systems have no obligation to take cultural imperatives and preferences into account in their treatment of Indigenous people (see O'Sullivan, 2015). However, the recommendation was not accepted.

The argument for an Indigenous-health purchasing agency is not necessarily, or only, about the redistribution of resources but also about the redistribution of authority. To put this another way, it is about an Indigenous share in the sovereign authority of the state that is strong enough to allow Indigenous people to set their own healthcare priorities. At present, ACCHOs operate in a context of 'dependent autonomy'. If Indigenous people do not take their place within the state, they cannot avoid dependence, for it is the state that determines the political and legislative context in which people exercise their capacities as citizens. It is the state that appropriates public money to the indigenous shadow state.

As Mazel (2016) observed, governments have come and gone since 1971, but ACCHOs have stood firm as examples of what self-determination really looks like—they have remained. Rowse (2000) described them as the most important contemporary expression of self-determination because 'the politics of Indigenous citizenship is a struggle not only over notions of right but also about ways of being present and effective, that is, about capacities for Indigenous participation' (p. 86).

Inequities in policy outcomes transcend the unfortunate to raise important questions of justice. Daniels (2008) asked, 'Why should some people be at such a health disadvantage through no fault of their own, losers in a natural and social lottery assigning them from birth to an unhealthy place?' (pp. 109–110). For indigenous people, health inequities are the outcome of unjust terms of association. If indigenous people 'are justified in claiming a right to health care only if it is derivable from an acceptable general theory of distributive justice' (Daniels, 1979, p. 174), then that theory must be concerned with the distribution of political authority at least as much as it is concerned with the distribution of material resources. The questions of how, by whom and for whom decisions are made are important, as health outcomes tend 'to be a good guide to the underlying capabilities' (Sen, 2004, p. 23) that people enjoy. Health outcomes are a reflection of political capacity and of people's capacity as citizens.

The internationally sanctioned right to health is only progressively realisable (UN, 1966b, pt. II art. 2[1]). Jurisdictions such as Australia, Canada, New Zealand, Norway and the US have the capacity to address a policy problem that affects small percentages of the national populations and for which there are innumerable examples of policy success (O'Sullivan, 2015). Political decisions cannot remove the injustice of colonialism, but they can tend towards the creation of noncolonial relations for the present and future.

In 2016, the Australian Medical Association's annual report card on Aboriginal and Torres Strait Islander health considered the relationship between 'political will' and health outcomes, and explored measures to reduce the incidence of rheumatic heart disease among Indigenous Australians. The association asked:

> what medicine is required to prevent new cases of RHD [rheumatic heart disease]? Awareness and political will. For the former, there is growing public awareness about the terrible impact of RHD in Indigenous communities ... In relation to political will, the AMA [Australian Medical Association] makes a *Call to Action* to prevent new cases of RHD in Indigenous Australia by 2031. This is also the target year of the Council of Australian Governments (COAG) Closing the Gap Framework objective to improve the life expectancy of Indigenous Australians. Preventing new cases of RHD in Indigenous Australia by 2031 will make an important and necessary contribution to the achievement of this overarching life expectancy target. (AMA, 2016, p. 3)

There is a relationship between political will and more explicit state acceptance of the Declaration. Ornelas (2014) proposed the creation of agencies within state bureaucracies to oversee and coordinate the Declaration's implementation. Such agencies would not only signal the Declaration's desirability but also that states are willing to submit to international oversight; however, this is unlikely given the absence of political will in most states.

Nevertheless, it is worth defending a process of 'collective deliberation conducted rationally and fairly among free and equal individuals' (Benhabib, 1996, p. 69). The presumption that internal self-determination is less valuable than secession is valid only if the two are equally realistic possibilities and therefore comparable. When internal decolonisation is the only pragmatic possibility, it is more politically advantageous to examine the potential that exists within that context rather than to dwell on secession's hypothetically greater political value.

Contemporary postsettler states sometimes 'overtly reject and undermine indigenous social and political orders' (Champagne, 2013, p. 14), and sometimes they do not. Further, the extent to which they are willing to entertain those orders as ones of national political significance vary. Willingness is subject to significant change according to shifting domestic political values and to governments' perceptions of what they need to do to maintain broader electoral support. From an assimilationist perspective, there is a rhetorical attractiveness in the view that self-determination creates a 'tension between the democratic principle of majority rule and the disruptive potential of minority separatism' (Schulte-Tenckhoff, 2012, p. 81). However, the tension is overstated. The 'separation' of indigenous peoples from the nation-state imposes no restriction on the liberal political rights of other citizens.

Citizenship of the nation-state is not something to be undervalued. It is not necessarily assimilationist, and citizenship of an indigenous nation does not need to be traded off to hold meaningful state citizenship. Indigenous resistance to citizenship tends to focus on specific curtailments of the right to exist as indigenous, not the existence of the state per se. However, if the state is to avoid functioning as a neo-colonial entity, indigenous peoples must contribute to the shaping of its institutions and opportunities to participate at every level of its decision-making processes. In this way, citizenship becomes the embodiment of a set of political capacities, and the ways in which these are constrained and in which they may be exercised are important.

It is significant that in Canada, as in New Zealand, treaty rights extend to the urban diaspora (Belanger, 2010). However, if there is a duty 'to seek out urban Aboriginal leaders for their participation' (p. 14), then there is an assumption that arrangements are not already in place for aboriginal people to participate as a matter of course, even though the 'honour of the Crown' (*Haida Nation*, 2004, paras. 16–19) demands consultation and the accommodation of indigenous rights where this is found to be just. In 2014, the UN special rapporteur observed that consultation processes in Canada were 'generally inadequate' and that:

> There appears to be a lack of a consistent framework or policy for the implementation of this duty to consult, which is contributing to an atmosphere of contentiousness and mistrust that is conducive neither to beneficial economic development or social peace. (UN, 2014, p. 18)

Greater participation would assure an indigenous presence and capacity to propose new legislation.

Overall, Canada has a strong legislative and jurisprudential framework for addressing the indigenous right to self-determination. For its part, the TRC imagined the Declaration as having a significant role in domestic politics. However, indigenous people commonly lack the financial capacity to make governance arrangements work. There is also a tension in the sphere of indigenous land rights, such that Aboriginal title is often 'regarded as a burden on the Crown's sovereignty' (Schulte-Tenckhoff, 2012, p. 66). Yet self-determination can be conceptualised as a burden on Crown sovereignty only if that sovereignty is understood as existing in its own right and not proceeding from the collective sovereignty of the people. If sovereignty inheres in *all* and not just *some* of the people, there ought to be no conflict. Political tension emerges on this point because of the nature of indigenous belonging and because the nature of the share in political authority that belongs to them is unsettled.

Marginalising Citizenship or Indigenising the Bureaucracy?

Marginalisation through denial is a common state strategy of containment, even though the ongoing effects of residential schools in Canada and the stolen generations in Australia continue to explain social dysfunction and diminish people's capacities for meaningful citizenship. The Australian Indigenous Doctors' Association (2010) argued that:

> The policies of assimilation, elimination, forced child removal, protection and segregation that were imposed after colonisation resulted in a huge disruption of traditional social institutions and kinship ties. The damage to the intricate kinship systems and community cohesion of Aboriginal people through the stolen generations cannot be overemphasised. (p. 7)

The human right to be part of a family ought to be sacrosanct and precede the assimilationist intent of a state. In Australia, the denial of that right is hugely ironic when considered alongside the Howard Government's (1996–2007) privileging of family as the only legitimate subnational unit of identity, especially as that government's policy rhetoric was not supported by measures to rebuild those families rendered dysfunctional by state-sanctioned violence. Similarly, a politics of exclusion distinguishes the Indigenous Australian journalist Stan Grant's (2016) discussion of his grandfather's 'personal journey in the black migration from mission to town a distance of mere miles, but an epochal trek' (para. 2). Grant's grandfather's journey was meant to be a migration of opportunity; however, three generations later, that opportunity remains unobtainable for many Indigenous peoples. Describing an isolation and alienation that many Indigenous peoples face, Grant observed that 'we lived in Australia and Australia was for other people' (A cage in search of a bird, para. 3). His observation is reflected in Indigenous people's perceptions of public institutions, hospitals, schools, courts and, especially, parliaments, as being for other people. However, Grant (2016) also challenged the distinction that the anthropologist WEH Stanner made between the Indigenous and non-Indigenous to create a rigid binary world:

> Stanner once remarked that for Indigenous people the dreaming and the market are mutually exclusive. For Stanner … Indigenous people were fixed in time and place. (Redefining aboriginality, para. 3)

The market was elsewhere.

Referring to Australia as a 'parallel' society, Grant identified a different binary, one in which the number of Indigenous students completing secondary school was increasing markedly, while policy failures in health, criminal justice, housing, employment and economic development for Indigenous people continued, showing that 'life in the open society … can be lonely [and] alienating' for Indigenous Australians ('Leaving the shadow world', para. 4). Yet it need not be: through a process of indigenising the bureaucracy—that is, by allowing Indigenous aspirations and epistemologies to influence policymaking in secure and meaningful ways—life in the open society could be inclusive and respectful. This could be achieved in New Zealand by bringing the cultural values set out in *He whakairo here whakaumu* into public relationships, and in Canada by complementing and facilitating nation-to-nation policy cocreation.

In Canada, the National Indigenous Economic Development Board's 'hope for the future' rests on differentiated liberal citizenship:

> The massive expansion of Indigenous businesses, increased shared governance, the intersection of indigenous knowledge and science, the enhanced interest from the Federal and provincial governments and reconciliation, and especially the passion, dedication and intelligence of First Nations' children and youth. (Public Policy Forum, 2017, p. 10)

In 2012, the Harper Government's (2006–2015) special federal representative on West Coast energy infrastructure was commissioned 'to identify approaches that could meet Canada's goals of expanding energy markets and ensuring Aboriginal participation in the economy' (Eyford, 2013, p. 2). The resulting report, which emphasised trust, inclusion and reconciliation, represented a significant departure from prevailing indigenous policy. Significantly, it stressed 'reconciling interests' rather than differences (Eyford, 2013), presumed that indigenous peoples comprised a legitimate part of the public and argued that resource development ought to serve their interests. To this end, the report recommended that:

- Canada and Aboriginal communities need to build effective relationships and this is best achieved through sustained engagement;
- Aboriginal communities view natural resource development as linked to a broader reconciliation agenda;
- Aboriginal communities will consider supporting natural resource development if it is undertaken in an environmentally sustainable manner; and
- these projects would contribute to improving the socio-economic conditions of Aboriginal communities. (Eyford, 2013, p. 1)

The subject of the report was economically important to the government. Since energy exports require developing pipelines and shipping terminals on indigenous lands, the government's aspirations could not be pursued without considering constitutionally protected indigenous rights.

While 'equality in the process of public deliberation may well be intrinsically just' (Christiano, 1997, p. 244), the question of how political systems and institutions protect equality is distinguished by important differences of perspective between state and indigenous actors. An important difference of perspective is evident in the situation described by Belanger (2010) wherein:

> Canadian officials consider Aboriginal self-government a policy issue [and] Aboriginal leaders consider self-determination a complex set of relationships that incorporate provisions protecting historic lands, as well as a continued political interface respecting historic treaties. (p. 6).

Policy contradictions leave indigenous people unable to make long-term decisions with certainty and clarity, and ill-equipped to maximise the inherent economic advantages that transgenerational investment timeframes provide to their commercial entities.

Policy tensions also exist between the Canadian Government and First Nations over the status of health care as a treaty right. The issue rests on whether health care is a right in distributive justice or a right of indigeneity. The distinction has implications for how and by whom decisions are made and for which purposes. From a purely distributive perspective, it may be sufficient for the state to make decisions on its own after consultation. However, a politics of indigeneity would require substantive indigenous participation and help to address the philosophical questions set out by the UN special rapporteur in 2014, which also described the political context in which Trudeau came to office in 2015:

> The relationship of Canada with the indigenous peoples within its borders is governed by a well-developed legal framework and a number of policy initiatives that in many respects are protective of indigenous peoples' rights. But despite positive steps, daunting challenges remain. The numerous initiatives that have been taken at the federal and provincial/territorial levels to address the problems faced by indigenous peoples have been insufficient. The well-being gap between aboriginal and non-aboriginal people in Canada has not narrowed over the past several years; treaty and aboriginal claims remain persistently unresolved; indigenous women and girls remain vulnerable to abuse; and overall there appear to be high levels of distrust among indigenous peoples towards the government at both the federal and provincial levels. (UN, 2014, p. 1)

Canada was engaged in a process of negotiating new treaties with indigenous peoples. According to the special rapporteur, 'at least in the conception', these served as examples of 'good practices' in the realisation of indigenous human rights (UN, 2014, p. 6). However, the relationship between indigenous peoples and the state remained 'strained'. The special rapporteur found it 'difficult to reconcile Canada's well-developed legal framework and general prosperity with the human rights problems faced by indigenous peoples in Canada, which have reached crisis proportions in many respects' (p. 6).

The Declaration presumes that self-determination requires an active indigenous citizenship. It also presumes that the state can be indigenised. Therefore, attention must be paid to group rights and interests so that politics can attend to the common good, which 'cannot be realised as the aggregate outcome of individuals pursuing their private interests' (Elster, 1997, p. 14). For these reasons, the common good may not, in fact, be a commonly understood aspiration. People define commonality from their own vantage points, conditioned by different life experiences and aspirations that are mediated through culture and, for indigenous peoples, conditioned by colonialism itself. As Rawls (1971) proposed:

> Justice as fairness begins with the idea that where common principles are necessary and to everyone's advantage, they are to be worked out from the viewpoint of the suitably defined initial situation of equality in which each person is fairly represented. The principal of participation transfers this notion from the original position to the constitution … [thus] preserv[ing] the equal representation of the original position to the degree that this is feasible. (pp. 221–222)

There must be equal political capacity to work out a shared conception of the 'common'; yet the idea of a completely virtuous citizen is naive. Indigenous peoples' exclusion from substantive citizenship well illustrates the point, as 'normative consensus … has [not] been secured in advance through tradition and ethos' (Habermas, 1997, p. 245). How, then, do indigenous peoples find political voice in a system whose institutions are not structured to achieve political equality, especially because, in practical terms, there is no original position of equality?

The question is also one of how to reach points of equality without compromising indigenous distinctiveness. How might distinctiveness be reflected in political institutions? Political decision-making is not neutral.

Its biases must be open to scrutiny, not just from those with different biases, but also from those with fundamentally different views of the common good mediated by culture and colonial experience. Is it possible that 'sovereignty should express itself only under the discursive conditions of an internally differentiated process of opinion and will formation' (Habermas, 1997, p. 46)?

There must be accepted tests of reasonableness and procedures for removing unreasonableness from public decision-making. Indigenous voice depends on the acceptability of a plurality of reasons.

People's perspectives change through exposure to others' ideas. Reasoned deliberation requires that all who deliberate are, as a matter of course, exposed to indigenous ideas. Public reason consequently requires that all people are equally part of the 'public':

> to the extent that public deliberation calls upon a set of morally important qualities, such as rationality, autonomy and respect for others, there is some reason to think that these traits, which are important in politics, will be promoted more in a society that encourages deliberation among all of its citizens. (Christiano, 1997, pp. 248–249)

It may be idealistic, but it is still aspirationally important to consider that:

> If discussion is not in an egalitarian context, then many more points of view will have to be debated to the extent that previously neglected sections of society come to the fore
>
> ...
>
> we ought not be aiming at political consensus on moral and political matters. As long as public discussion acts as a process of trial and error for excluding forms of ignorance, it serves a useful purpose. (Christiano, 1997, pp. 248–250)

The point at which political agreement matters most is a procedural one and involves the steps that will be followed to make decisions and their underlying rationale.

Deliberation requires citizens to engage respectfully with one another and with concern for the common good; it is a 'condition of political justification' and 'outcomes are justified because they are brought about in certain ways' (Christiano, 1997, p. 246). Such deliberation strengthens democracy for indigenous peoples because it is 'able to root out policies based on unsubstantiated prejudices' (Christiano, 1997, p. 247). Ultimately, equal participation in discussion and debate depend on supporting institutional arrangements.

Conclusion

The Declaration affirms an indigenous people's right to separate itself from the colonial society established over its territories. An indigenous people need not presume equal citizenship of the colonial state or concern itself with the affairs of the state other than through a nation-to-nation relationship. For example, it may adopt a kind of bicultural binary to justify an independent—though isolationist—self-determination as *He whakairo here whakaumu* proposes for New Zealand. However, this is a limited and constraining approach to politics, as it overlooks the political value of claiming a share in public sovereignty.

In contrast, differentiated liberal citizenship recognises sovereignty's dispersed character and presumes substantive indigenous voice as a right of citizenship belonging to indigenous persons as much as to anyone else. It is reasonable that arrangements are made for that voice to be expressed in ways that demonstrate participatory parity.

Self-determination is a relative and relational power that the Declaration allows indigenous peoples to exercise within the state as liberal citizens and beyond the state as members of indigenous nations. The close relationships between these two spheres of political authority means that the capacity for self-determination is maximised by a politics that is equally attentive to both.

.

Conclusion

The Declaration does not guarantee justice. Instead, it is an instrument of significant moral standing that indigenous peoples use to assert their claim to self-determination. It is a codification of rights that follow from prior occupancy. Its point of greatest political significance is that it prevents an exclusive neo-colonial state sovereignty by ensuring substantive indigenous capacity to make decisions over their own affairs and to share in the decision-making of the state itself. It thus requires reimagining where power lies and how it is dispersed—a reimagination of the liberal state's normative structure and underlying political values.

The Declaration supports the argument that liberal democracy should work for indigenous peoples as effectively as it works for anybody else. It shows how and why this might occur through political frameworks that are attentive to the presumption that self-determination belongs to all and not just some citizens. In doing so, it helps to create an indigenous affairs policy discourse of human dignity and equality that functions as a claim to culture and to meaningful political authority.

The presumption that human rights belong to indigenous people is inherently and necessarily anticolonial. However, the further presumption that these rights belong to indigenous peoples collectively as well as individually gives the Declaration potentially transformative significance, reframing debates about the meaning of liberal freedom and placing liberal freedom into a collective context. The rights that the Declaration enunciates demonstrate relationships between culture and personal freedom and show why indigenous claims to the autonomy and agency that liberal political theory promises cannot be realised unless and until the colonial context is also recognised.

The liberal concepts of citizenship, democracy, self-determination and sovereignty are not routinely available to indigenous peoples. Indeed, liberalism's exclusive capacity is as powerful as its inclusive and transformative potential, which explains why indigenous people may not instinctively turn to Western liberal democratic theories of justice to support their own claims to self-determination. However, the critiques that indigenous scholars and political actors have reasonably laid against liberal democracy are not inherent to the theory itself. They are the product of human choices and subjective theoretical interpretations. The Declaration helps us to understand how and why. As a liberal instrument of different and potentially transformative potential, its political value is the theoretical possibilities it develops for expressing indigenous claims in the liberal language that frames the politics of Australia, Canada, New Zealand and the US, and in the liberal language that the international community seeks to impose on all states. The Declaration's intent is to help democracy to work better.

Indigenous self-determination requires reconciliation based on trust and political inclusivity. Reconciliation is a significant moral and political challenge to the prevailing order of Australia, Canada, New Zealand and the US—four states that were initially opposed to the Declaration but came to support it when they realised that it could be interpreted as aspirational and did not threaten their territorial integrity or democratic presumptions. Yet as an instrument of reconciliation, the Declaration is not a politically benign statement of symbolic principle.

Reconciliation requires reparation or restitution. It also requires a strong and obvious connection between the state's sorrow for its transgressions of justice and policy outcomes that show a public commitment to correcting the consequences of injustice and ensuring that unjust policy measures do not recur. Reconciliation is an essential precursor to just terms of political association that, in turn, serve as a precursor to a postcolonial politics of self-determination.

The purpose of reconciliation is to improve people's lives. For reconciliation to occur, indigenous peoples must be able to identify good reasons for setting aside their mistrust of the state. Ensuring that indigenous peoples may claim a distinctive share in public sovereignty is therefore important. Constructing a state that is not the colonial entity that once usurped indigenous self-determination is difficult. It is, perhaps, an unlikely aspiration; yet it remains a morally defensible goal that is worth pursuing using the supporting principles set out in the Declaration.

Parties in a political relationship can only accept each other's legitimacy on the strength of trust. For indigenous peoples, this may mean the right to presence; to participatory parity in public affairs; to an equal say in setting out what constitutes just terms of association; and to having a substantive voice in the development of the society that has emerged over their lands, often without their consent.

However, mistrust runs deeply into the indigenous experience of the colonial state. Schools, hospitals, police forces and welfare agencies have been used consciously and systematically to undermine indigenous societies. They continue to obstruct the creation of a politics of trust. Yet they are all potentially important sites of the right to self-determination, and their transformation into institutions that work for indigenous peoples and not against them is important. A reconciled state is one in which indigenous peoples may influence what schools do and why, and shape them to support, not impede, self-determination. A reconciled state is one in which indigenous people have the political and professional capacity to ensure that hospitals recognise relationships between culture and wellbeing, and police forces and welfare agencies fulfil their protective functions equally well for all people.

Canada's initial objection to the Declaration was grounded in the argument that it was a noncolonial state and that its prevailing political institutions, values and cultures gave indigenous people equal capacity for citizenship. New Zealand took this argument further, suggesting that the Declaration was inconsistent with universal citizenship and with the Treaty of Waitangi. There was a fear that the Declaration would raise new and more far-reaching rights that would disturb the negotiated political settlement of claims for breaches of the treaty.

The idea that the Declaration provided indigenous peoples with veto powers over resource development was especially worrisome for the four dissenting states, which responded by trying to position indigenous peoples beyond the national public. A 'them' and 'us' binary politics was promoted that excluded or denied the proposition that indigenous people might be part of the national polities as equal liberal citizens. However, all four states eventually 'read down' the Declaration's significance and agreed that it should be given aspirational value. Their initial opposition reflected colonialism's continuing presence and highlighted the importance of the claim to more inclusive liberal democratic politics. In doing so, it showed the value of pluralism in public affairs, for the alternative to pluralism is exclusion.

When state-based arguments against the Declaration are set alongside indigenous arguments that universal human rights are incompatible with self-determination because they privilege the individual over the collective, one finds an intellectual conflict resolvable with reference to a liberal theory of indigeneity. The argument against extending universal human rights to indigenous people shows the value of bringing liberal political theories into debates over the nature and purpose of the indigenous right to self-determination. There is considerable political value in the liberal argument that all people's freedoms are inherent to their humanity, that all people are fundamentally equal and that one person's humanity is not inferior to another's simply because they are the physically weaker party in a contest over collective cultural values. Self-determination is enhanced by a liberal theory of indigeneity grounded in the view that equal human worth belongs to all, not just some, indigenous people, just as it belongs equally to indigenous people vis-a-vis all others.

Indigeneity is a theory of fundamental human equality. This means that, while self-government may be an important constituent of self-determination, it cannot express the concept's full potential. Self-government over a defined territory is not a substitute for the claim to shared national sovereignty. In Canada, the constitutional right to self-government is conditional. It is not the inherent right that the Declaration promises nor is it a right that, on its own, can protect indigenous peoples against an all-powerful and constraining state. That right is partly protected by the right to exist and to deliberate, as indigenous, inside the state. This is politically important because the state is not a neutral construct that instinctively or naturally represents all citizens equally. It is only through having a substantive presence in its deliberations that all may share in the formation of collective values and political priorities.

Self-determination is the outcome of a wider capacity to share sovereignty. Working out how sovereignty should be shared is a complex, complicated and contested matter. However, the underlying principle of human equality is a simple one. It is a matter of justice that indigenous people have the political capacity to exercise that equality in whichever spheres are required to allow people to lead lives that they have reason to value. Therefore, self-determination is as much a political capacity as it is a political right. However, the capacities that it embodies come from the wider political values and institutional structures that determine where power resides. The capacity for self-determination is facilitated or constrained according to sovereignty's prevailing character, shape and form.

The New Zealand Waitangi Tribunal's finding that the Treaty of Waitangi was not a cession of sovereignty to the British Crown as successive New Zealand governments have insisted is a finding that creates new theoretical possibilities for inclusive understandings of political power. However, the right to equal liberal citizenship is compromised by the bicultural 'them' and 'us' binary that confuses the sovereign for the Pakeha polity.

Biculturalism positions Maori as the political 'other' distinct from the *kāwanatanga* of the New Zealand state. Although there are many important examples of Maori participation in the state—most significantly as members of the executive—there remain alternative strands in Maori political thought that privilege bicultural distinction and separation. For example, Matike Mai Aotearoa's (2016) position paper, *He whakairo here whakaumu*, claimed independent indigenous authority (as justified by the Declaration and Treaty of Waitangi) but surrendered any claim to national citizenship. The paper, discussed in Chapter 9, helps to illuminate the merits of a liberal theory of indigeneity realised through differentiated citizenship as an alternative of more far-reaching potential.

The Declaration not only proposes ways in which differentiated liberal citizenship might be realised but also has the capacity to support self-determination's translation from political right to political capacity. Political arrangements do not arise from an intellectual void. Their capacity to support or constrain indigenous self-determination arises from prevailing theories of the state: what it is, to whom it belongs, and by whom and by what means decisions should be made in its name. Indigeneity is, then, a liberal theory of the state. Its contribution to indigenous political aspirations is a presumption that there is a political gap to be closed between conditional accounts of indigenous citizenship and citizenship as the expression of fundamental political equality. It provides a theoretical justification for culturally meaningful inclusion, self-determination and just terms of association. Further, it is a theory that allows indigenous politics to transcend colonial victimhood. As a politics of potential, it presumes procedural fairness in the ways that public decisions are made. It presumes that indigenous voice is procedurally fair. It is not a guarantee of justice. However, by allowing independent indigenous political authority, it rationalises a liberal citizenship capable of helping people to live lives that they have reason to value. A liberal theory of indigeneity uses the Declaration to help democracy work better because of the simple fact that 'we are all here to stay' (*Delgamuukw*, 1997, para. 186).

References

Abrams, P. (2006). Notes on the difficulty of studying the state. In A. Sharma & A. Gupta (Eds), *The anthropology of the state: A reader* (pp. 58–89). Oxford, UK: Blackwell.

Alfred, T. (1999). *Peace, power, righteousness: An indigenous manifesto.* Ontario, Canada: Oxford University Press.

Alfred, T. (2005). Sovereignty. In P. Deloria & N. Salisbury (Eds), *A companion to American Indian history* (pp. 460–474). Oxford, UK: Blackwell. doi.org/10.1002/9780470996461.ch26

Alfred, T. (2009). Colonialism and state dependency. *Journal of Aboriginal Health,* 5(2), 42–60.

Altamirano-Jiménez, I. (2004). North American first peoples: Slipping up into market citizenship? *Citizenship Studies,* 8(4), 349–365. doi.org/10.1080/1362102052000316963

Altman, J. C. (2009). *Beyond Closing the Gap: Valuing diversity in Indigenous Australia* (CAEPR Working Paper No. 54/2009). Retrieved from caepr.cass.anu.edu.au/sites/default/files/docs/CAEPRWP54_0.pdf

Anaya, J. (1993). The native Hawaiian people and international human rights law: Toward a remedy for past and continuing wrongs. *Georgia Law Review,* 28, 309–363.

Anaya, S. J. (2008, 11 August). *Promotion and protection of all human rights, civil, political, economic, social and cultural rights, including the right to development: Report of the special rapporteur on the situation of human rights and fundamental freedoms of indigenous people, S. James Anaya* (Report No. A/HRC/9/9). doi.org/10.2139/ssrn.1242451

Anaya, S. J. (2009). The right of indigenous peoples to self-determination in the post-declaration era. In C. Charters and R. Stavenhagen (Eds), *Making the declaration work: The United Nations Declaration on the Rights of Indigenous Peoples* (IWGIA Doc. No. 127; pp. 184–198). Copenhagen, Denmark: International Work Group for Indigenous Affairs.

Anaya, J. (2010, 15 July). *Statement on the United Nations Declaration on the Rights of Indigenous Peoples, to the EMRIP* [Statement of the special rapporteur]. Retrieved from unsr.jamesanaya.org/?p=354

Anderson, I. (2004). Recent developments in national Aboriginal and Torres Strait Islander health strategy. *Australia and New Zealand Health Policy, 1*(3), 1–7. doi.org/10.1186/1743-8462-1-3

Anderson, P. (2014). *Launching 2030 – A vision for Aboriginal and Torres Strait Islander health* [Speech delivered 6 March, 2014, Canberra]. Retrieved from www.lowitja.org.au/content/Document/PDF/Futures-6-March-2014-Pat-Anderson.pdf

Aristotle. (1988). *The politics* (S. Everson, Ed.). Cambridge, UK: Cambridge University Press.

Aristotle. (1995). *Aristotle: Selections* (T. Irwin & G. Fine, Eds & Trans.). Indianapolis, IN: Hackett.

Aristotle. (2010). *The politics* (C. Lord, Trans.). Chicago, IL: University of Chicago Press.

Assembly of First Nations. (2017). *Implementing the United Nations Declaration on the Rights of Indigenous Peoples.* Retrieved from www.afn.ca/wp-content/uploads/2018/02/17-11-27-Implementing-the-UN-Declaration-EN.pdf

Australian Human Rights Commission. (2013). The Declaration dialogue series: Paper No.2 - self-determination – the fundamental right of Aboriginal and Torres Strait Islander peoples to shape our own lives. Retrieved from www.human rights.gov.au/sites/default/files/2014_AHRC_DD_2_Self-determination.pdf

Australian Human Rights Commission. (2017). *Violence against women in Australia.* Retrieved from www.humanrights.gov.au/submissions/violence-against-women-australia-2017

Australian Indigenous Doctors' Association. (2010). *Health impact assessment of the Northern Territory emergency response.* Canberra, ACT: Author.

Australian Institute of Health and Welfare. (2009). *Aboriginal and Torres Strait Islander health performance framework 2008 report.* Canberra, ACT: Author.

Australian Medical Association. (2016). *Aboriginal and Torres Strait Islander health report card.* Retrieved from ama.com.au/system/tdf/documents/2016-AMA-Report-Card-on-Indigenous-Health.pdf?file=1

Australian National Audit Office. (2017). *Indigenous advancement strategy* (Report No. 35 2016–17 Performance Audit). Retrieved from www.anao. gov.au/work/performance-audit/indigenous-advancement-strategy

Axelby, C. & Wanganeen, K. (2017, 20 April). Constitutional recognition must make Indigenous lives better. Otherwise what's the point? *The Guardian.* Retrieved from www.theguardian.com/commentisfree/ 2017/apr/20/constitutional-recognition-must-make-indigenous-lives-better-otherwise-whats-the-point

Banks, R. (2007). United Nations General Assembly Declaration on the Rights of Indigenous Peoples explanation of vote by New Zealand permanent representative H. E. Ms Rosemary Banks. Retrieved from www.nzembassy. com/info.cfm?c=51&l=124&CFID=7984901&CFTOKEN=19347722&s =to&p=63315 (site discontinued).

Beatty, B. (2014). Indigenous health governance and UNDRIP. In T. Mitchell (Ed.), *The internationalization of Indigenous rights: UNDRIP in the Canadian context* (pp. 49–53). Waterloo, Canada: Centre for International Governance Innovation.

Beck, A. (2016). Aboriginal consultation in Canadian water negotiations: The Mackenzie bilateral water management agreements. *Dalhousie Law Journal, 39*(2), 487–523.

Belanger, Y. D. (2010). *The United Nations Declaration on the Rights of Indigenous Peoples (UNDRIP) and urban Aboriginal self-determination in Canada* (Final report prepared for the National Association of Friendship Centres). Ottawa, Canada: National Association of Friendship Centres.

Bellamy, R. (2007). *Political constitutionalism: A republican defence of the constitutionality of democracy.* Cambridge, UK: Cambridge University Press. doi.org/10.1017/CBO9780511490187

Belot, H. & Laurence, E. (2017, 5 November). Malcolm Turnbull defends decision to abandon constitutional recognition of Indigenous Australians. *ABC News.* Retrieved from www.abc.net.au/news/2017-11-05/malcolm-turnbull-defends-decision-on-indigenous-recognition/9120252

Benhabib, S. (1996). Introduction. In S. Benhabib (Ed.), *Democracy and difference: Contesting the boundaries of the political* (pp. 3–18). Princeton, NJ: Princeton University Press.

Bishop, R., O'Sullivan, D. & Berryman, M. (2010). *Scaling up education reform: Addressing the politics of disparity.* Wellington, New Zealand: NZCER Press.

Black, K. & McBean, E. (2016). Increased indigenous participation in environmental decision-making: A policy analysis for the improvement of indigenous health. *International Indigenous Policy Journal, 7*(4), art. 5. doi.org/10.18584/iipj.2016.7.4.5

Bohman, J. (1997). Deliberative democracy and effective social freedom: Capabilities, resources and opportunities. In J. Bohman & W. Rehg (Eds), *Deliberative democracy: Essays on reason and politics* (pp. 321–348). Cambridge, MA: MIT Press. doi.org/10.7551/mitpress/2324.003.0014

Bohman, J. & Rehg. W. (1997). Introduction. In J. Bohman & W. Rehg (Eds), *Deliberative democracy: Essays on reason and politics* (pp. ix–xiv). Cambridge, MA: MIT Press. doi.org/10.7551/mitpress/2324.003.0002

Boldt, M. & Long, J. A. (1984). Tribal philosophies and the Canadian Charter of Rights and Freedoms. *Ethnic and Racial Studies, 7*(4), 478–493. doi.org/10.1080/01419870.1984.9993463

Borrows, J. (2017). Revitalizing Canada's indigenous constitution: Two challenges. In O. Fitzgerald (Ed.), *UNDRIP implementation braiding international, domestic and indigenous law* (pp. 20–28). Waterloo, Canada: Centre for International Governance Innovation.

Boston, J. (1996). *Public management: The New Zealand model.* New York, NY: Oxford University Press.

Boutilier, S. (2017). Free, prior, and informed consent and reconciliation in Canada: Proposals to implement articles 19 and 32 of the UN Declaration on the Rights of Indigenous Peoples. *Western Journal of Legal Studies, 7*(1), 1–21.

Bowen, J. (2000). Should we have a universal concept of 'indigenous peoples' rights'?: Ethnicity and essentialism in the twenty-first century. *Anthropology Today, 16*(4), 12–16. doi.org/10.1111/1467-8322.00037

Boxill, B. (1995). The morality of reparation. In S. Cahn (Ed.), *The affirmative action debate* (pp. 107–113). Oxford, UK: Routledge.

Boyer, Y. (2014). *Using the UN framework to advance and protect the inherent rights of indigenous peoples in Canada.* In T. Mitchell (Ed.), *The internationalization of indigenous rights: UNDRIP in the Canadian context* (pp. 11–15). Waterloo, Canada: Centre for International Governance Innovation.

Brands, J. (2014). *The shape of things to come: Visions for the future of Aboriginal and Torres Strait Islander health research.* Melbourne, Vic.: The Lowitja Institute.

Brash, D. (2004). *Nationhood* [Speech delivered to the Orewa Rotary Club, 27 January, 2004]. Retrieved from www.scoop.co.nz/stories/PA0401/S00220/nationhood-don-brash-speech-orewa-rotary-club.htm

Brayboy, B., Fann, A., Castagno, A. & Solyom, J. A. (2012). Postsecondary education for American Indian and Alaska natives: Higher education for nation building and self-determination [Special issue]. *ASHE Higher Education Report, 37*(5). doi.org/10.1002/aehe.v37.5

Brett, J. (2005). Relaxed and comfortable: The Liberal Party's Australia. *Quarterly Essay, 19.*

Broderstad, E. G. (2014). Implementing indigenous self-determination: The case of the Sámi in Norway. In M. Woons (Ed.), *Restoring indigenous self-determination: Theoretical and practical approaches* (pp. 80–87). Bristol, UK: e-International Relations.

Carroll, C. (2012). Articulating indigenous statehood: Cherokee state formation and implications for the UN Declaration on the Rights of Indigenous Peoples. In E. Pulitano (Ed.), *Indigenous rights in the age of the UN Declaration* (pp. 143–171). Cambridge, UK: Cambridge University Press.

Champagne, D. (2013). UNDRIP (United Nations Declaration on the Rights of Indigenous Peoples): Human, civil and indigenous rights. *Wicazo Sa Review, 28*(1), 9–22. doi.org/10.5749/wicazosareview.28.1.0009

Chapple, S. (2000). Maori socio-economic disparity. *Political Science, 52*(2), 101–115. doi.org/10.1177/003231870005200201

Charge D'Affaires, Australian Permanent Mission. (2016). [Letter to Office of the UN High Commissioner for Human Rights, Geneva].

Christiano, T. (1997). The significance of public deliberation. In J. Bohman & W. Rehg (Eds), *Deliberative democracy: Essays on reason and politics* (pp. 243–277). Cambridge, MA: MIT Press.

Christie, G. (2017). Indigenous legal orders, Canadian law and UNDRIP. In O. Fitzgerald (Ed.), *UNDRIP implementation braiding international, domestic and indigenous law* (pp. 48–55). Waterloo, Canada: Centre for International Governance Innovation.

Clark defends refusal to meet hikoi. (2004, 5 May). *New Zealand Herald.* Retrieved from www.nzherald.co.nz/treaty-of-waitangi/news/article.cfm?c_id=350&objectid=3564678

Clarke, J. (2006). Desegregating the 'Indigenous rights' agenda. *Australian Journal of Legal Philosophy, 31*, 119–126.

Coates, K. & Holroyd, C. (2014). Indigenous internationalism and the emerging impact of UNDRIP in aboriginal affairs in Canada. In T. Mitchell (Ed.), *The internationalization of indigenous rights: UNDRIP in the Canadian context* (pp. 5–9). Waterloo, Canada: Centre for International Governance Innovation.

Coates, K. & Newman, D. (2014). *The end is not nigh: Reason over alarmism in analysing the Tsilhqot'in decision.* Retrieved from ssrn.com/abstract=2517041

Cohen, J. (1994). A more democratic liberalism [Review of the book *Political liberalism*, by J. Rawls]. *Michigan Law Review, 92*(6), 1503–1546. doi.org/10.2307/1289593

Cohen, J. (1997). Deliberation and democratic legitimacy. In D. Matravers & J. Pike (Eds), *Debates in contemporary political philosophy: An anthology* (pp. 41–53). London, UK: Routledge.

Collingwood-Whittick, S. (2012). Australia's Northern Territory intervention and Indigenous rights on language education. In E. Pulitano (Ed.), *Indigenous rights in the age of the UN Declaration* (pp. 110–142). Cambridge, UK: Cambridge University Press. doi.org/10.1017/CBO9781139136723.005

Commonwealth of Australia, Department of the Prime Minister and Cabinet. (2018a). *Annual evaluation workplan: Indigenous advancement strategy.* Retrieved from www.pmc.gov.au/sites/default/files/publications/2018-19-evaluation-work-plan.pdf

Commonwealth of Australia, Department of the Prime Minister and Cabinet. (2018b). *Closing the Gap: Report 2019.* Retrieved from ctgreport.pmc.gov.au/sites/default/files/ctg-report-2019.pdf?a=1 (site discontinued).

Constitución Política del Estado [Political Constitution of the State] 2009 (Bolivia) (Max Planck Institute, Trans.). Retrieved from www.constituteproject.org/constitution/Bolivia_2009.pdf

Conway-Long, D. (2016). Indigenous peoples and human rights. *Human Rights Review, 17*, 115–120. doi.org/10.1007/s12142-016-0394-6

Cook, L. (2017, 19 April). Reflections on whānau – the bigger picture [Blog post]. Retrieved from superublogsite.wordpress.com/2017/04/19/reflections-on-whanau-the-bigger-picture-and-what-the-future-implications-are-for-maori-and-government/

Corntassel, J. (2008). Toward sustainable self-determination: Rethinking the contemporary Indigenous-rights discourse. *Alternatives: Global, Local, Political, 33*(1), 105–132. doi.org/10.1177/030437540803300106

Corntassel, J. (2012). Re-envisioning resurgence: Indigenous pathways to decolonization and sustainable self-determination. *Decolonization: Indigeneity, Education & Society, 1*(1), 86–101.

Corrigan, P. (1990). *Social forms/human capacities: Essays in authority and difference.* London, UK: Routledge.

Coulthard, G. S. (2007). Subjects of empire: Indigenous peoples and the 'politics of recognition' in Canada. *Contemporary Political Theory, 6*(4), 437–460. doi.org/10.1057/palgrave.cpt.9300307

Cowan, A. (2013). UNDRIP and the intervention: Indigenous self-determination, participation, and racial discrimination in the Northern Territory of Australia. *Pacific Rim Law and Policy Journal, 22*(2), 247–310.

Cranston, M. (1967). Liberalism. In P. Edwards (Ed.), *The encyclopedia of philosophy* (pp. 458–461). New York, NY: Macmillan and the Free Press.

Cultural Survival. (n.d.). *Canada endorses the UN Declaration on the Rights of Indigenous Peoples.* Retrieved from www.culturalsurvival.org/news/canada-endorses-un-declaration-rights-indigenous-peoples

Cultural Survival. (2016). *Observations on the state of indigenous human rights in Ecuador.* Retrieved from www.culturalsurvival.org/sites/default/files/ECUADOR%20UPR2016%20final.pdf

Cultural Survival. (2018). *Observations on the state of indigenous human rights in Malaysia.* Retrieved from www.culturalsurvival.org/sites/default/files/Malaysia%202018%20UPR%20Report.pdf

Cutler, L. (2016). Tribal sovereignty, tribal court legitimacy and public defense. *UCLA Law Review, 63,* 1752–1816.

Daes, E.-I. A. (2008). An overview of the history of indigenous peoples: Self-determination and the United Nations. *Cambridge Review of International Affairs, 21*(1), 7–26. doi.org/10.1080/09557570701828386

Dahl, A. (2016). Nullifying settler democracy: William Apess and the paradox of settler sovereignty. *Polity, 48*(2), 279–304. doi.org/10.1057/pol.2016.2

Daniels, N. (1979). Rights to health care and distributive justice: Programmatic worries. *Journal of Medicine & Philosophy, 4*(2), 174–191. doi.org/10.1093/jmp/4.2.174

Daniels, N. (2008). International health inequalities and global justice. In M. Boylan (Ed.), *International public health policy and ethics* (pp. 109–129). New York, NY: Springer Science and Business Media. doi.org/10.1007/978-1-4020-8617-5_7

Davey, M. (2017, 9 January). Ration days again: Cashless welfare card ignites shame. *The Guardian.* Retrieved from www.theguardian.com/australia-news/2017/jan/09/ration-days-again-cashless-welfare-card-ignites-shame

Davis, M. (2007). The United Nations Declaration on the Rights of Indigenous Peoples. *Indigenous Law Bulletin, 6*(30), 50. Retrieved from www5.austlii.edu.au/au/journals/IndigLawB/2007/50.html

Davis, M. (2013). Community control and the work of the national aboriginal community controlled health organisation: Putting meat on the bones of the 'UNDRIP'. *Indigenous Law Bulletin, 8*(7), 11–14.

Deloria, V., Jr (1999). Self-determination and the concept of sovereignty. In J. R. Wunder (Ed.), *Native American sovereignty* (pp. 107–114). New York & London: Garland.

Devlin, B. (2009, June). Bilingual education in the Northern Territory and the continuing debate about its effectiveness and value. In *Bilingual education in the Northern Territory: Principles, policy and practice.* Symposium conducted at the meeting of AIATSIS, Canberra, ACT.

Dorfmann, J. (2015). Undermining paternalism: UNDRIP and Aboriginal rights in Australia. *Harvard International Review, 37*(1), 13–14.

Durie, M. (1998). *Te mana, te kāwanatanga: The politics of Maori self-determination.* Auckland, New Zealand: Oxford University Press.

Durie, M. (2001). *The Hui Taumata Mātauranga and a framework for considering Māori educational advancement: An address to the Ministry of Education, 9 August 2001, National Library Auditorium, Wellington.* Palmerston North, New Zealand: Author.

Duthu, B. (2013). *Shadow nations: Tribal sovereignty and the limits of legal pluralism.* Oxford, UK: Oxford University Press. doi.org/10.1093/acprof:oso/9780199735860.001.0001

Dwyer, J., Kelly, J., Willis, E., Glover, J., Mackean, T., Pekarsky, B. & Battersby, M. (2011). Managing two worlds together: City hospital care for country Aboriginal people—Project report. Retrieved from www.lowitja.org.au/content/Document/Lowitja-Publishing/M2WT_Project_Report.pdf

Elster, J. (1997). Alchemies of the mind: Transmutation and misrepresentation. *Legal Theory*, *3*(2), 133–176. doi.org/10.1017/S1352325200000707

Engle, K. (2011). On fragile architecture: The UN Declaration on the Rights of Indigenous Peoples in the context of human rights. *European Journal of International Law*, *22*(1), 141–163. doi.org/10.1093/ejil/chr019

Espiner, G. (2017, 7 April). The reformer—Geoffrey Palmer. *Radio New Zealand*. Retrieved from www.radionz.co.nz/programmes/the-9th-floor/story/201839427/the-reformer-geoffrey-palmer

Estlund, D. (1997). Beyond fairness and deliberation: The epistemic dimensions of democratic authority. In J. Bohman & W. Rehg (Eds), *Deliberative democracy: Essays on reason and politics* (pp. 173–204). Cambridge, MA: MIT Press.

Eyford, D. R. (2013). *Forging partnerships, building relationships: Aboriginal Canadians and energy development* (Report to the prime minister). Retrieved from www.nrcan.gc.ca/sites/www.nrcan.gc.ca/files/www/pdf/publications/ForgPart-Online-e.pdf

Fitzgerald, O. & Schwartz, R. (2017). Introduction. In O. Fitzgerald (Ed.), *UNDRIP implementation braiding international, domestic and indigenous law* (pp. 1–9). Waterloo, Canada: Centre for International Governance Innovation.

Fleras, A. (2000). The politics of jurisdiction: Pathway or predicament. In D. Long & O. P. Dickason (Eds), *Visions of the heart: Canadian Aboriginal issues* (2nd ed., pp. 107–142). Toronto, Canada: Harcourt Canada.

Foley, G. (1991). Redfern Aboriginal medical service: 20 years on. *Aboriginal and Islander Health Worker Journal*, *15*(4), 4–8.

Forman, M. (2016). [Review of the book *On sovereignty and other political delusions*, by J. Cocks]. *New Political Science*, *38*(2), 283–285. doi.org/10.1080/07393148.2016.1153196

Fraser, N. & Honneth, A. (2003). *Redistribution or recognition? A political-philosophical exchange*. London, UK: Verso Books.

Garrow, C. (2012). The freedom to pass and repass: Can the UN Declaration on the Rights of Indigenous Peoples keep the US–Canadian border ten feet above our heads? In E. Pulitano (Ed.), *Indigenous rights in the age of the UN Declaration* (pp. 172–197). Cambridge, UK: Cambridge University Press.

Gaus, G. F. (1997). Reason, justification, and consensus: Why democracy can't have it all. In J. Bohman & W. Rehg (Eds), *Deliberative democracy: Essays on reason and politics* (pp. 172–197). Cambridge, MA: MIT Press.

Gover, K. (2015). Settler–state political theory, 'CANZUS' and the UN Declaration on the Rights of Indigenous Peoples. *European Journal of International Law, 26*(2), 345–373. doi.org/10.1093/ejil/chv019

Government of Canada. (1995). *The Government of Canada's approach to implementation of the inherent right and the negotiation of Aboriginal self-government*. Retrieved from www.rcaanc-cirnac.gc.ca/eng/1100100031843/ 1539869205136

Government of Canada, Department of Indian Affairs and Northern Development. (1969). *Government statement on Indian policy June 25, 1969: Comparison with remarks recorded at consultation meetings on the Indian Act.* Retrieved from publications.gc.ca/site/eng/9.840343/publication.html

Grant, S. (2016). *New Indigenous middle class finds place in modern economy* [Edited extract of a lecture delivered at the University of Melbourne, November 2016]. Retrieved from pursuit.unimelb.edu.au/articles/new-indigenous-middle-class-finds-place-in-modern-economy

Gunn, B. L. (2017). Beyond van der Peet: Bringing together international, indigenous and constitutional law. In J. Borrows, L. Chartrand, O. E. Fitzgerald & R. Schwartz (Eds), *Braiding legal orders: Implementing the United Nations Declaration on the Rights of Indigenous Peoples* (pp. 29–37). Waterloo, Canada: Centre for International Governance Innovation.

Gupta, J., Hildering, A. & Misiedjan, D. (2014). Indigenous people's right to water under international law: A legal pluralism perspective. *Current Opinion in Environmental Sustainability, 11*, 26–33. doi.org/10.1016/j.cosust.2014. 09.015

Gussen, B. (2016). A comparative analysis of constitutional recognition of aboriginal peoples. *Melbourne University Law Review, 40*, 867–905.

Gutmann, A. (1993). The challenge of multiculturalism in political ethics. *Philosophy & Public Affairs, 22*, 171–206.

Gutmann, A. (1994). Introduction. In C. Taylor (A. Gutmann, Ed.), *Multiculturalism* (Expanded ed., pp. 3–24). Princeton, NJ: Princeton University Press.

Habermas, J. (1997). Popular sovereignty as procedure. In J. Bohman & W. Rehg (Eds), *Deliberative democracy: Essays on reason and politics* (pp. 35–65). Cambridge, MA: MIT Press.

Hattrem, T. (2017). *Joint Nordic statement by Denmark, together with Greenland, Finland, Iceland, Norway and Sweden. delivered by Ambassador and Permanent Representative Tore Hattrem on rights of indigenous peoples, 12 October 2017.* Retrieved from www.norway.no/en/missions/un/statements/general-assembly-committees/3c-rights-of-indigenous-peoples/ (site discontinued).

Hegtvedt, K. A. (2005). Doing justice to the group: Examining the roles of the group in justice research. *Annual Review of Sociology, 31,* 25–45. doi.org/10.1146/annurev.soc.31.041304.122213

Heim, J. (2017, 3 March). U.N. Human Rights Official Criticizes federal relationships with Indian tribes. *Washington Post.* Retrieved from www.washingtonpost.com/national/un-human-rights-official-criticizes-federal-relationship-with-indian-tribes/2017/03/03/81cff046-0034-11e7-99b4-9e613afeb09f_story.html

Held, D. (1995). *Democracy and the global order: From the modern state to cosmopolitan governance.* Cambridge, MA: Polity Press.

Henderson, J. (2008). *Indigenous diplomacy and the rights of peoples: Achieving UN recognition.* Saskatoon: Purich.

Henderson, J. Y. (2017). The art of braiding indigenous peoples' inherent human rights into the law of nation-states. In O. Fitzgerald (Ed.), *UNDRIP Implementation: Braiding international, domestic and indigenous law* (pp. 10–19). Waterloo, Canada: Centre for International Governance Innovation.

Hill, R. (2004). *State authority, indigenous autonomy: Crown–Maori relations in New Zealand/Aotearoa 1900–1950.* Wellington, New Zealand: Victoria University Press.

Hindess, B. (2000). Limits to citizenship. In W. Hudson & J. Kane (Eds), *Rethinking Australian citizenship* (pp. 66–74). Cambridge, UK: Cambridge University Press.

Hindess, B. (2002). Neo-liberal citizenship. *Citizenship Studies, 6*(2), 127–143. doi.org/10.1080/13621020220142932

Hobbes, T. (1946). *Leviathan* (M. Oakeshott, Ed.). Oxford, UK: Basil Blackwell.

Hobbes, T. (1998). *Leviathan.* Oxford, UK: Oxford University Press.

Holder, C. L. & Corntassel, J. (2002). Indigenous peoples and multicultural citizenship: Bridging collective and individual rights. *Human Rights Quarterly, 24*(1), 126–151. doi.org/10.1353/hrq.2002.0012

Hoʻomanawanui, K. (2012). Contested ground: Aina, identity, and nationhood in Hawaii. In E. Pulitano (Ed.), *Indigenous rights in the age of the UN Declaration* (pp. 276–298). Cambridge, UK: Cambridge University Press.

Horscroft, V. (2002). The politics of ethnicity in the Fiji islands: Competing ideologies of indigenous paramountcy and individual equality in political dialogue (Unpublished master's thesis). University of Oxford, UK.

Howard-Hassman, R. (2014). A defence of the international human rights regime. In T. Mitchell (Ed.), *The internationalization of indigenous rights: UNDRIP in the Canadian context* (pp. 23–27). Waterloo, Canada: Centre for International Governance Innovation.

Human Rights and Equal Opportunity Commission. (1997). *Bringing them home: Report of the National Inquiry into the Separation of Aboriginal and Torres Strait Islander Children from Their Families.* Retrieved from www.human rights.gov.au/sites/default/files/content/pdf/social_justice/bringing_them_home_report.pdf

Human Rights Commission of Malaysia. (2017). *UN permanent forum on indigenous issues: Questionnaire to national human rights institutions.* Retrieved from www.un.org/development/desa/indigenouspeoples/wp-content/uploads/sites/19/2018/02/Malaysia.pdf

Hunt, P. & Blackman, G. (2009). *Health systems and the right to the highest attainable standard of health.* Essex, UK: University of Essex, Human Rights Centre. Retrieved from repositories.lib.utexas.edu/bitstream/handle/2152/18926/Health_Systems_Univ_of_Essex_OCR.pdf?sequence=2

Independent Sovereign State of Hawaiʻi. (2017). *UNFPII Questionnaire to Indigenous Peoples' Organizations.* Retrieved from www.un.org/development/desa/indigenouspeoples/wp-content/uploads/sites/19/2016/08/Nation_of_Hawaii.pdf

Indigenous Peoples Network of Malaysia. (2013). *Universal Periodic Review of Malaysia by the Indigenous Peoples Network of Malaysia (JOAS) – 2013.* Retrieved from www.forestpeoples.org/en/topics/un-human-rights-system/publication/2013/universal-periodic-review-malaysia-indigenous-peoples

International Council on Mining and Metals. (2013). *Indigenous peoples and mining* [Position statement]. Retrieved from www.commdev.org/pdf/publications/ICMM-Indigenous-Peoples-and-Mining-Position-Statement.pdf

International Work Group for Indigenous Affairs. (2018). In. P. Jacquelin-Anderson (Ed.), *The indigenous world 2018.* Retrieved from www.iwgia.org/images/documents/indigenous-world/indigenous-world-2018.pdf

The Inuit Circumpolar Council. (2009). *A Circumpolar Inuit declaration on sovereignty in the Arctic.* Retrieved from iccalaska.org/wp-icc/wp-content/uploads/2016/01/Signed-Inuit-Sovereignty-Declaration-11x17.pdf

Iorns, C. I. (1993). The draft declaration on the rights of indigenous peoples. *Murdoch University Electronic Journal of Law, 1*(1). Retrieved from classic.austlii.edu.au/au/journals/MurUEJL/1993/2.html

Ivison, D. (2002). *Postcolonial liberalism.* Cambridge, UK: Cambridge University Press.

Ivison, D., Patton, P. & Sanders, W. (Eds). (2000). *Political theory and the rights of indigenous peoples.* Melbourne, Vic.: Cambridge University Press.

Jackman, S. (1998). Pauline Hanson, the mainstream, and political elites: The place of race in Australian political ideology. *Australian Journal of Political Science, 33*(2), 167–186. doi.org/10.1080/10361149850598

Jackson, N. (2011). Maori and the [potential] demographic dividend. *New Zealand Population Review, 37*, 65–88.

Jenkins, M. (2016). *Evaluation of partnership schools, Kura Hourua policy: Year 2—focus on delivery approaches and assessment final report.* Retrieved from www.educationcounts.govt.nz/__data/assets/pdf_file/0019/181450/Martin Jenkins-Report-Evaluation-of-Partnership-Schools-Kura-Hourua-Policy.pdf

Jenkins, M. (2018). *Multi-year evaluation of partnership schools. Kura Hourua policy, summary of findings across years.* Retrieved from www.educationcounts.govt.nz/__data/assets/pdf_file/0008/184841/Multi-Year-Evaluation-of-Partnership-Schools-Kura-Hourua-Policy-Final-Evaluation-Report.pdf

Jones, C. (2014). A Maori constitutional tradition. *New Zealand Journal of Public and International Law, 12*(1), 187–203.

Josefsen, E., Mörkenstam, U. & Saglie, J. (2015). Different institutions within similar states: The Norwegian and Swedish Sámediggis. *Ethnopolitics, 14*(1), 32–51. doi.org/10.1080/17449057.2014.926611

Kant, I. (1970). *Kant's political writings* (H. Reiss, Ed., H. B. Nisbet, Trans.). Cambridge, UK: Cambridge University Press.

Keim, S. & Reddy, S. (2015). *Free, prior and informed consent: A Just accommodation demands no less.* Retrieved from www.academia.edu/19620322/Free_Prior_and_Informed_Consent_A_Just_Accommodation_Demands_No_Less

Kenny, K. (2014, 14 November). Maori did not give up sovereignty: Waitangi Tribunal. *Stuff.* Retrieved from www.stuff.co.nz/national/politics/63196127/null

Khalil, S. (2018, 5 November). Senator Hanson said she gets really upset when people say this is Aboriginal land. Retrieved from www.news.com.au/national/politics/senator-hanson-said-she-gets-really-upset-when-people-say-this-is-aboriginal-land/news-story/e9f031f065d649f4871480f5512f1ca3

King, T. (2012). *The inconvenient Indian: A curious account of native people in North America.* Anchor, Canada: Random House.

Kingsbury, B. (1992). Claims by non-state groups in international law. *Cornell International Law Journal, 25*, 481–513.

Kingsbury, B. (2002). Competing conceptual approaches to indigenous group issues in New Zealand law. *The University of Toronto Law Journal, 52*(1), 101–134. doi.org/10.2307/825929

Kingsbury, B. & Grodinsky, W. (1992). Self-determination and 'indigenous peoples'. *Proceedings of the Annual Meeting (American Society of International Law), 86*, 383–397. Retrieved from www.jstor.org/stable/25658664

Klausen, J. C. (2014). Jeremy Waldron's partial Kant: Indigenous proximity, colonial injustice, cultural particularism. *Polity, 46*(1), 31–55. doi.org/10.1057/pol.2013.38

Knight, J. & Johnson, J. (2011). *The priority of democracy: The political consequences of pragmatism.* Princeton, NJ: Princeton University Press. doi.org/10.23943/princeton/9780691151236.001.0001

Kommunal Landspensjonskasse (KLP). (2017). *Decision to exclude energy transfer partners, Phillips 66, Enbridge Inc., and Marathon Petroleum Corporation.* Retrieved from www.klp.no/en/english-pdf/Decision%20to%20exclude%20ETP%20Phillips%2066%20Enbridge%20and%20Marathon%20Petroleum.pdf

Kukutai, T., Sporle, A. & Roskruge, M. (2017). *Subjective whānau wellbeing in Te Kupenga.* Wellington, New Zealand: Superu.

Kulchyski, P. (2013). *Aboriginal rights are not human rights.* Winnipeg, Canada: ARP Books.

Kuokkanen, R. (2012). Self-determination and indigenous women's rights at the intersection of international human rights. *Human Rights Quarterly, 34*(1), 225–250. doi.org/10.1353/hrq.2012.0000

Kymlicka, W. (1995). *Multicultural citizenship: A liberal theory of minority rights.* New York, NY: Oxford University Press.

Kymlicka, W. & Norman, W. (1994). Return of the citizen: A survey of recent work on citizenship theory. *Ethics, 104*(2), 352–381. doi.org/10.1086/293605

Langton, M. & Longbottom, J. (2012). Introduction. In M. Langton & J. Longbottom (Eds), *Community futures, legal architecture: Foundations for indigenous peoples in the global mining boom* (pp. 1–20). London, UK: Routledge. doi.org/10.4324/9780203123119

Lee, P., Fasoli, L., Ford, L., Stephenson, P. & McInerne, D. (2014). *Indigenous kids and schooling in the Northern Territory: An introductory overview and brief history of Aboriginal education in the Northern Territory.* Darwin, NT: Batchelor Institute.

Lipsky, M. (2010). *Street-level bureaucracy: Dilemmas of the individual in public service.* New York, NY: Russell Sage Foundation.

Little, A. (2003). Multiculturalism, diversity and liberal egalitarianism in Northern Ireland. *Irish Political Studies, 18*(2), 23–29. doi.org/10.1080/1364298042000227631

Locke, J. (1887). *Locke on civil government* (2nd ed., H. Morley, Ed.). London, UK: George Routledge and Sons.

Maaka, R. & Fleras, A. (2000). Engaging with indigeneity: Tino rangatiratanga in Aotearoa. In D. Ivison, P. Patton & W. Sanders (Eds), *Political theory and the rights of indigenous peoples* (pp. 89–109). Melbourne, Vic.: Cambridge University Press.

Maaka, R. & Fleras, A. (2005). *The politics of indigeneity: Challenging the state in Canada and Aotearoa New Zealand.* Dunedin, New Zealand: University of Otago Press.

Maaka, R. & Fleras, A. (2009). Towards an indigenous grounded analysis (IGA) policy framework as participatory constitutional governance. *Australasian Canadian Studies, 27*(1–2), 55–84. Retrieved from www.acsanz.org.au/archives/acs27-1-2-2009.pdf

MacDonald, L. T. & Muldoon, P. (2006). Globalisation, neoliberalism and the struggle for indigenous citizenship. *Australian Journal of Political Science, 41*(2), 209–223. doi.org/org/10.1080/10361140600672477

Maciel, R. (2014). Conflicting ontologies and balancing perspectives. In T. Mitchell (Ed.), *The internationalization of indigenous rights: UNDRIP in the Canadian context* (pp. 37–41). Waterloo, Canada: Centre for International Governance Innovation.

Mallard, T. (2004, 29 July). *We are all New Zealanders now* [Speech delivered to the Stout Research Centre for NZ Studies, Victoria University, Wellington]. Retrieved from www.beehive.govt.nz/speech/we-are-all-new-zealanders-now

Mansbridge, J. (1996). Using power/fighting power: The polity. In S. Benhabib (Ed.), *Democracy and difference. Contesting the boundaries of the political* (pp. 46–66). Princeton, NJ: Princeton University Press.

Mansell, M. (2011). Will the Declaration make any difference to Australia's treatment of Aborigines? *Griffith Law Review, 20*(3), 659–672. doi.org/10.1080/10383441.2011.10854715

Martin, B. (2005, 28 September). Chief Justice Brian Martin's sentencing remarks [Transcript of proceedings]. *Sydney Morning Herald.* Retrieved from www.smh.com.au/news/national/chief-justice-brian-martins-sentencing-rem arks/2005/09/27/1127804478319.html

Martinez Cobo, J. (1981). *Study of the problem of discrimination against indigenous populations.* New York, NY: United Nations. Retrieved from www.un.org/development/desa/indigenouspeoples/publications/martinez-cobo-study.html

Matike Mai Aotearoa. (2016). *He whakairo here whakaumu mō Aotearoa: The report of Matike Mai Aotearoa – the independent working group on constitutional transformation.* Retrieved from www.converge.org.nz/pma/iwi.htm

Maya Leaders Alliance. (2018, 7 September). *Maya leaders alliance – Update report to the human rights committee of the ICCPR for the 124th session review of Belize.* Retrieved from tbinternet.ohchr.org/Treaties/CCPR/Shared%20Documents/BLZ/INT_CCPR_CSS_BLZ_32402_E.pdf

Mazel, O. (2016). Self-determination and the right to health: Australian Aboriginal community controlled health services. *Human Rights Law Review, 16*(2), 323–355. doi.org/10.1093/hrlr/ngw010

Mazzuoli, V. O. & Ribeiro, D. (2015). Indigenous rights before the inter-American court of human rights: A call for a pro individual interpretation. *Harvard International Law Journal.* Retrieved from harvardilj.org/wp-content/uploads/sites/15/Indigenous-Rights-before-the-Inter-American-Court-of-Human-Rights-Valerio-Mazzzuoli-Dilton-Ribeiro_Final.pdf

McCarty, T. & Lee, T. (2014). Critical culturally sustaining/revitalizing pedagogy and Indigenous education sovereignty. *Harvard Educational Review, 84*(1), 101–124. doi.org/10.17763/haer.84.1.q83746nl5pj34216

McCue, J. (2007). New modalities of sovereignty: An indigenous perspective. *Intercultural Human Rights Law Review, 2*, 19–29.

McIvor, S. (2004). Aboriginal women unmasked: Using equality litigation to advance women's rights. *Canadian Journal of Women and the Law, 16*, 106–136.

Merkel, R., Newhouse, G. & Schokman, B. (2009). *Request for urgent action under the international convention on the elimination of all forms of racial discrimination* (Submission in relation to the Commonwealth Government of Australia). Retrieved from www.uts.edu.au/sites/default/files/RequestforUrgentAction_28Jan09.pdf

Métis Nation. (2017). *Defining the nation-to-nation relationship*. Retrieved from www.metisnation.ca/wp-content/uploads/2017/03/March-18-2017-GA-defining-nation-to-nation-relationship.pdf

Michelman, F. (1997). How can the people ever make the laws? A critique of liberal democracy. In J. Bohman & W. Rehg (Eds), *Deliberative democracy: Essays on reason and politics* (pp. 145–171). Cambridge, MA: MIT Press.

Mill, J. S. (1843). *A system of logic*. London, UK: Parker.

Miller, J. R. (2016). *Lethal legacy: Current native controversies in Canada*. Toronto, Canada: McClelland & Stewart.

Mitchell, T. (2014). Introduction. In T. Mitchell (Ed.), *The internationalization of indigenous rights: UNDRIP in the Canadian context* (pp. 1–3). Waterloo, Canada: Centre for International Governance Innovation.

Moore, D., Scott, G., Drew, R., Smith, J. & Whelen, C. (2014). *Decentralising welfare—te manamotuhake o tuhoe* (Report to the Ministry of Social Development). Retrieved from www.srgexpert.com/wp-content/uploads/2015/11/Decentralising-welfare-te-mana-motuhake-o-tuhoe.pdf

Moreton-Robinson, A. (2003). I still call Australia home: Indigenous belonging and place in a white postcolonizing society. In S. Ahmed, C. Castada, A.-M. Fortier & M. Sheller (Eds), *Uprootings/regroundings: Questions of home and migration* (pp. 131–149). New York, NY: Berg.

Moreton-Robinson, A. (2004). Whiteness, epistemology and Indigenous representation. In A. Moreton-Robinson (Ed.), *Whitening race: Essays in social and cultural criticism* (pp. 75–88). Canberra, ACT: Aboriginal Studies Press.

Murphy, M. (2008). Representing Indigenous self-determination. *The University of Toronto Law Journal, 58*(2), 185–216. doi.org/10.3138/utlj.58.2.185

Nakata, M. (2001). Introduction. In M. Nakata (Ed.), *Indigenous peoples, racism and the United Nations* (pp. 11–23). Sydney, NSW: Common Ground.

National Congress of Australia's First Peoples. (2013). *National congress education policy.* Retrieved from nationalcongress.com.au/advocacy/education/national-congress-education-policy/ (site discontinued).

National Congress of Australia's First Peoples. (2018). *Submission on the Closing the Gap refresh strategy discussion paper.* Retrieved from nationalcongress.com.au/advocacy/general/national-congress-ctgr-submission-final/ (site discontinued).

National Health and Medical Research Council. (2016). *NHMRC translating research into policy and practice (TRIPP) forum.* Retrieved from naccho communique.files.wordpress.com/2017/03/final_tripp_forum_report_pcic_approved.pdf

Neville, A. O. (1947). *Australia's coloured minority.* Sydney, NSW: Currawong.

New South Wales Aboriginal Land Council. (2017). *Aboriginal Land Rights Act key to delivering better outcomes in NSW* [Press release]. Retrieved from alc.org.au/newsroom/media-releases/aboriginal-land-rights-act-key-to-delivering-better-outcomes-in-nsw.aspx

New Zealand History. (n.d.). *Read the treaty.* Retrieved from nzhistory.govt.nz/politics/treaty/read-the-treaty/english-text

Newcomb, S. T. (2011). The UN Declaration on the Rights of Indigenous Peoples and the paradigm of domination. *Griffith Law Review, 20*(3), 578–607. doi.org/10.1080/10383441.2011.10854711

Newhouse, D. (2016). Indigenous peoples, Canada and the possibility of reconciliation. *IRPP Insight, 11*, 1–18. Retrieved from irpp.org/wp-content/uploads/2016/11/insight-no11.pdf

Northern Territory Government. (2007). *Ampe akelyernemane meke mekarle: 'Little children are sacred'* (Report of the Northern Territory Board of Inquiry into the Protection of Aboriginal Children from Sexual Abuse). Retrieved from www.inquirysaac.nt.gov.au/pdf/bipacsa_final_report.pdf

Nussbaum, M. (1987). *Nature, function, and capability: Aristotle on political distribution* (Working Paper No. 31). Retrieved from www.wider.unu.edu/sites/default/files/WP31.pdf

Nussbaum, M. (2008). Human rights and human capabilities: Twentieth anniversary reflections. *Harvard Human Rights Journal, 20*, 20–24.

Orange C. (1987). *The Treaty of Waitangi.* Wellington, New Zealand: Allen & Unwin.

Organization of American States. (1948). *American declaration of the rights and duties of man.* Retrieved from www.cidh.oas.org/Basicos/English/Basic2. american%20Declaration.htm

Ornelas, R. T. (2014). Implementing the policy of the UN Declaration on the Rights of Indigenous Peoples. *The International Indigenous Policy Journal, 5*(1), 1–22. doi.org/10.18584/iipj.2014.5.1.4

O'Sullivan, D. (2005). *Faith politics and reconciliation: Catholicism and the politics of indigeneity.* Adelaide, SA: The Australian Theological Forum.

O'Sullivan, D. (2007). *Beyond biculturalism.* Wellington, New Zealand: Huia.

O'Sullivan, D. (2008). The Treaty of Waitangi in contemporary New Zealand politics. *Australian Journal of Political Science, 43*(2), 317–331. doi.org/ 10.1080/10361140802035804

O'Sullivan, D. (2014). Māori self-determination and a liberal theory of indigeneity. In M. Woons (Ed.), *Restoring indigenous self-determination: Theoretical and practical approaches* (pp. 64–71). Bristol, UK: e-International Relations.

O'Sullivan, D. (2015). *Indigenous health: Power, politics and citizenship.* Melbourne, Vic.: Australian Scholarly Publishing.

O'Sullivan, D. (2017). *Indigeneity: A politics of potential: Australia, Fiji and New Zealand.* Bristol, UK: Policy Press. doi.org/10.2307/j.ctt1t89hxx

O'Sullivan, D. (2018a). Between indigenous paramountcy and democracy: How differentiated citizenship and the UN Declaration on the Rights of Indigenous Peoples could help Fijian self-determination. *Australian Journal of Politics & History, 64*(1), 129–141. doi.org/10.1111/ajph.12424

O'Sullivan, D. (2018b, 18 January). Indigenous recognition in our constitution matters—and will need greater political will to achieve. *The Conversation.* Retrieved from theconversation.com/indigenous-recognition-in-our-constitution-matters-and-will-need-greater-political-will-to-achieve-90296

Palmer, G. (1995). Where to from here. *Victoria University of Wellington Law Review, 25*, 153–154.

Paradies, Y. (2006). Race, racism, stress and indigenous health (Unpublished doctoral dissertation). University of Melbourne, Victoria, Australia.

Paterson, J. (2017, 9 May). Jackson at odds with Labour's charter schools policy. *Radio New Zealand*. Retrieved from www.radionz.co.nz/news/political/330414/jackson-at-odds-with-labour%27s-charter-schools-policy

Patton, P. (2005). Historic injustice and the possibility of supersession. *Journal of Intercultural Studies, 26*(3), 255–266. doi.org/10.1080/07256860500153526

Phillips, A. (1995). *The politics of presence: Issues in democracy and group representation.* Oxford, UK: Oxford University Press.

Philpott, D. (2016). Sovereignty. In E. N. Zalta (Ed.), *The Stanford encyclopedia of philosophy* (Summer 2016 ed.). Retrieved from plato.stanford.edu/archives/sum2016/entries/sovereignty/

Picq, M. L. (2014). Self-determination as anti-extractivism: How indigenous resistance challenges world politics. In M. Woons (Ed.), *Restoring indigenous self-determination: Theoretical and practical approaches* (pp. 26–33). Bristol, UK: e-International Relations.

Pihama, L., Te Nana, R., Cameron, N., Smith, C., Reid, J. & Southey, K. (2016). Maori cultural definitions of sexual violence. *Sexual Abuse in Australia and New Zealand, 7*(1), 43–50.

Pop Ac, A. (2017). *End of year statement by chair of the UN permanent forum on indigenous issues.* Retrieved from www.humanrightscolumbia.org/news/end-year-statement-chair-un-permanent-forum-indigenous-issues

Public Policy Forum. (2017). *Expanding the circle: What reconciliation and inclusive economic growth can mean for First Nations and Canada.* Ottawa, Canada.

Quane, H. (2011). New directions for self-determination and participatory rights? In S. Allen & P. Xanthaki (Eds), *Reflections on the UN Declaration on the Rights of Indigenous Peoples* (pp. 259–287). Oxford, UK: Hart.

Quitian, A. & Rodríguez, G. (2016). Guidelines for inclusion: Ensuring Indigenous peoples' involvement in water planning processes across South Eastern Australia. *Journal of Hydrology, 542*, 828–835. doi.org/10.1016/j.jhydrol.2016.09.050

Ratima, M. M., Brown, R. M., Garrett, N. K., Wikaire, E. I., Ngawati, R. M., Aspin, C. S. & Potaka, U. K. (2007). Strengthening Maori participation in the New Zealand health and disability workforce. *Medical Journal of Australia, 186*(10), 541–543. doi.org/10.5694/j.1326-5377.2007.tb01034.x

Rawls, J. (1971). *A theory of justice.* Cambridge, MA: Harvard University Press.

Rawls, J. (1993). *Political liberalism.* New York, NY: Columbia University Press.

Rawls, J. (1997). The idea of public reason revisited. *The University of Chicago Law Review*, *64*(3), 765–807. doi.org/10.2307/1600311

Rawls, J. (1999). *A theory of justice*. Cambridge, MA: Harvard University Press.

Raya, M. (2006). *Indigenous women stand against violence: A companion report to the United Nations' secretary-general's study on violence against women*. New York, NY: United Nations.

Referendum Council. (2017). *Uluru statement from the heart*. Retrieved from www.referendumcouncil.org.au/sites/default/files/2017-05/Uluru_Statement_From_The_Heart_0.PDF

Reynolds, H. (1996). *Aboriginal sovereignty. Three nations, one Australia?* Sydney, NSW: Allen & Unwin.

Rice, R. (2014). UNDRIP and the 2009 Bolivian constitution: Lessons for Canada. In T. Mitchell (Ed.), *The internationalization of indigenous rights: UNDRIP in the Canadian context* (pp. 59–63). Waterloo, Canada: Centre for International Governance Innovation.

Richmond, C. A. & Cook, C. (2016). Creating conditions for Canadian Aboriginal health equity: The promise of healthy public policy. *Public Health Reviews*, *37*(1), 2–16. doi.org/10.1186/s40985-016-0016-5

Rousseau, J. (1984). *On the social contract* (C. M. Sherover, Trans.). New York, NY: Harper and Row.

Rowse, T. (2000). Indigenous citizenship. In W. Hudson & J. Kane (Eds), *Rethinking Australian citizenship* (pp. 86–98). Cambridge, UK: Cambridge University Press.

Royal Commission on Aboriginal Peoples (Canada) (Final Report, October 1996), vol 2.

Ruger, J. (2006). Toward a theory of a right to health: Capability and incompletely theorized agreements. *Yale Journal of Law & the Humanities*, *18*(2), 273–326.

Schulte-Tenckhoff, I. (2012). Treaties, peoplehood and self-determination: Understanding the language of indigenous rights. In E. Pulitano (Ed.), *Indigenous rights in the age of the UN Declaration* (pp. 64–86). Cambridge, UK: Cambridge University Press. doi.org/10.1017/CBO9781139136723.003

Scott. C. (1996). Indigenous self-determination and decolonization of the international imagination: A plea. *Human Rights Quarterly*, *18*(4), 814. doi.org/10.1353/hrq.1996.0049

Scott, D. (2003). Culture in political theory. *Political Theory, 31*(1), 92–115. doi.org/10.1177/0090591702239440

Sen, A. (1979). Equality of what? In S. M. McMurrin (Ed.), *The Tanner lectures on human values* (vol. 1). Cambridge, UK: Cambridge University Press.

Sen, A. (1999a). Democracy as a universal value. *Journal of Democracy, 10*(3), 3–17. doi.org/10.1353/jod.1999.0055

Sen, A. (1999b). *Development as freedom*. Oxford, UK: Oxford University Press.

Sen, A. (2002). Response to commentaries. *Studies in Comparative International Development, 37*(2), 78–86. doi.org/10.1007/BF02686264

Sen, A. (2004). Why health equity? In S. Anand, P. Fabienne & A. Sen (Eds), *Public health, ethics and equity* (pp. 21–33). Oxford, UK: Oxford University Press.

Shaw, K. (2008). *Indigeneity and political theory: Sovereignty and the limits of the political*. London, UK: Routledge. doi.org/10.4324/9780203891148

Slezack, M. (2017, 4 December). Adani coalmine project: China construction bank won't grant loan, PR firm says. *The Guardian*. Retrieved from www.theguardian.com/business/2017/dec/02/adani-group-china-construction-bank-wont-grant-loan-pr-firm-says

Smith, A. (2013, 7 April). Indigenous feminism without apology. *New Socialist: Ideas for Radical Social Change*. Retrieved from newsocialist.org/indigenous-feminism-without-apology/

Social Policy Evaluation and Research Unit. (2016). *The Whānau Rangatiratanga Frameworks: Approaching whānau wellbeing from within Te Ao Māori* (Research report). Retrieved from thehub.swa.govt.nz/assets/Uploads/Whanau-rangatiratanga-frameworks-summary.pdf

Solano, E. (2002). To break the silence! Freedom of expression and indigenous peoples in Guatemala from a human rights law perspective (Unpublished master's thesis). University of Oslo, Norway.

Statistics New Zealand. (2013). *2013 census QuickStats about Māori*. Retrieved from archive.stats.govt.nz/Census/2013-census/profile-and-summary-reports/quickstats-about-maori-english.aspx

Stephens, M. (2017). The Crown isn't just Pākehā. It is also Māori. *E-Tanagata*. Retrieved from e-tangata.co.nz/comment-and-analysis/the-crown-isnt-just-pakeha-it-is-also-maori/

Sweetgrass, S. N. (2015, 8 December). Trudeau outlines five-point plan to chiefs. *Ammsa.com.* Retrieved from ammsa.com/publications/alberta-sweetgrass/trudeau-outlines-five-point-plan-chiefs

Sworn to no master, of no sect am I. (1838, 7 November). *The Sydney Herald,* p. 2. Retrieved from nla.gov.au/nla.news-article12861179

Tasker, J. P. (2016, 15 December). Justin Trudeau announces 3 steps to help enact truth and reconciliation calls to action. *CBC News.* Retrieved from www.cbc.ca/news/politics/trudeau-indigenous-leaders-trc-1.3897902

Tawhai, V. & Gray-Sharp, K. (Eds). (2011). *Always speaking. The Treaty of Waitangi and public policy.* Wellington, New Zealand: Huia.

Taylor, C. (1989). *Sources of the self: The making of the modern identity.* Cambridge, MA: Harvard University Press.

Taylor, C. (1994). *Multiculturalism* (Expanded ed., A. Gutmann, Ed.). NJ: Princeton University Press. doi.org/10.2307/j.ctt7snkj

Thompson, A. (2017). *On the side of the angels: Canada and the United Nations Commission on Human Rights.* Vancouver, Canada: UBC Press.

Thornberry, P. (2002). *Indigenous peoples and human rights.* Manchester, UK: Manchester University Press. doi.org/10.7228/manchester/9780719037931.001.0001

Thrupp, M. (2016). The political rhetoric and everyday realities of citizenship in New Zealand society and schools. In A. Peterson, R. Hattam, M. Zembylas & J. Arthur (Eds), *The Palgrave international handbook of education for citizenship and social justice* (pp. 509–521). London, UK: Palgrave MacMillan. doi.org/10.1057/978-1-137-51507-0_24

Trask, H.-K. (1999). *From a native daughter: Colonialism and sovereignty in Hawai'i.* Honolulu: University of Hawaii Press.

Trask, M. (2012). Implementing the Declaration. In E. Pulitano (Ed.), *Indigenous rights in the age of the UN Declaration* (pp. 327–336). Cambridge, UK: Cambridge University Press.

Truth and Reconciliation Commission of Canada (TRC). (2015). *Final report of the Truth and Reconciliation Commission of Canada. Volume one: Summary. Honouring the truth, reconciling for the future.* Toronto, Canada: James Lorimer.

Trudeau, J. (2015, 8 December). *Prime minister Justin Trudeau delivers a speech to the Assembly of First Nations Special Chiefs Assembly* [Transcript of speech]. Retrieved from pm.gc.ca/en/news/speeches/2015/12/08/prime-minister-justin-trudeau-delivers-speech-assembly-first-nations

Tsutsui, K. (2018). *Rights make might: Global human rights and minority social movements in Japan.* New York, NY: Oxford University Press. doi.org/10.1093/oso/9780190853105.001.0001

Tully, J. (1995). *Strange multiplicity: Constitutionalism in an age of diversity.* Cambridge, UK: Cambridge University Press. doi.org/10.1017/CBO9781139170888

Tully, J. (1999). Aboriginal peoples: Negotiating reconciliation. In J. Bickerton & A. Gagnon (Eds), *Canadian politics* (pp. 413–441). Peterborough, Canada: Hadleigh.

Tully, J. (2000). The struggles of indigenous peoples for and of freedom. In D. Ivison, P. Patton & W. Sanders (Eds), *Political theory and the rights of indigenous peoples* (pp. 257–288). Port Melbourne, Vic.: Cambridge University Press.

United Nations. (1948). *Universal declaration of human rights.* Retrieved from www.un.org/en/udhrbook/pdf/udhr_booklet_en_web.pdf

United Nations. (1966a). *International covenant on civil and political rights.* Retrieved from www.ohchr.org/en/professionalinterest/pages/ccpr.aspx

United Nations. (1966b). *International covenant on economic, social and cultural rights.* Retrieved from www.ohchr.org/en/professionalinterest/pages/cescr.aspx

United Nations. (1994). *Standard-setting activities: Evolution of standards concerning the rights of indigenous populations, UN working group on indigenous populations,* 12th Sess., UN Doc. E/ CN.4/Sub.2/AC.4/1994/4/Add.1.

United Nations. (1996). *Report of the working group established in accordance with Commission on Human Rights resolution 1995/32 of 3 March 1995,* 52nd Sess., Provisional Agenda Item 3, UN Doc. E/CN.4/1996/84.

United Nations. (1997). *Working group on indigenous populations to hold annual session in Geneva* [Press release]. Retrieved from www.un.org/press/en/1997/19970725.HR4332.html

United Nations. (2001). *Mandate of the working group on indigenous populations.* Retrieved from www.ohchr.org/en/Issues/IPeoples/Pages/MandateWGIP.aspx

United Nations. (2006a). *Report of the special rapporteur on contemporary forms of racism, racial discrimination, xenophobia and related intolerance, Doudou Diène,* 62nd Sess., Provisional Agenda Item 6, UN Doc. E/CN.4/2006/16/Add.2.

United Nations. (2006b). *Report of the working group established in accordance with Commission on Human Rights resolution 1995/32 of 3 March 1995 on its eleventh session.* 62nd Sess., Provisional Agenda Item 15, UN Doc. E/CN.4/2006/79.

United Nations. (2007a, 13 September). *General assembly adopts declaration on rights of indigenous peoples; 'Major step forward' towards human rights for all, says president* [Press release]. Retrieved from www.un.org/press/en/2007/ga10612.doc.htm

United Nations. (2007b). *Universal Declaration on the Rights of Indigenous Peoples.* Retrieved from www.un.org/esa/socdev/unpfii/documents/DRIPS_en.pdf

United Nations. (2007c). United Nations Declaration on the Rights of Indigenous Peoples [Webpage]. Retrieved from www.un.org/development/desa/indigenous peoples/declaration-on-the-rights-of-indigenous-peoples.html

United Nations. (2011). *Report of the special rapporteur on the rights of indigenous peoples, James Anaya. Addendum. The situation of Māori people in New Zealand.* Retrieved from www2.ohchr.org/english/issues/indigenous/rapporteur/docs/A.HRC.18_NewZealand.pdf

United Nations. (2012a). *Report of the special rapporteur on the rights of indigenous peoples, James Anaya. Addendum: The situation of indigenous peoples in the United States of America,* 21st Sess., Agenda Item 3, UN Doc. A/HRC/21/47/Add.1.

United Nations. (2012b). *Report of the working group on the universal periodic review: Ecuador,* 21st Sess., Agenda Item 6, UN Doc. A/HRC/21/4.

United Nations. (2013). *Implementing declaration on indigenous rights will be difficult or impossible without greater awareness of human rights values, third committee told* [Press release]. Retrieved from www.un.org/press/en/2013/gashc4074.doc.htm

United Nations. (2014). *Report of the special rapporteur on the rights of indigenous peoples, James Anaya. Addendum: The situation of indigenous peoples in Canada,* 27th Sess., Agenda Item 3, UN Doc. A/HRC/27/52/Add.2.

United Nations. (2016a). *End of year statement by UNPFII chair* [Press release]. Retrieved from www.un.org/development/desa/indigenouspeoples/news/2016/12/end-of-year-statement-by-unpfii-chair/ (site discontinued).

United Nations. (2016b). *Report of the special rapporteur on the rights of indigenous peoples on the human rights situation of the Sami people in the Sámpi region of Norway, Sweden and Finland,* 33rd Sess., Agenda Item 3, UN Doc A/ HRC/33/42/Add.3.

United Nations. (2017a). *Australian Indigenous people's caucus response questionnaire on Indigenous issues.* Retrieved from www.un.org/esa/socdev/ unpfii/documents/2017/16-session/Indigenous_Peoples/Aboriginal_Rights_ Coalition_response.pdf

United Nations. (2017b). *End of mission press conference & statement by UN special rapporteur on the rights of indigenous peoples on her visit to Australia.* Retrieved from www.ohchr.org/EN/NewsEvents/Pages/DisplayNews.aspx? NewsID=21473&LangID=E

United Nations. (2017c). *End of mission statement by the United nations special rapporteur on the rights of indigenous peoples, Victoria Tauli-Corpuz of her visit to the United States of America.* Retrieved from www.ohchr.org/EN/ NewsEvents/Pages/DisplayNews.aspx?NewsID=21274

United Nations Committee on the Elimination of Racial Discrimination. (2007). *Consideration of reports submitted by states parties under article 9 of the convention: Concluding observations of the committee on the elimination of racial discrimination,* 80th Sess., UN Doc. CERD/C/VNM/CO/10-14.

United States of America. (2011). *Announcement of U.S. support for the United Nations Declaration on the Rights of Indigenous Peoples.* Retrieved from 2009-2017.state.gov/s/srgia/154553.htm

Universities New Zealand. (2018). *Building Māori success.* Retrieved from www. universitiesnz.ac.nz/sector-research-issues-facts-and-stats/building-māori-and-pasifika-success/building-māori-success

van Bekhoven, J. (2016). Identity crisis: Taiwan's laws and regulations on the status of indigenous peoples. *Asia Pacific Law Review, 24*(2), 202–232. doi.org/ 10.1080/10192557.2016.1245399

Villeneuve, L. (2016). Could the progressive 'hardening' of human rights soft law impair its further expansion? Insights from the UN Declaration of the Rights of Indigenous Peoples. In S. Lagoutte, T. Gammeltoft-Hansen & J. Cerone (Eds), *Tracing the roles of soft law in human rights* (pp. 213–233). Oxford, UK: Oxford University Press. doi.org/10.1093/acprof:oso/9780198791409. 003.0011 von der Porten, S., Lepofsky, D., McGregor, D. & Silver, J. (2016). Recommendations for marine herring policy change in Canada: Aligning with indigenous legal and inherent rights. *Marine Policy, 74,* 68–76. doi.org/ 10.1016/j.marpol.2016.09.007

Vos, T., Barker, B., Begg, S., Stanley, L. & Lopez, A. D. (2009). Burden of disease and injury in Aboriginal and Torres Strait Islander Peoples: the Indigenous health gap. *International Journal of Epidemiology, 38*(2), 470–477. doi.org/ 10.1093/ije/dyn240

Waikato-Tainui. (2015). *Ko te mana matauranga.* Hamilton, New Zealand: Waikato-Tainui. Retrieved from versite.co.nz/~2015/18510/files/assets/basic-html/page-1.html

Waitangi Tribunal, *He Whakaputanga me te Tiriti = The Declaration and the Treaty: The report on stage 1 of the Te Paparahi o te Raki Inquiry* (Wai 1040, 2014).

Waitangi Tribunal, *Te reo Māori* [Prepublication copy of Chapter 5 of *Ko Aotearoa tēnei*] (Wai 262, 2010).

Waldron, J. (2003). Indigeneity? First Peoples and last occupancy. *New Zealand Journal of Public and International Law, 1*(1), 55–82.

Waldron, J. (2004). Settlement, return and the supersession thesis. *Theoretical Inquiries in Law, 5*(2), 237–268. doi.org/10.2202/1565-3404.1093

Ward, C. (2011). A travesty of a mockery of a sham: Colonialism as 'self-determination' in the UN Declaration on the Rights of Indigenous Peoples. *Griffith Law Review, 20*(3), 526–556. doi.org/10.1080/10383441. 2011.10854709

Watson, I. & Venne, S. (2012). Talking up Indigenous peoples' original intent in a space dominated by state interventions. In E. Pulitano (Ed.), *Indigenous rights in the age of the UN Declaration* (pp. 87–109). Cambridge, UK: Cambridge University Press. doi.org/10.1017/CBO9781139136723.004

Wereta, W. (2001). *Towards a Maori statistics framework.* Wellington, New Zealand: Statistics New Zealand.

Westpac New Zealand. (2014). *Maori business is New Zealand business.* Retrieved from www.westpac.co.nz/rednews/business/maori-business-is-new-zealand-business/ (site discontinued).

Wiessner, S. (2008). Indigenous sovereignty: A reassessment in light of the UN Declaration on the Rights of Indigenous Peoples. *Vanderbilt Journal of Transnational Law, 41*(4), 1141–1176.

Wiessner, S. (2009). United Nations Declaration on the Rights of Indigenous Peoples. *United Nations audio visual library of international law*. Retrieved from legal.un.org/avl/pdf/ha/ga_61-295/ga_61-295_e.pdf

Williams, M. (2004). [Review of the book *The claims of culture: Equality and diversity in the global era*, by S. Benhabib]. *Ethics: An International Journal of Social, Political and Legal Philosophy, 114*(2), 337–339. doi.org/10.1086/379902

Wilson, R. (2008). Making rights meaningful for Mayas: Reflections on culture, rights, and power. In P. Pitarch, S. Speed & X. Solano (Eds), *Human rights in the Maya region: Global politics, cultural contentions, and moral engagements* (pp. 305–321). Durham, NC: Duke University Press.

Wilson-Raybauld, J. (2017). *Investing in Canada's future: The next 150 years* [Speech to the Public Policy Forum Reconciliation and Inclusive Economic Growth Conference]. Retrieved from nationtalk.ca/story/speech-investing-in-canadas-future-the-next-150-years

Woons, M. (2014). Introduction: On the meaning of restoring indigenous self-determination. In M. Woons (Ed.), *Restoring indigenous self-determination: Theoretical and practical approaches* (pp. 8–17). Bristol, UK: e-International Relations.

Xanthaki, A. (2008). *Indigenous rights and United Nations standards*. Cambridge, UK: Cambridge University Press. doi.org/10.1017/CBO9780511494468

Yabaki, A. (2011). *Indigenous rights are human rights* [Transcript of speech delivered 10 December 2008]. Retrieved from news.ccf.org.fj/indigenous-rights-are-human-rights/

Young, I. (1989). Polity and group difference: A critique of the ideal of universal citizenship. *Ethics, 99*(2), 250–274. doi.org/10.1086/293065

Legislation

Australian Constitution.

Bill C-262, An Act to ensure that the laws of Canada are in harmony with the United Nations Declaration on the Rights of Indigenous Peoples. 1st Sess., 42nd Parl., 2018 (Canada).

Canada Act 1982 (UK).

Explanatory Memorandum, Northern Territory Emergency Response Bill 2007 (Cth).

Human Rights Act 2004 (ACT).

Indian Act 1876 (Canada).

Local Government Act 2002 (Canada).

Native Title Act 1993 (Cth).

Racial Discrimination Act 1975 (Cth).

Treaty of Waitangi Act 1975 (NZ).

Waikato Raupatu Claims Settlements Act 1995 (NZ).

Legal Authorities

Cherokee Nation v Georgia, 30 US 1 (1831).

Delgamuukw v British Columbia [1997] 3 SCR 1010.

Haida Nation v British Columbia (Minister of Forests) [2004] 3 SCT 511.

Mabo v Queensland [No. 2] (1992) 175 CLR 1.

Wi Parata v Bishop of Wellington (1877) 1 NZLRLC 14 (Supreme Court of New Zealand).

Yorta Yorta v The State of Victoria (1998) 214 CLR 422.

www.ingramcontent.com/pod-product-compliance
Lightning Source LLC
Chambersburg PA
CBHW040820280326
41926CB00093B/4623